Microsoft®

Exam Ref 70-417: Upgrading Your Skills to MCSA Windows Server® 2012

J.C. Mackin

D1377144

PUBLISHED BY
Microsoft Press
A Division of Microsoft Corporation
One Microsoft Way
Redmond, Washington 98052-6399

Library of Congress Control Number: 2012950444
ISBN: 978-0-7356-7304-5

Printed and bound in the United States of America.

First Printing

Microsoft Press books are available through booksellers and distributors worldwide. If you need support related to this book, email Microsoft Press Book Support at mspinput@microsoft.com. Please tell us what you think of this book at http://www.microsoft.com/learning/booksurvey.

Microsoft and the trademarks listed at http://www.microsoft.com/about/legal/en/us/IntellectualProperty /Trademarks/EN-US.aspx are trademarks of the Microsoft group of companies. All other marks are property of their respective owners.

The example companies, organizations, products, domain names, email addresses, logos, people, places, and events depicted herein are fictitious. No association with any real company, organization, product, domain name, email address, logo, person, place, or event is intended or should be inferred.

Acquisitions Editor: Anne Hamilton
Developmental Editor: Karen Szall
Project Editor: Valerie Woolley
Editorial Production: nSight, Inc.
Technical Reviewer: Mitch Tulloch; Technical Review services provided by Content Master, a member of CM Group, Ltd.
Copyeditor: Teresa Horton
Indexer: Lucie Haskins

Contents at a glance

Contents

What do you think of this book? We wan~~~ ~~~ ~~~ ~~~ cu!

Microsoft is interested in hearing your feedback s~ w~ ~an ~ ~ ~ ~ve c
books and learning resources for you. To participa~ ~ ~riet ~ ~ ~ ~ease ~ ~t.

www.microsoft~ ~m/lea~ ~ ~sur~

Chapter 2   Configure server roles and features   37

Chapter 3   Configure Hyper-V   55

Chapter 4   Install and administer Active Directory   89

Chapter 5   Deploy, manage, and maintain servers   107

Chapter 11 File and storage solutions   245

Chapter 12 Implement business continuity and disaster recovery 271

Chapter 13   Configure network services   309

Chapter 14   Configure identity and access solutions   335

Introduction

This book is written for IT professionals who want to earn the MCSA: Windows Server 2012 certification by passing the Microsoft exam "Exam 70-417: Upgrading Your Skills to MCSA Windows Server 2012." Exam 70-417 serves as a path to the Windows Server 2012 MCSA for those who have already earned the Windows Server 2008 certification that is named alternately "MCITP: Server Administrator" and "MCSA: Windows Server 2008." The book is therefore written specifically for IT professionals who have already earned this Windows Server 2008 certification and maintain the associated level of expertise in Windows Server 2008 or Windows Server 2008 R2.

Exam 70-417 also serves as an upgrade path to the Windows Server 2012 MCSA from certifications other than the Windows Server 2008 MCSA. These other certifications include MCITP: Virtualization Administrator, MCITP: Enterprise Messaging Administrator, MCITP: Lync Server Administrator, MCITP: SharePoint Administrator, and MCITP: Enterprise Desktop Administrator certifications. However, the assumed knowledge for this book is only MCSA-level expertise in Windows Server 2008 or Windows Server 2008 R2.

One of the first things you need to understand about Exam 70-417 is that it is a condensed version of three others: Exam 70-410, Exam 70-411, and Exam 70-412. This set of three exams allows you to earn the Windows Server 2012 MCSA from scratch, without any prior certification. Together, these three exams include 18 domains of broader skills and 62 more specific objectives. Because the exams are intended for people who haven't yet earned Windows Server certification, they test both new features in Windows Server 2012 and features that haven't changed since Windows Server 2008 or even earlier.

On the 70-417 exam, just 14 of the original 18 domains and 22 of the original 62 objectives have been taken from these three source exams. This smaller subset of material corresponds generally to the features that are new in Windows Server 2012. Approximately 80 percent of the questions you will encounter on the 70-417 exam in fact will involve new Windows Server 2012 features in some way. The remaining 20 percent will be "review"-type questions about features that have not changed since Windows Server 2008, questions you could have seen when you earned your existing certification. *This 20 percent can be taken from any of the 62 original objectives on Exams 70-410, 70-411, or 70-412.*

To keep this book brief, we've focused on the 80 percent of material that is new to Windows Server 2012 and that forms the core of Exam 70-417. After all, the remaining 20 percent draws on knowledge in which you have already demonstrated expertise by earning your Windows Server 2008 certification. However, it's possible you will need to brush up on some of these older topics, and when appropriate we've provided guidance throughout the book about which of these older features might require special review.

This book covers every exam objective, but it does not cover every exam question. Only the Microsoft exam team has access to the exam questions themselves and Microsoft regularly adds new questions to the exam, making it impossible to cover specific questions. You should consider this book a supplement to your relevant real-world experience and other study materials. If you encounter a topic in this book with which you do not feel completely comfortable, use the links you'll find in the text to find more information and take the time to research and study the topic. Great information is available on MSDN, TechNet, and in blogs and forums.

Microsoft certifications

Microsoft certifications distinguish you by proving your command of a broad set of skills and experience with current Microsoft products and technologies. The exams and corresponding certifications are developed to validate your mastery of critical competencies as you design and develop, or implement and support, solutions with Microsoft products and technologies both on-premise and in the cloud. Certification brings a variety of benefits to the individual and to employers and organizations.

> **MORE INFO** **ALL MICROSOFT CERTIFICATIONS**
>
> For information about Microsoft certifications, including a full list of available certifications, go to *http://www.microsoft.com/learning/en/us/certification/cert-default.aspx*.

Acknowledgments

I'd like to thank Anne Hamilton for her patience; Travis Jones, Adnan Ijaz, and Osama Sajid for their generous technical contribution; Mitch Tulloch for his always-phenomenal review; Karen Szall and Valerie Woolley for their expert and amiable management styles; Teresa Horton for her sharp editing; Chris Norton at nSight, Inc. for his diligence; and Neil Salkind and Stacey Czarnowski at Studio B for their ability to deftly maneuver through a treacherous course.

Errata & book support

We've made every effort to ensure the accuracy of this book and its companion content. Any errors that have been reported since this book was published are listed on our Microsoft Press site at Oreilly.com:

http://go.microsoft.com/FWLink/?Linkid=263535

If you find an error that is not already listed, you can report it to us through the same page.

If you need additional support, email Microsoft Press Book Support at *mspinput@microsoft.com.*

Please note that product support for Microsoft software is not offered through the addresses above.

We want to hear from you

At Microsoft Press, your satisfaction is our top priority, and your feedback our most valuable asset. Please tell us what you think of this book at:

http://www.microsoft.com/learning/booksurvey

The survey is short, and we read every one of your comments and ideas. Thanks in advance for your input!

Stay in touch

Let's keep the conversation going! We're on Twitter: *http://twitter.com/MicrosoftPress.*

Preparing for the Exam

Microsoft certification exams are a great way to build your resume and let the world know about your level of expertise. Certification exams validate your on-the-job experience and product knowledge. While there is no substitution for on-the-job experience, preparation through study and hands-on practice can help you prepare for the exam. We recommend that you round out your exam preparation plan by using a combination of available study materials and courses. For example, you might use the Training Kit and another study guide for your "at home" preparation, and take a Microsoft Official Curriculum course for the classroom experience. Choose the combination that you think works best for you.

CHAPTER 1

Install and configure servers

The Install and Configure Servers domain originates from the 70-410 exam. Unlike that exam, the 70-417 upgrade exam avoids basic installation concepts that aren't new to Windows Server 2012. Instead, you'll mostly see questions about *new features* related to the initial configuration of Windows Server (such as Features on Demand, full installation/Server Core convertibility, and the remote deployment of server roles) or to server hardware (such as NIC teaming and Storage Spaces).

Objectives in this chapter:

- Objective 1.1: Install servers
- Objective 1.2: Configure servers
- Objective 1.3: Configure local storage

> **IMPORTANT**
>
> *Have you read page xvi?*
>
> It contains valuable information regarding the skills you need to pass the exam.

Objective 1.1: Install servers

"Installing servers" might sound like an easy topic that you don't need to study, but there's a bit more to this objective than meets the eye. Yes, you should certainly review the hardware requirements for Windows Server 2012, but just as important, a new feature that you are likely to see on the 70-417 exam makes an appearance here: Features on Demand.

> **This section covers the following topics:**
> - Windows Server 2012 minimum hardware requirements
> - Migrating roles from previous versions of Windows Server
> - Optimizing resource utilization by using Features on Demand

Minimum hardware requirements

You already know you won't see questions on any Microsoft exam that ask you, for example, "What are the processor requirements for Windows?" But sometimes hardware require-ments sneak into exam questions indirectly. For example, you might see a scenario in which a new feature that is available only in Windows Server 2012 is needed, and the existing server hardware (based on, say, an x86 processor) requires an upgrade to support the new operating system. Fortunately, in this case the hardware requirements are easy to learn: the minimum hardware requirements for Windows Server 2012 are the same as those for Windows Server 2008 R2. Here's a recap:

- Processor: 1.4 GHz 64-bit processor
- RAM: 512 MB (allocate more for the Chinese version)
- Disk space: 32 GB

Don't miss the obvious here. Windows Server 2012 requires a 64-bit processor, unlike Windows Server 2008 (but like Windows Server 2008 R2). This fact could easily form the basis of a test question. If a question states you need to upgrade to Windows Server 2012 on an existing server, make sure the server has a 64-bit processor. If it doesn't, you need to replace the hardware. If the hardware is compatible, you can perform an in-place upgrade (as opposed to a fresh installation) from Windows Server 2008 SP2 or later.

Migrating server roles by using the Windows Server Migration Tool

Don't forget about the Windows Server Migration Tool (WSMT), a command-line tool that helps you migrate certain roles to servers running Windows Server. WSMT is a built-in, installable feature of Windows Server 2012. When you use WSMT, the source computer can be running Windows Server 2003 (SP2 or later), Windows Server 2008, Windows Server 2008 R2, or Windows Server 2012.

You don't need to remember the specifics of how to use WSMT for the 70-417 exam. However, it's a good idea to review the procedure for setting up a role migration from a server running Windows Server 2008 R2. Some of these elements, such as Install-WindowsFeature Migration, SmigDeploy.exe, or Get-SmigServerFeature, could possibly appear in a test question.

To set up a role migration from a server running Windows Server 2008 R2, take the following steps:

1. Install WSMT on the destination server running Windows Server 2012. At an elevated Windows PowerShell prompt, type the following:

    ```
    Install-WindowsFeature Migration
    ```

2. Create deployment folders on the destination server running Windows Server 2012. For this step, use the SmigDeploy.exe command at an elevated command prompt. For example, to create a deployment folder to migrate from Windows Server 2008 R2, type the following:

    ```
    SmigDeploy.exe /package /architecture amd64 /os WS08R2 /path <deployment folder path>
    ```

3. Copy the deployment folders from the destination server to the source server.

4. Register WSMT on source servers by typing the following at an elevated command prompt in the copied directory on the source server:

```
.\Smigdeploy.exe
```

5. Load WSMT into your Windows PowerShell session. To load WSMT, type the following and then press Enter.

```
Add-PSSnapin Microsoft.Windows.ServerManager.Migration
```

6. Type **Get-SmigServerFeature** at an elevated Windows PowerShell prompt to find out which features can be exported from the local server.

At this point, you would use cmdlets such as Export-SmigServerSettings, Import-SmigServerSettings, Send-SmigServerData, and Receive-SmigServerData to migrate data and settings to the destination server.

> **MORE INFO**   For more information about using WSMT to migrate to Windows Server 2012, visit *http://technet.microsoft.com/en-us/library/jj134202*. For cmdlets that apply to Windows Server 2008 R2, visit *http://technet.microsoft.com/en-us/library/dd871125*.

Features on Demand

A copy of the binary files for all features and roles that are installed during Windows Setup is stored in a directory called the *side-by-side store*, located in Windows\WinSxS. Keeping a copy of the feature files available on disk in this way enables you to add a role or enable a feature after Windows Server installation without needing to access Windows Server media. In previous versions of Windows Server, these features files remained on disk for the life of the operating system. The disadvantage of this approach was that these files took up space on the disk even if you never wanted to install the associated feature or role. In addition, you weren't able to reduce the size of the installation image, which you might want to do when creating custom installation media for your organization.

In Windows Server 2012, you can minimize the footprint of your installation by deleting the files for features you're not using from the side-by-side store. This ability to delete feature files is called Features on Demand. To later reinstall a role or feature for which files have been deleted, you need access to the Windows Server 2012 source files.

To completely remove all files for a role or feature from disk, use the Uninstall-WindowsFeature cmdlet of Windows PowerShell and specify the name of the feature by using the –Remove option. For example, to delete the DHCP server binaries from server storage, run the following Windows PowerShell command:

```
Uninstall-WindowsFeature DHCP –Remove
```

EXAM TIP

Windows PowerShell is heavily emphasized on the 70-417 exam.

Figure 1-1 shows the result after you run the Get-WindowsFeature cmdlet. The DHCP Server install state is described as Removed.

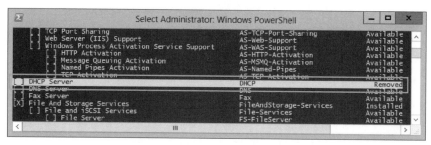

FIGURE 1-1 Removing feature files.

You can reinstall these feature files at any point. To install a role or feature for which the binaries have been deleted, you can use the Install-WindowsFeature cmdlet in Windows PowerShell with the –Source option to specify any of the following:

- A path to a local Windows Imaging (WIM) file (for example, the product DVD)

  The path for a WIM file should be in the following format: *WIM:[drive letter]:\sources \install.wim:[image index]*, for example, *WIM:e:\sources\install.wim:4*.

- A Universal Naming Convention (UNC) path to a WIM file on a network share, using the WIM: prefix before the path

- A UNC path to a network share that contains the WinSxS folder for the appropriate version of Windows Server 2012

If you do not specify a –Source option, Windows will attempt to access the files by performing the following tasks in order:

1. Searching in a location that has been specified by users of the Add Roles And Features Wizard or Deployment Image Servicing and Management (DISM) installation commands.

2. Evaluating the configuration of the Group Policy setting, Computer Configuration \Administrative Templates\System\Specify settings for optional component installation and component repair.

3. Searching Windows Update. (Note that this can be a lengthy process for some features.)

Alternatively, you can reinstall the feature by using Server Manager. When you get to the final page of the Add Roles And Features Wizard, choose the option to specify an alternate source path, as shown in Figure 1-2. Then provide a path to source files when prompted.

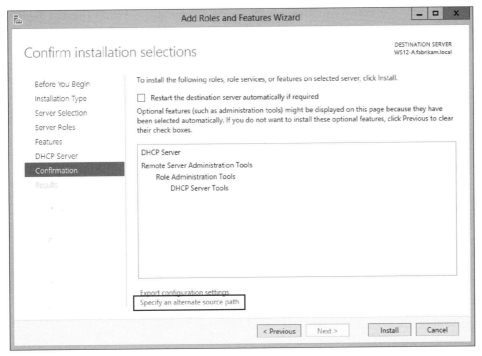

FIGURE 1-2 Reinstalling feature files that have been removed.

The source path or file share must grant Read permissions either to the Everyone group (not recommended for security reasons) or to the computer account of the destination server; granting user account access is not sufficient.

> **MORE INFO** For more information on Features on Demand, visit *http://technet.microsoft .com/en-us/library/jj127275.aspx.*

Objective summary

- The minimum hardware requirements for Windows Server 2012 are the same as those for Windows Server 2008 R2: a 1.4 GHz 64-bit processor, 512 MB of RAM, and 32 GB of storage.

- The Uninstall-WindowsFeature cmdlet uninstalls and removes specified roles, role services, and features from a computer that is running Windows Server 2012 or an offline VHD that has Windows Server 2012 installed on it.

- You can reduce the storage footprint of your Windows Server 2012 installation by removing from disk the files for unused roles or features. To remove feature files, use the following Windows PowerShell command:

```
Uninstall-WindowsFeature feature name -Remove
```

- To reinstall a feature for which files have been removed from the local disk, use the following Windows PowerShell command:

```
Install-WindowsFeature feature name [-Source path to a WIM file or share
containing a WinSxS folder from an appropriate version of Windows Server 2012]
```

Objective review

Answer the following questions to test your knowledge of the information in this objective. You can find the answers to these questions and explanations of why each answer choice is correct or incorrect in the "Answers" section at the end of the chapter.

1. You work for a large company named Contoso.com. A server in the finance department named Server1 is running Windows Server 2008. The server includes a 2.0 GHz 32-bit CPU and 4 GB of RAM.

   Management has issued the requirement that every server should be reduced to a minimal footprint and the files of all unused features should be completely removed from server storage. What should you do? (Choose all that apply.)

   A. Keep the existing server and install Windows Server 2012.

   B. Replace the existing server and install Windows Server 2012.

   C. Use the Uninstall-WindowsFeature cmdlet.

   D. Use the DISM utility.

2. You want to reduce the amount of space taken up by Windows Server 2012 for a Server Message Block (SMB) file server named Server1. Server1 is a member of the Contoso.com domain but doesn't perform any functions beyond those of an SMB file server. Which of the following commands, entered at a Windows PowerShell prompt, are acceptable methods to reduce the size of the Windows Server 2012 installation on Server1? (Choose all that apply.)

   A. Uninstall-WindowsFeature Web-Server -Remove

   B. Dism /online /disable-feature /featurename:iis-webserverrole /remove

   C. Uninstall-WindowsFeature FS-FileServer -Remove

   D. Dism /online /disable-feature /featurename:File-Services /remove

3. Web1 is a web server on your network connected to the Internet. You have used the Uninstall-WindowsFeature cmdlet in Windows PowerShell to remove from disk the feature files for Active Directory Domain Services on Web1. Which of the following commands provides a valid method to reinstall these feature files if you insert the product media into the D drive?

   A. Install-WindowsFeature –Source WIM:D:\sources\install.wim:1

   B. Install-WindowsFeature –Source D:\sources\install.wim:1

   C. Install-WindowsFeature –Source WIM:D:\sources\install.wim

   D. Install-WindowsFeature –Source D:\sources\install.wim

Objective 1.2: Configure servers

Within this objective, there are three major feature changes in Windows Server 2012. First are the improvements to the process of adding or removing server roles and features. You can now perform these functions locally or remotely, through the GUI or by using Windows PowerShell. Next is the new possibility of converting between a Server Core installation of Windows Server 2012 and full installation of Windows Server 2012. Finally, Windows Server 2012 introduces network interface card (NIC) teaming, a fault resiliency feature that you are likely to configure soon after installation.

This section covers the following topics:
- Deploying roles on remote servers
- Configuring online and offline images by using the DISM.exe utility
- Converting between Server Core and full graphical user interface (GUI)
- Configuring the Minimal Server Interface
- Configuring NIC teaming

Installing roles and features

You already know you can use Server Manager to add or remove roles or features locally. As we saw in the last objective, you can also now use the new Install-WindowsFeature and Uninstall-WindowsFeature cmdlets to achieve these same tasks in Windows PowerShell.

EXAM TIP

Add-WindowsFeature is an alias of the Install-WindowsFeature cmdlet, and Remove-WindowsFeature is an alias of the Uninstall-WindowsFeature cmdlet. You can see all of these versions on the 70-417 exam.

Even more interesting, you can now use either Windows PowerShell or Server Manager to perform these tasks remotely.

Deploying features and roles on remote servers through Windows PowerShell

In Windows Server 2012, you can deploy roles and features on remote servers. This feature is an important new functionality that is sure to be tested on the 70-417 exam.

To install roles and features on a remote server by using Windows PowerShell, follow these steps:

1. Type **Get-WindowsFeature** and then press Enter to view a list of available and installed roles and features on the local server. If the local computer is not a server, run Get-WindowsFeature -ComputerName <computer_name>, where *computer_name* represents the name of a remote computer that is running Windows Server 2012. The results of the cmdlet contain the command names of roles and features that you add to your cmdlet in step 4.

2. Type **Get-Help Install-WindowsFeature** and then press Enter to view the syntax and accepted parameters for the Install-WindowsFeature cmdlet.

3. Type the following and then press Enter, where *feature_name* represents the command name of a role or feature that you want to install (obtained in step 2), and *computer_name* represents a remote computer on which you want to install roles and features. Separate multiple values for *feature_name* by using commas. The Restart parameter automatically restarts the destination server if required by the role or feature installation.

   ```
   Install-WindowsFeature –Name <feature_name> -ComputerName <computer_name> -Restart
   ```

Figure 1-3 shows an example of using this cmdlet to install a feature (NFS-Client) on a remote server (WS12-B).

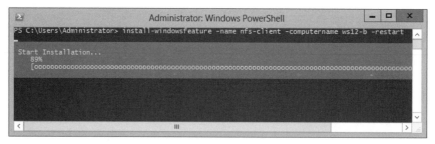

FIGURE 1-3 Installing a feature on a remote server.

Deploying features and roles on remote servers by using Server Manager

If you prefer to use Server Manager to deploy roles and features to a remote server, you must first add the remote server to the Server Manager server pool.

To add a remote server in Server Manager, follow these steps:

1. From the Manage menu, select Add Servers, as shown in Figure 1-4.

FIGURE 1-4 Adding a remote server to manage in Server Manager.

2. Do one of the following:

   - On the Active Directory tab, select servers that are in the current domain. Press Ctrl while selecting multiple servers. Click the right-arrow button to move selected servers to the Selected list.

   - On the DNS tab, type the first few characters of a computer name or IP address and then press Enter or click Search. Select servers that you want to add and then click the right-arrow button.

   - On the Import tab, browse for a text file that contains the DNS names or IP addresses of computers that you want to add, one name or IP address per line.

3. When you are finished adding servers, click OK.

The new server will appear in Server Manager when you select All Servers in the navigation pane, as shown in Figure 1-5.

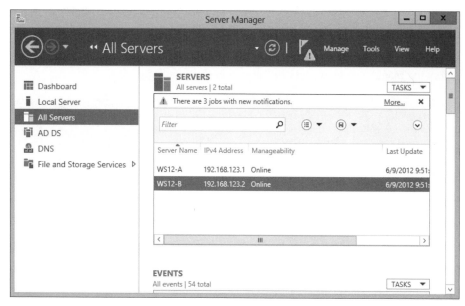

FIGURE 1-5 The remote server WS12-B has been added in Server Manager.

After you have added the remote server to the server pool, you can deploy features to it as you would to the local server.

To install roles and features on a remote server by using Server Manager, follow these steps:

1. From the Manage menu of Server Manager, select Add Roles And Features.

2. On the Before You Begin page, verify that your destination server and network environment are prepared for the role and feature you want to install. Click Next.

3. On the Select Installation Type page, select Role-Based Or Feature-Based Installation to install all parts of roles or features on a single server, or Remote Desktop Services Installation to install either a virtual machine–based desktop infrastructure or a session-based desktop infrastructure for Remote Desktop Services. The Remote Desktop Services Installation option distributes logical parts of the Remote Desktop Services role across different servers as needed by administrators. Click Next.

4. On the Select Destination Server page, select a server from the server pool. After you have selected the destination server, click Next.

5. Select roles, select role services for the role if applicable, and then click Next to select features.

6. On the Confirm Installation Selections page, review your role, feature, and server selections. If you are ready to install, click Install.

   You can also export your selections to an XML-based configuration file that you can use for unattended feature installations with Windows PowerShell. To export the configuration you specified in this Add Roles And Features Wizard session, click Export Configuration Settings, as shown in Figure 1-6, and then save the XML file to a convenient location.

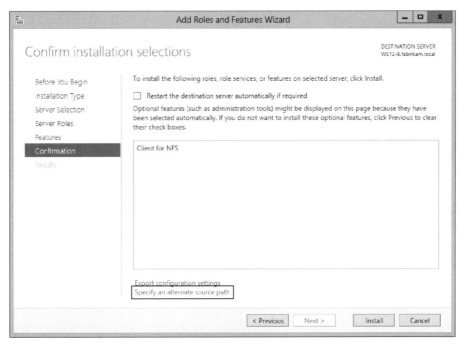

FIGURE 1-6 Exporting an XML configuration file for use with Windows PowerShell.

7. After you click Install, the Installation Progress page displays installation progress, results, and messages such as warnings, failures, or postinstallation configuration steps that are required for the roles or features that you installed. In Windows Server 2012, you can close the Add Roles And Features Wizard while installation is in progress and view installation results or other messages in the Notifications area at the top of the Server Manager console. Click the Notifications flag icon to see more details about installations or other tasks that you are performing in Server Manager.

Deployment Image Servicing and Management

If you received your MCTS certification for Windows Server 2008 before the release of Windows Server 2008 R2, you might have missed hearing about the Deployment Image Servicing and Management (DISM) utility. DISM is an image configuration tool that first appeared in Windows 7 and Windows Server 2008 R2, and its functionality has expanded in

Windows Server 2012. DISM replaces several deployment tools that were used in Windows Server 2008 and Windows Vista, including PEimg, Intlcfg, ImageX, and Package Manager.

In Windows 8 and Windows Server 2012, DISM helps you service WIM, VHD, and the new VHDX file types.

You can use DISM with .wim files to do the following:

- Capture and apply Windows images
- Append and delete images in a .wim file
- Split a .wim file into several smaller files

You can use DISM with .wim, .vhd, or .vhdx files to do the following:

- Add, remove, and enumerate packages
- Add, remove, and enumerate drivers
- Enable or disable Windows features
- Upgrade a Windows image to a different edition
- Prepare a Windows PE image

An important thing to know about DISM is that you can use it to service online images and offline images. Servicing online images is essentially the same as configuring the local running installation of Windows.

> **MORE INFO**   Windows PowerShell in Windows 8 and Windows Server 2012 includes a new module for DISM. You can review the cmdlets in this new module by typing the command **Get-Command -Module Dism** at a command prompt. For more information about the new DISM module in Windows 8 and Windows Server 2012, visit *http://technet.microsoft .com/en-us/library/hh852126*.

Add features to and remove features from an offline image with DISM

Before you can service an offline image, you need to mount the image in the file structure, specifying the image by index or name. In Windows Server 2012, you can find the image names and indexes within an image file by using DISM with the /Get-ImageInfo switch. For example, to see the images within an image file named Install.wim that is stored in C:\images, type the following:

```
Dism /Get-ImageInfo /ImageFile:C:\images\install.wim
```

The output of this command is shown in Figure 1-7.

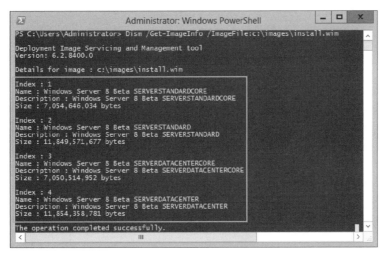

FIGURE 1-7 Obtaining image information from an image file.

Once you know the name or index of the desired image, you can mount it in a specified directory. For example, use the following command to mount the image with index 2 in the C:\images\offline directory:

```
Dism /Mount-Image /ImageFile:C:\images\install.wim /index:2 /MountDir:C:\images\offline
```

At this point, you can use the /Get-Features switch if necessary to determine the command name of the relevant features or to determine which features are enabled on the image:

```
Dism /Image:C:\images\offline /Get-Features
```

Finally, you can use DISM to point to the mounted image and enable a desired feature. You can use the /All argument to enable all the parent features in the same command. For example, to enable the Remote-Desktop-Services role and all parent features, type the following:

```
Dism /Image:C:\images\offline /Enable-Feature /FeatureName:Remote-Desktop-Services /All
```

If you want to remove a feature from or disable a feature on an offline image, use the /Disable-Feature switch. For example:

```
Dism /Image:C:\images\offline /Disable-Feature /FeatureName:Remote-Desktop-Services
```

EXAM TIP

You can use Dism and the /Add-Package option to apply to an image an update in the form of a .cab or .msu package. Use the /IgnoreCheck option if you don't want to verify the applicability of each package before installing. Use the /PreventPending option to skip the installation of the package if a system restart is required.

MORE INFO For more information on DISM in Windows Server 2012, visit *http://technet .microsoft.com/en-us/library/hh825236.aspx.*

Converting a server with a GUI to or from Server Core

As in Windows Server 2008 and Windows Server 2008 R2, Windows Setup in Windows Server 2012 allows you to choose one of two installation types: Server Core Installation or Server With A GUI (also called a full installation), as shown in Figure 1-8. One of the more interesting new features in Windows Server 2012 is the ability to convert a full installation to a Server Core Installation and vice versa.

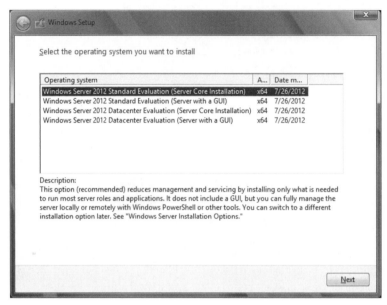

FIGURE 1-8 Windows Server 2012 includes a Server Core option and a Server with a GUI option.

You can switch between a Server Core installation and full installation in Windows Server 2012 because the difference between these installation options is contained in two specific Windows features that can be added or removed. The first feature, Graphical Management Tools and Infrastructure (Server-Gui-Mgmt-Infra), provides a minimal server interface and server management tools such as Server Manager and the Microsoft Management Console (MMC). The second feature, Server Graphical Shell (Server-Gui-Shell), is dependent on the first feature and provides the rest of the GUI experience, including Windows Explorer. In Figure 1-9, you can see these two features in the Add Roles And Features Wizard, on the Select Features page, beneath User Interfaces And Infrastructure.

To convert a full installation to a Server Core installation, just remove these two features in Server Manager. Note that removing the first feature will automatically remove the second, dependent feature.

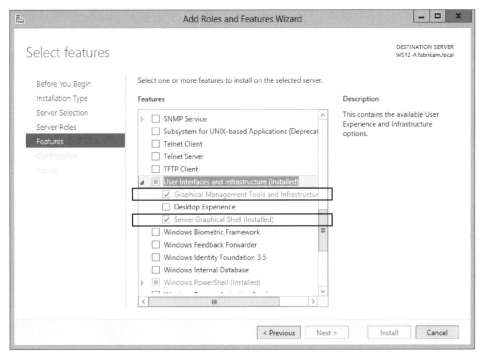

FIGURE 1-9 Two features are responsible for the difference between the full installation and Server Core installation.

> **NOTE**   As shown in Figure 1-9, Desktop Experience is a third available GUI feature. It builds on the Server Graphical Shell feature and is not installed by default in the Server with a GUI installation of Windows Server 2012. Desktop Experience makes available Windows 8 client features such as Windows Media Player, desktop themes, and photo management.

You can also remove these graphical interface features in Windows PowerShell. If you have deployed a full installation of Windows Server 2012 and want to convert it to a Server Core installation, run the following Windows PowerShell command:

```
Uninstall-WindowsFeature Server-Gui-Mgmt-Infra -restart
```

Remember that you only need to specify Server-Gui-Mgmt-Infra for removal to remove both this feature and Server-Gui-Shell. Once the graphical management tools and graphical shell have been removed, the server restarts. When you log back on, you are presented with the Server Core user interface.

The process can be reversed by replacing both features. You can do this from a remote server by using the Add Roles And Features Wizard in Server Manager. You can also do it locally by running the following Windows PowerShell command:

```
Install-WindowsFeature Server-Gui-Mgmt-Infra,Server-Gui-Shell -Restart
```

Note that when you install these two features from Windows PowerShell, you must specify them both.

> **NOTE** If you just want to configure basic settings in a **Server Core** installation of **Windows Server 2012** as opposed to adding or removing entire features, you can use the Sconfig utility. This utility, which appeared in Windows Server 2008 R2, enables you to set the domain/workgroup, computer name, Remote Desktop, network settings, date and time, Windows activation, Windows Update, and other similar settings.

Configuring a server with Minimal Server Interface

The Server With A GUI option is made of two cumulative features in Windows Server 2012 that are built on top of Server Core. You have the option of installing only the first of these graphical features: Graphical Management Tools and Infrastructure, or Server-Gui-Mgmt-Infra. Doing so results in what is called the Minimal Server Interface, shown in Figure 1-10. This form is not available when you install Windows Server 2012, but you can configure it through Server Manager or Windows PowerShell. To configure a server with the Minimal Server Interface in Server Manager, begin with a full installation and then just remove the Server Graphical Shell feature by using the Remove Roles And Features Wizard. In Windows PowerShell, you can either begin with a full installation and remove only the Server-Gui-Shell feature or begin with a Server Core installation and add only the Server-Gui-Mgmt-Infra feature.

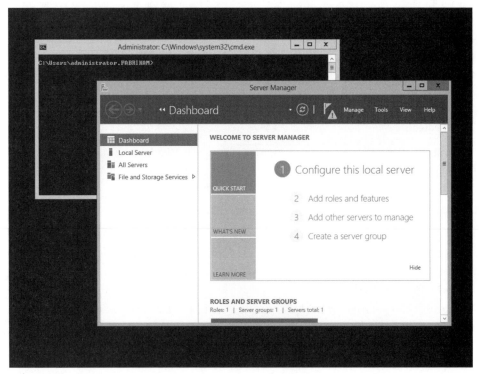

FIGURE 1-10 The new Minimal Server Interface option makes Server Manager and other administrative tools available without a desktop or Start screen.

The relationship between the Minimal Server Interface and the Server with a GUI installation levels is illustrated in Figure 1-11.

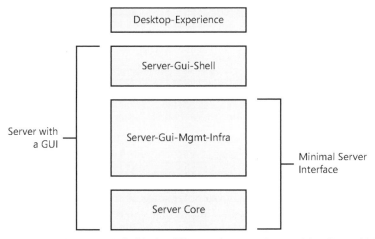

FIGURE 1-11 Server-Gui-Shell is the difference between Server with a GUI and Minimal Server Interface.

When you configure the Minimal Server Interface, the following elements are removed from the full installation:

- Desktop
- Start screen
- Windows Explorer
- Windows Internet Explorer

The following management tools *are* available in the Minimal Server Interface:

- Server Manager
- Microsoft Management Console (MMC) and snap-ins
- Subset of Control Panel

The Minimal Server Interface is a good option if you want to reduce the footprint of your installation but prefer not to be restricted to command-line–based management.

EXAM TIP

Expect to see questions on the 70-417 exam about converting between a Server Core, Server with a GUI, and Minimal Server Interface. Be sure to remember the command names of the features Server-Gui-Mgmt-Infra and Server-Gui-Shell, as well as how to remove the GUI by using Server Manager.

MORE INFO   For more information about converting between installation options in Windows Server 2012, see "Server Core and Full Server Integration Overview" at *http://technet.microsoft.com/en-us/library/hh831758.aspx* and "Windows Server Installation Options" at *http://technet.microsoft.com/en-us/library/hh831786.aspx*.

Configuring NIC teaming

NIC teaming, also known as Load Balancing and Failover (LBFO), is a new feature included in Windows Server 2012 that enables multiple network adapters on a server to be grouped into a team. NIC teaming has two purposes:

- Ensuring the availability of network connectivity if one adapter fails
- Aggregating network bandwidth across multiple network adapters

Before Windows Server 2012, implementing network adapter teaming on Windows Server required using third-party solutions from independent hardware vendors. However, network adapter teaming is now built into the Windows Server operating system and can therefore work across different NIC hardware types and manufacturers.

Windows NIC teaming supports up to 32 network adapters in a team and runs in three modes:

- **Static Teaming**   Also called Generic Teaming, this mode is based on IEEE 802.3ad draft v1 and is supported by most server-class Ethernet switches. It requires manual configuration of the switch and the server to identify which links form the team.

- **Switch Independent**   This mode allows each NIC in a team to connect to different switches.

- **LACP**   Also called Dynamic Teaming, this mode is based on IEEE 802.1ax and is supported by most enterprise-class switches. It allows teams to be automatically created through the Link Aggregation Control Protocol (LACP). LACP dynamically identifies links between the server and a specific switch. To use this mode, you generally need to enable LACP manually on the port of the switch.

NIC teaming can be enabled from Server Manager or by using Windows PowerShell. In Server Manager, you can begin by right-clicking the server you want to configure and selecting Configure NIC Teaming, as shown in Figure 1-12.

In the NIC Teaming dialog box that opens, select the network adapters you want to team and then right-click and select Add To New Team, as shown in Figure 1-13.

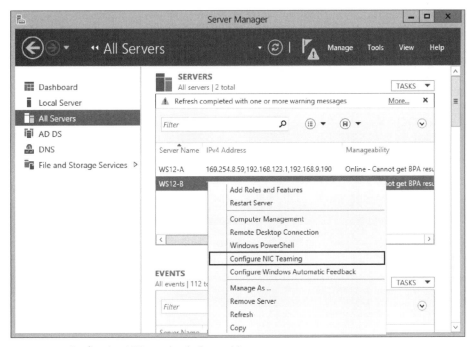

FIGURE 1-12 Configuring NIC teaming in Server Manager.

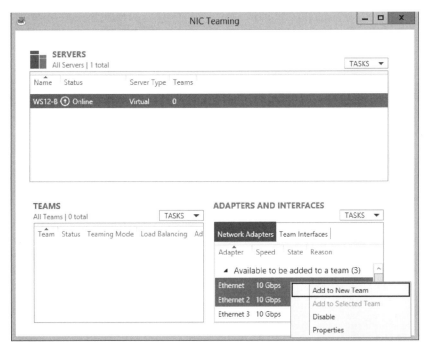

FIGURE 1-13 Adding network adapters to a new team.

In the New Team dialog box, shown in expanded mode in Figure 1-14, you can configure the teaming mode and other settings.

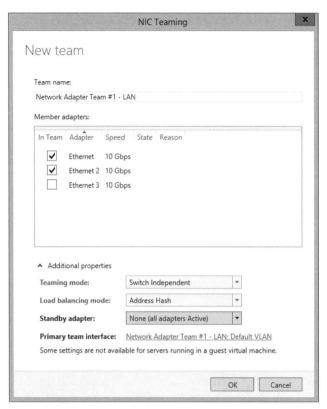

FIGURE 1-14 Configuring team properties.

Clicking OK completes the process and, if the process is successful, the new team will be displayed in both the Teams area and the Adapters And Interfaces area of the NIC Teaming dialog box, shown in Figure 1-15.

> **MORE INFO** For more information about NIC teaming in Windows Server 2012, see the NIC teaming overview at *http://technet.microsoft.com/en-us/library/hh831648.aspx*. For more in-depth information, search for the white paper titled "NIC Teaming (LBFO) in Windows Server 8 Beta" on *http://technet.microsoft.com*.

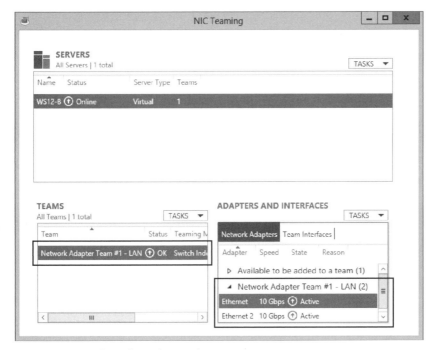

FIGURE 1-15 A newly configured network team.

To configure and manage NIC teaming in Windows PowerShell, use cmdlets such as New-NetLbfoTeam to add a new team or Get-NetLbfoTeam to display the properties of a team. The cmdlets for managing NIC teaming are defined in the Windows PowerShell module named NetLbfo. As Figure 1-16 shows, you can use the Get-Command cmdlet to display all the cmdlets defined in this module. You can then use the Get-Help cmdlet to learn the syntax for any of the functions displayed. For example, type **Get-Help New-NetLbfoTeam** to find out more about the New-NetLbfoTeam cmdlet.

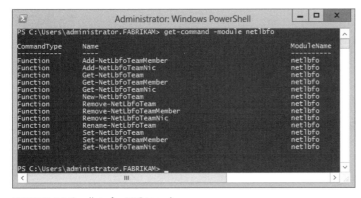

FIGURE 1-16 Cmdlets for NIC teaming.

EXAM TIP

Remember that each network adapter team is assigned a single IP address..

Objective summary

- The DISM.exe utility was introduced in Windows 7 and Windows Server 2008 R2. It enables you to service WIM files, VHD files, VHDX files, and online installations of Windows, including adding and removing features, packages, and drivers.

- New to Windows Server 2012 is the ability to deploy roles and features to remote servers.

  To perform this task in Windows PowerShell, use the following command:

  ```
  Install-WindowsFeature –Name <feature_name> -ComputerName <computer_name> -Restart
  ```

  To perform this task in Server Manager, you first need to add the remote server to the server pool. Then install the role or feature as you would to the local server.

- In Windows Server 2012, you can convert between a Server Core installation and a full (Server With A GUI) installation. To do so, you can begin from a full installation and then type the following command in Windows PowerShell:

  ```
  Uninstall-WindowsFeature Server-Gui-Mgmt-Infra -restart
  ```

  If you later want to reinstall the full graphical interface, type the following command in Windows PowerShell:

  ```
  Install-WindowsFeature Server-Gui-Mgmt-Infra,Server-Gui-Shell –Restart
  ```

- NIC teaming is a new feature in Windows Server 2012 that allows you to group two or more NICs to aggregate bandwidth and help ensure the availability of network connectivity. You can configure NIC teaming by using Server Manager or the New-NetLbfoTeam cmdlet.

Objective review

Answer the following questions to test your knowledge of the information in this objective. You can find the answers to these questions and explanations of why each answer choice is correct or incorrect in the "Answers" section at the end of the chapter.

1. You work in the IT department for Contoso.com, which has approximately 200 employees. Your manager has created a new image named Basic.wim that will be used to deploy Windows Server 2012. She has asked you to modify the image with an index of 1 within this image file so that the IIS-WebServer feature is disabled. You move

the Basic.wim file from network storage to your server, which is running Windows Server 2012. Which of the following actions should you take next?

   A.   Use DISM with the /Mount-Image option.

   B.   Use DISM with the /Disable-Feature option.

   C.   Use the Uninstall-WindowsFeature cmdlet without the –Remove option.

   D.   Use the Uninstall-WindowsFeature cmdlet with the –Remove option.

2.   You want to install Windows Server 2012 and configure an interface that includes Server Manager but not Windows Explorer. What should you do? (Choose two.)

   A.   Choose the Server Core installation of Windows Server 2012.

   B.   Choose the Server with a GUI installation of Windows Server 2012.

   C.   Remove the Graphical Management Tools and Infrastructure feature.

   D.   Add the Graphical Management Tools and Infrastructure feature.

3.   You have built a new server with network adapters from two different manufacturers. You want to use these two adapters to provide resiliency for the server's network connectivity, so that if one adapter fails, the other will continue to operate with the same configuration settings. What should you do?

   A.   Install the Network Load Balancing feature.

   B.   Install the Multipath I/O feature.

   C.   Use the New-NetLbfoTeam cmdlet.

   D.   Use the Set-NetConnectionProfile cmdlet.

Objective 1.3: Configure local storage

For the 70-417 exam, this objective is likely to focus on Storage Spaces, an interesting new feature that adds SAN-like flexibility to your storage. The topic of Storage Spaces can be broken down into primordial pools, new storage pools, and virtual disks.

This section covers the following topics:

   ■   Creating and configuring storage pools

   ■   Provisioning virtual disks

   ■   Designing Storage Spaces

Introducing Storage Spaces

Storage Spaces is a new feature in Windows Server 2012 that provides for a single server the same storage flexibility provided by a storage area network (SAN) by using inexpensive locally attached disks. Storage Spaces enables you to create storage pools from which you can provision storage as needed.

Once you've created a storage pool by using Storage Spaces, you can provision storage from the pool by creating virtual disks, also called logical unit numbers (LUNs). A virtual disk behaves like a physical disk except that it can span multiple physical disks within the storage pool.

Storage Spaces has the following requirements:

- Windows Server 2012.
- One physical drive is required to create a storage pool; a minimum of two physical drives is required to create a resilient mirror storage space.
- A minimum of three physical drives is required to create a storage space with resiliency through parity or three-way mirroring.
- Drives must be unpartitioned and unformatted.
- Drives must have at least 10 GB capacity.
- Drives can be attached either internally or externally (individually or in a just-a-bunch-of-disks [JBOD] enclosure). The following bus technologies are supported:
  - SATA (not possible to use in a failover cluster)
  - SCSI (not supported in a failover cluster)
  - Serial Attached SCSI (SAS) arrays that support SCSI Enclosure Services (SES)
  - USB (external drives for local storage only; not possible to use in a failover cluster or recommended for file servers)

Installing Storage Spaces

To install Storage Spaces, use the Add Roles And Features Wizard to add the File Server role service. This role service is found under File and iSCSI Services in the File and Storage Services role. You can also install the File Server role service by using Windows PowerShell as follows:

```
Install-WindowsFeature -Name FS-FileServer
```

> **NOTE** Storage Services, another role service of the File and Storage Services role, is always installed by default on Windows Server 2012 and provides general storage management functionality needed by other server roles.

Creating a storage pool

To create a storage pool, Storage Spaces requires a server to have at least one attached physical disk of at least 10 GB without any partitions or volumes. Any physical disks that meet these two criteria are automatically added to what is called the server's *primordial pool*. The *primordial pool* is the complete set of locally available disks from which a storage pool can be created. Figure 1-17 shows in Server Manager the primordial pools available to the server named WS12-A and WS12-B, respectively.

EXAM TIP

Physical disks that are initialized in Server Manager are automatically configured with the GUID Partition Table (GPT) partition style, not the Master Boot Record (MBR) partition style.

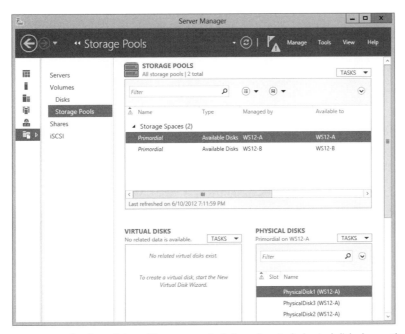

FIGURE 1-17 A primordial pool is composed of all unallocated physical disks larger than 10 GB available to a server.

You can use Server Manager or Windows PowerShell to configure your storage pools from a primordial pool. To create a storage pool in Windows PowerShell, use the New-StoragePool cmdlet. To create a new storage pool by using Server Manager, first make sure that you have navigated to File and Storage Services\Volumes\Storage Pools. Then select New Storage Pool from the Tasks menu in the Storage Pools area, as shown in Figure 1-18.

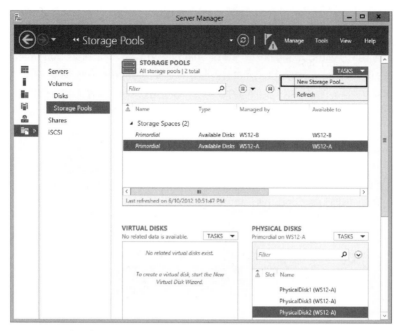

FIGURE 1-18 Creating a new storage pool.

This step opens the New Storage Pool Wizard. After specifying a server (primordial pool) and name for your new pool, you can select the physical disks you want to include in your pool, as shown in Figure 1-19.

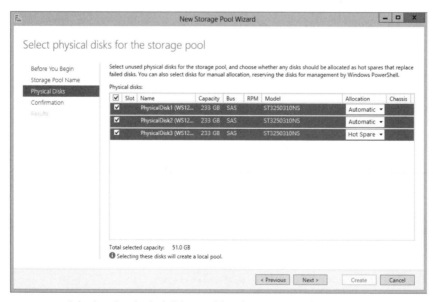

FIGURE 1-19 Selecting the physical disks to add to the storage pool.

EXAM TIP

Remember that if you want the storage pool to support failover clusters, you have to use SAS storage arrays that support SES.

For each disk that you add to the pool, you can choose one of the following allocation types:

- **Automatic**   This is the default setting. For this allocation type, the capacity on drives is set automatically.
- **Hot Spare**   Physical disks added as hot spares to a pool act as reserves that are not available for provisioning in the creation of virtual disks. If a failure occurs on a drive in a pool that has an available hot spare, the spare will be brought online to replace the failed drive.

Creating virtual disks

After a storage pool is created, you can use Server Manager to provision new virtual disks from this new available storage. These new virtual disks will appear as unallocated disks in Disk Management, from which you can then create volumes. Note that a virtual disk is the representation of virtualized storage and should not be confused with the VHD that is used in the context of Hyper-V or the iSCSI Target Server.

To create a virtual disk in Windows Powershell, use the New-VirtualDisk cmdlet.

To create a virtual disk in Server Manager, complete the following steps:

1. In Server Manager, choose File And Storage Services and then Storage Pools.
2. Locate a storage pool (not a primordial pool) that you want to use to support the new virtual disk.
3. Right-click the storage pool and select New Virtual Disk to start the New Virtual Disk Wizard, as shown in Figure 1-20.

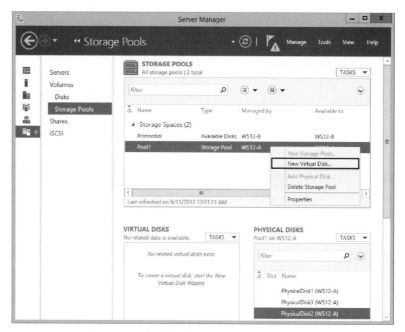

FIGURE 1-20 Creating a new virtual disk in a storage pool.

4. On the first pages of the wizard, verify that the correct server and storage pool are selected and provide a name and description for the new virtual disk.

5. On the Select The Storage Layout page (Figure 1-21), specify one of the following three data redundancy types for the virtual disk:

- **Simple**   A simple virtual disk provides data striping across physical disks but does not provide redundancy. Administrators should not host irreplaceable user data on a simple space. A simple space maximizes capacity and throughput and therefore can be good for hosting temp files or easily re-created data at a reduced cost.

- **Parity**   A parity virtual disk is similar to a hardware redundant array of inexpensive disks (RAID-5). Data, along with parity information, is striped across multiple physical disks. Parity enables Storage Spaces to continue to service read and write requests even when a drive has failed, and it provides this fault tolerance with efficient use of storage. A minimum of three physical disks is required for a parity virtual disk. Note that a parity disk cannot be used in a failover cluster.

- **Mirror**   A mirror virtual disk maintains either two or three copies of the data it hosts: two data copies for two-way mirror spaces and three data copies for three-way mirror spaces. All data writes are repeated on all physical disks to ensure that the copies are always current. Mirror spaces are attractive due to their greater data throughput and lower access latency compared to parity disks.

Make sure you understand the advantages and disadvantages of simple, parity, and mirror spaces.

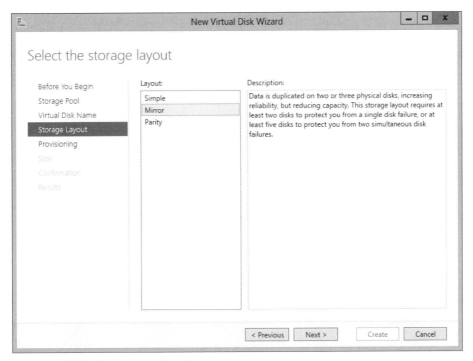

FIGURE 1-21 Selecting a storage layout.

6. On the Specify The Provisioning Type page, choose one of the following provisioning types:

   ■ **Thin**   Thin provisioning is a mechanism that enables storage capacity to remain unallocated until datasets require the storage. You specify a maximum size for the virtual disk, and the capacity of the virtual disk grows as needed. Thin provisioning optimizes utilization of available storage, but it adds a few extra I/Os that can cause an occasional latency increase.

   ■ **Fixed**   A fixed provisioned space allocates storage capacity upfront at the time the space is created.

7. On the Specify The Size Of The Virtual Disk page, choose a size for the virtual disk.

8. Confirm all the selections and then click Create.

   The new virtual disk appears in both Server Manager and Disk Management. The view in Server Manager is shown in Figure 1-22.

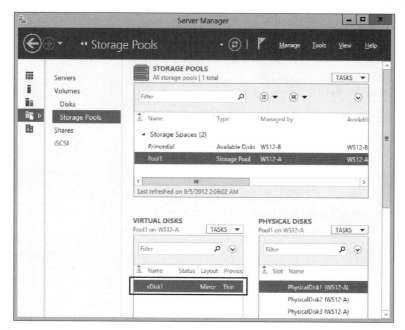

FIGURE 1-22 A new virtual disk created from a storage pool in Server Manager.

Objective summary

- Storage Spaces is a new feature in Windows Server 2012 that provides flexible provisioning of local storage to a server.

- All locally attached, unpartitioned physical disks with a capacity of at least 10 GB are automatically added to a server's primordial pool. A primordial pool is the complete set of locally available disks from which a storage pool can be created.

- Storage pools can be created from one or more physical disks. If you want to be able to create a mirrored virtual disk later from a storage pool, you need to add at least two physical disks to that storage pool. If you want to be able to create a virtual disk with parity later from a storage pool, you need to add at least three physical disks to that storage pool. In addition to these requirements, you need to add one physical disk to a storage pool for each hot spare you want to be available to the storage.

- Thin provisioning is a new feature in Windows Server 2012 that enables you to create drives that don't require all their storage capacity to be allocated immediately. Thin provisioning optimizes available storage capacity for virtual disks.

- When you create new virtual disks from a storage pool, they appear in Disk Management as new, unallocated disks.

Objective review

Answer the following questions to test your knowledge of the information in this objective. You can find the answers to these questions and explanations of why each answer choice is correct or incorrect in the "Answers" section at the end of the chapter.

1. You want to create a storage pool that can be used with a failover cluster. Which of the following disk types can you use?

   A. Internal SCSI

   B. Serial Attached SCSI

   C. Internal SATA

   D. iSCSI

2. You want to create a storage pool that maximizes available storage capacity and includes built-in fault tolerance and data resiliency. You also want to include a hot spare so that if a physical disk fails, another will be brought online to replace it.

   Which configuration should you choose for your storage pool? Assume you want to use the minimum number of physical disks possible.

   A. Three physical disks and a mirror layout

   B. Three physical disks and a parity layout

   C. Four physical disks and a mirror layout

   D. Four physical disks and a parity layout

3. You want to increase the size of a server's primordial pool. Which of the following disks can you use? (Choose all that apply.)

   A. A 20-GB external USB drive

   B. A 12-GB internal SCSI drive

   C. An 8-GB SATA drive

   D. A 5-GB Serial Attached SCSI drive

Thought experiment

You work as a network administrator in a company named Fabrikam.com. The Fabrikam Finance department requires a new server to support a web application that runs on Windows Server 2012. Your manager asks you to help design and plan for the server. She specifies the following requirements:

- **Operating system installation and configuration** The application requires a GUI to be installed. The server should not be limited to command-line administration, but it can be managed through remote administration. Within these limitations, the attack surface of the server must be minimized, and performance must be optimized.

- **Network** The network requires a single network connection with fault tolerance, so if one adapter fails there will be no loss in connectivity, and the IP address will not change.

- **Storage** You have an 8-bay disk array and eight 1-TB SATA disks available to attach to the new server. The disk array will be reserved for data storage. Your manager wants to use as few of these disks as possible while using the Storage Spaces feature to meet the following storage requirements:

  - Virtual Disk 1: Triple mirrored with a capacity of 100 GB

  - Virtual Disk 2: Parity disk with a capacity of 200 GB

  - One hot spare for each storage pool

How do you answer the following design questions from your manager? You can find the answers to these questions in the "Answers" section at the end of the chapter.

1. How should you reconcile the requirement for a GUI during installation with the need to minimize the attack surface?

2. Is this server an ideal candidate for a Minimal Server Interface configuration? Why or why not?

3. What are two possible solutions to meet the needs for fault-tolerant network connectivity?

4. What is the minimum number of physical disks you need to reserve for the application? What is the minimum number of storage pools you need?

Answers

This section contains the answers to the Objective Reviews and the Thought Experiment.

Objective 1.1: Review

1. **Correct Answers:** B, C
   A. **Incorrect:** You cannot install Windows Server 2012 on the existing server because Windows Server 2012 requires a 64-bit CPU.
   B. **Correct:** You need to replace the existing server with another that has a 64-bit CPU.
   C. **Correct**: You can use the Uninstall-WindowsFeature cmdlet with the –Remove option in Windows PowerShell to delete the binaries of unused roles and features.
   D. **Incorrect**: The DISM utility does not completely remove feature files from disk.

2. **Correct Answers:** A, B
   A. **Correct:** This command will delete from disk all the feature files for the Web Server role.
   B. **Correct:** This command will delete from disk all the feature files for the Web Server role except the Manifest file.
   C. **Incorrect:** You should not execute this command because it will remove the File Server role service from the server, and the server's only stated function is that of a file server.
   D. **Incorrect:** You should not execute this command because it will remove the File Server role service from the server, and the server's only stated function is that of a file server.

3. **Correct Answer:** A
   A. **Correct:** When you specify a path to source files with the Install-WindowsFeature cmdlet, you need to use the WIM: prefix at the beginning and specify an image index at the end.
   B. **Incorrect:** You need to use the WIM: prefix before the path to the source.
   C. **Incorrect:** You need to specify an image index after the path.
   D. **Incorrect:** You need to use the WIM: prefix before the path and specify an image index after the path.

Objective 1.2: Review

1. **Correct Answer:** A

   A. **Correct:** You need to mount the image file before you can service it.

   B. **Incorrect:** You need to mount the image before you can disable any feature in it.

   C. **Incorrect:** You can use Uninstall-WindowsFeature on a VHD file, but not on a WIM file.

   D. **Incorrect:** You can use Uninstall-WindowsFeature on a VHD file, but not on a WIM file.

2. **Correct Answers:** A, D

   A. **Correct:** The interface requirements describe the Minimal Server Interface. To configure this interface type, you can either start with a Server Core installation and add Graphical Management Tools and Infrastructure or start with a Server with a GUI and remove Server Graphical Shell. Removing Server Graphical Shell is not an answer choice, so you have to start with a Server Core.

   B. **Incorrect:** Removing Server Graphical Shell is not an answer choice, so you cannot start with a full installation of Windows Server 2012.

   C. **Incorrect:** Removing the Graphical Management Tools and Infrastructure feature would transform a full installation into a Server Core installation. The Server Core installation would not make Server Manager available.

   D. **Correct:** The Graphical Management Tools and Infrastructure feature includes Server Manager and some other basic administrative tools, but it does not include Windows Explorer. Adding this feature to a Server Core installation would result in the desired configuration.

3. **Correct Answer:** C

   A. **Incorrect:** Network Load Balancing is used to configure many different servers to answer requests for a service at a single address.

   B. **Incorrect:** Multipath I/O is used to provide multiple data paths to a storage device.

   C. **Correct:** This cmdlet is used to create a new NIC team. NIC teaming is used to provide failure resiliency to physical network connections.

   D. **Incorrect:** This cmdlet is used to set a profile to a network connection. It is not used to provide failure resiliency to physical network connections.

Objective 1.3: Review

1. **Correct Answer:** B

   A. **Incorrect:** SCSI disks cannot be used in failover clusters.

   B. **Correct:** Serial Attached SCSI (SAS) disks can be used to create a storage pool that can support a failover cluster.

   C. **Incorrect:** SATA disks cannot be used in failover clusters.

   D. **Incorrect:** iSCSI disks cannot be used to create a storage pool that can support a failover cluster.

2. **Correct Answer:** D

   A. **Incorrect:** You want a parity layout so that the storage capacity is maximized.

   B. **Incorrect:** You need four physical disks: three to support the parity layout and a fourth for the hot spare.

   C. **Incorrect:** You want a parity layout so that the storage capacity is maximized.

   D. **Correct:** You want a parity layout so that the storage capacity is maximized, and you need four physical disks: three to support the parity layout and a fourth for the hot spare.

3. **Correct Answers:** A, B

   A. **Correct:** You can use external USB drives in storage pools as long as they are at least 10 GB.

   B. **Correct:** You can use SCSI drives in storage pools as long as they are at least 10 GB.

   C. **Incorrect:** You can use SATA drives in storage pools, but they need to be at least 10 GB.

   D. **Incorrect:** You can use Serial Attached SCSI drives in storage pools, but they need to be at least 10 GB.

Thought experiment

1. You can first install Windows Server 2012 with a full GUI and then install the application. After you install the application, you can remove the GUI features.

2. This is not an ideal candidate for a Minimal Server Interface configuration because even though its administration should not be restricted to the command line, it can be managed through a GUI on remote computers. The requirements of a minimal attack surface and optimal performance suggest that a Server Core installation is a better fit for this scenario.

3. Two possible solutions to meet the requirements for network fault tolerance are the built-in NIC teaming feature of Windows Server 2012 and NIC teaming provided by an independent hardware vendor of network adapters.

4. You need four disks to meet the requirements of this configuration. You can create both virtual disks from one storage pool. Both these virtual disks require three physical disks, but they can be provisioned from the same pool. The hot spare requires a fourth, separate physical disk to be assigned to the storage pool.

CHAPTER 2

Configure server roles and features

The 70-417 exam distills three other exams (70-410, 70-411, and 70-412) into one exam that is largely concentrated on new features in Windows Server 2012. This chapter is a case in point. The Configure Server Roles and Features domain is taken from the 70-410 exam, but only one of the three original objectives in this domain includes significant changes since the last version of Windows Server. Therefore, the questions you see from the Configure Server Roles and Features domain on the 70-417 exam will fall entirely or almost entirely within Objective 2.1: the topic of remote management.

Objectives in this chapter:

- Objective 2.1: Configure servers for remote management.

Objective 2.1: Configure servers for remote management

Windows Server 2012 is much better suited to administering remote servers on the network than any of its predecessors. It's not only because Windows Server 2012 offers new capabilities in remote management; it's also because, behind the scenes, existing technologies have been revised to simplify remote management.

As you study this section for the exam, above all do not rely on what you learned for Windows Server 2008 and Windows Server 2008 R2. Some features might look the same, but they have changed. Examples include the inbound rules you may use to enable various types of remote management, the function of a particular command, and the names of the relevant Group Policy settings.

> **This section covers the following topics:**
> - Remote management with Server Manager
> - Configuring various server types for remote management
> - Configuring Group Policy to enforce remote management settings

Managing multiple servers by using Server Manager

The new Server Manager in Windows Server 2012 reveals big changes, both cosmetic and functional, and some of these changes are relevant to the 70-417 exam. The most significant of these new features is that you can now use Server Manager to manage multiple servers, as shown in Figure 2-1. One way you can use Server Manager to manage multiple servers is through the All Servers option in the navigation pane. You can also use the Create Server Group option on the Manage menu to create server groups, which are custom pages in Server Manager that allow you to manage subsets of your servers, such as all your DNS servers. Finally, you can multiselect servers on Server Manager pages, which enables you to perform some actions simultaneously on all the servers you selected.

FIGURE 2-1 Server Manager is a multiserver management tool in Windows Server 2012.

> **MORE INFO** See Chapter 1, "Install and configure servers," for information about how to add servers to the All Servers page in Server Manager.

Remote management tasks through All Servers

After you add remote servers to Server Manager, you can manage those servers from your local Server Manager console as long as they are enabled for remote management. Figure 2-2 shows a menu of management tasks you can perform on remote servers listed in the All Servers – Servers section in Server Manager. (These servers could also be added to a custom server group you create.) These tasks include adding roles and features, opening Computer Management (to review event logs, for example), opening a Windows PowerShell prompt on the remote server, and configuring NIC teaming.

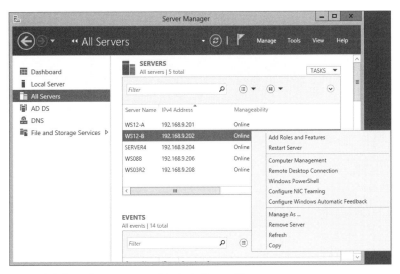

FIGURE 2-2 Remote management tasks in Server Manager.

If you right-click a server that is a domain controller, you can access a much larger set of administrative options, including the option to run many diagnostic tools, as shown in Figure 2-3.

EXAM TIP

None of the utilities shown in the shortcut menu in Figure 2-3 are new to Windows Server 2012, but make sure you review them all before taking the exam.

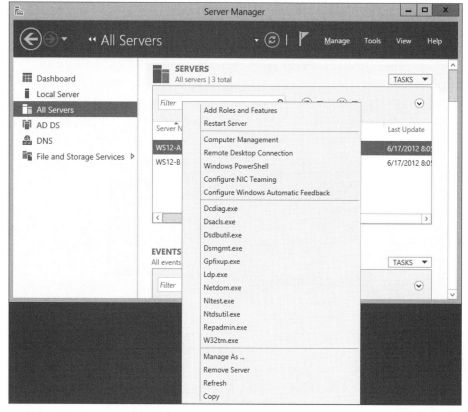

FIGURE 2-3 Remote management options on a domain controller.

On the All Servers page in Server Manager, you can use the following sections to perform everyday maintenance on the status of your servers:

- **Events** Use this section to check for errors and warnings on your servers without having to open a console on the remote machine.

- **Services** Use this section to check for stopped services.

- **Best Practices Analyzer** Use this section to compare the server configuration to a Best Practices standard.

- **Performance** Use this section to monitor CPU and memory usage data of a server over time. To start CPU and memory performance monitoring, first right-click a server and select Start Performance Counters, as shown in Figure 2-4.

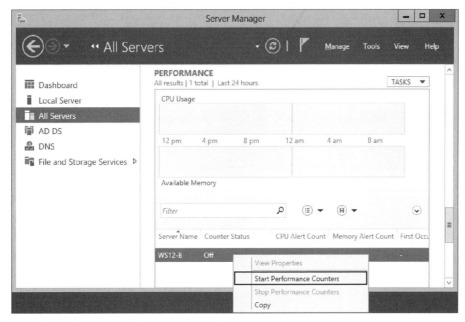

FIGURE 2-4 Monitoring CPU and memory performance.

- **Roles And Features**   Use this section to verify the installed roles and features on your servers. You can also use this section to remove roles and features.

The good news about remote management in Windows Server 2012 is that it's enabled and configured by default. You can start remotely managing servers out of the box as long as they are running Windows Server 2012, they are in the same domain, and you have the proper administrative privileges. This ease of remote management is a welcome change from both Windows Server 2008 and Windows Server 2008 R2, in which you needed to configure a server to manage it remotely with administrative tools.

Now the bad news. The fact that remote management is easy in Windows Server 2012 doesn't mean that questions about this topic on the exam will be easy. It's the exam writers' job to think of problems that require a reasonable amount of expertise to solve. For remote management, these problems are likely to include scenarios in which you need to reenable Windows Server 2012 for remote management at the command line, enforce remote management settings through Group Policy, and create proper firewall settings on downlevel servers such as those running Windows Server 2008.

Remote management types: DCOM and WinRM

A brief review of remote management technologies in Windows networks is helpful for exam preparation. Generally speaking, it's important to remember that remote management in Windows networks is an umbrella term. Different remote management tools use different underlying technologies and require different preconfiguration steps.

For both local and remote management, Windows Management Instrumentation (WMI) provides an administrative interface to scripts, programs, and built-in Windows tools. For remote management, WMI-based queries and configuration commands are typically passed through one of two protocols: Distributed Component Object Model (DCOM) or Windows Remote Management (WinRM). DCOM is an older, proprietary technology for software component communication across networks, and WinRM is the Microsoft implementation of an independent standard called WS-Management Protocol.

WMI OVER DCOM

Traditional console-based tools such as Microsoft Management Console (MMC) snap-ins and Computer Management rely on WMI over DCOM when used for remote management. When used remotely, DCOM tools require only that you open certain ports on the firewall of the server you want to manage. If you don't open those ports, you get a message like the one shown in Figure 2-5. This particular error message is helpful because it informs you exactly which predefined inbound rules you need to enable by using either the Windows Firewall with Advanced Security tool or the Enable-NetFirewallRule cmdlet on the remote server:

- COM+ Network Access (DCOM-In)
- All rules in the Remote Event Log Management group

These two sets of rules enable you to connect to most MMC consoles in Windows Server 2012. Other inbound rules you might need to create are Remote Volume Management (to use Disk Management remotely) and Windows Firewall Remote Management (to use Windows Firewall with Advanced Security remotely).

If you see a question about these DCOM-based remote management tools on the 70-417 exam, it's unlikely it will mention DCOM by name. Instead, the question will probably mention Computer Management or the name of another MMC console or snap-in.

EXAM TIP

Remember that if you need to remotely manage a computer running Windows Server 2012 by using Computer Management, you should enable certain firewall rules either by using Windows Firewall with Advanced Security or the Enable-NetFirewallRule cmdlet. (Enabling the remote management property is not sufficient.) This statement is true for both Server Core installations and Server with a GUI installations.

FIGURE 2-5 If you get this message, you have likely tried to use an MMC console for remote management without opening the proper ports.

WMI OVER WINRM

The second type of protocol for accessing WMI is WinRM. WinRM isn't new, but within Windows Server there's been a movement toward WinRM-based tools and away from DCOM since Windows Server 2008. WinRM, as you might remember, is a Windows service. The most notable tools that use WinRM for remote management are Windows PowerShell, WinRS (Windows Remote Shell), and Server Manager in Windows Server 2012.

EXAM TIP

Even though it's not new, you should remember the WinRS command for the exam. Use WinRS with the /r switch to specify the target computer on which you want to run another command. For example, type **winrs /r:myserver ipconfig** to run Ipconfig on a server named Myserver.

From an exam standpoint, it's important to know that because WinRM is a service, when a WinRM tool fails, the underlying cause could be that the WinRM service has stopped. (Note that WinRM by default starts automatically in Windows Server 2008, Windows Server 2008 R2, and Windows Server 2012.)

There are a few other important points to remember about WinRM. WinRM tools are firewall-friendly because they communicate over a single port: either 5985 over HTTP or 5986 over HTTPS. (Yes, you read that right: the usual ports 80 and 443 are avoided for security reasons.) Besides requiring a single port to be open for communication, WinRM also requires a WinRM listener to be enabled on the server you want to manage remotely. As you might remember, both the listener and the port can be configured at the same time by running the simple command Winrm Quickconfig at an elevated command prompt on the server you want to manage. (On servers running Windows Server 2012, however, this step is normally not required because WinRM is enabled by default.)

Reenabling Windows Server 2012 for remote management through Server Manager

As mentioned earlier in this chapter, remote management is enabled by default in Windows Server 2012. This behavior is governed in the GUI by the Remote Management property in Server Manager. However, this property enables only WinRM-based remote management, not DCOM-based administration. As a result, by default you can open a Windows PowerShell prompt on a remote server running Windows Server 2012 or restart a remote server running Windows Server 2012 because both of these options rely on WinRM. However, you receive an error message if you attempt to open Computer Management without opening the needed ports on the remote server, even though this option appears on the shortcut menu of a server that has been added to Server Manager (as shown in Figure 2-2 and Figure 2-3).

If you discover that you aren't able to use Server Manager to remotely manage a server running Windows Server 2012, it's possible that remote management has been disabled manually. If the server is running either a Server with a GUI installation or Minimal Server Interface, you can reenable this functionality in the Server Manager interface on that remote server. To do so, perform the following steps:

1. In Server Manager, in the Properties area of the Local Server page, click the hyperlink for the Remote Management property, as shown in Figure 2-6.

FIGURE 2-6 Reenabling remote management for Server Manager.

2. In the dialog box that opens, select Enable Remote Management Of This Server From Other Computers and then click OK.

Although you need to know how to perform this quick procedure, it might be a bit too straightforward to appear in an exam question. It's more likely you will see a question in which you need to know how to reenable remote management at the command prompt:

```
Configure-SMRemoting.exe -Enable
```

If you want to disable remote Server Manager management, type the following:

```
Configure-SMRemoting.exe -Disable
```

> **NOTE** You can also use Configure-SMRemoting -Get to view the current remote management setting on the server.

Note also that in previous versions of Windows Server, remote Server Manager management required many open ports, and Configure-SMRemoting was a Windows PowerShell script that opened all those ports. In Windows Server 2012, remote Server Manager management relies only on WinRM for most features (such as deploying roles, restarting, and Windows PowerShell) and on DCOM for some additional features (such as Computer Management). Consistent with this more efficient remote management method, Configure-SMRemoting configures only WinRM in Windows Server 2012, and is now the equivalent of the command Winrm Quickconfig. As when you enable remote management in the interface or by using Winrm Quickconfig, if you enable remote management by using Configure-SMRemoting, you still need to enable the DCOM ports manually later if you want more complete remote management functionality by using MMC consoles.

ENABLING REMOTE MANAGEMENT ON SERVER CORE WITH SCONFIG

Sconfig is a text-based configuration tool that is available in the Server Core version of Windows Server. Sconfig first appeared in Windows Server 2008 R2, so if you received your MCTS in Windows Server 2008, you might have missed this handy utility.

Using Sconfig is easy. Just type **Sconfig** at the command prompt in Server Core, and you get a menu of self-explanatory configuration options, one of which (choice 4) is to configure remote management, as shown in Figure 2-7.

FIGURE 2-7 The Sconfig tool makes it easy to enable remote management in Server Core.

Again, like Winrm Quickconfig and Configure-SMRemoting, enabling remote management in Sconfig configures only WinRM-based remote management.

> **NOTE** Local administrator accounts other than the built-in Administrator account might not have rights to manage a server remotely, even if remote management is enabled. The Remote User Account Control (UAC) LocalAccountTokenFilterPolicy registry setting must be configured to allow local accounts of the Administrators group other than the built-in Administrator account to remotely manage the server.

Configuring remote management of earlier versions of Windows Server

Server Manager can be used to remotely administer computers running versions of Windows Server older than Windows Server 2012. For Windows Server 2008 and Windows Server 2008 R2, Server Manager can be used to perform many of the tasks available in Server Manager, with the notable exception of adding or removing roles. To manage remote servers that are running Windows Server 2008 or Windows Server 2008 R2, you must first install the following updates, in the order shown:

1. .NET Framework 4

2. Windows Management Framework 3.0

   The Windows Management Framework 3.0 download package updates WMI providers on Windows Server 2008 and Windows Server 2008 R2. The updated WMI providers enable Server Manager to collect information about roles and features that are installed on the managed servers.

3. The performance update associated with Knowledge Base (KB) article 2682011 (or a superseding update), which enables Server Manager to collect performance data from Windows Server 2008 and Windows Server 2008 R2.

EXAM TIP

The first two updates—.NET Framework 4 and Windows Management Framework 3.0—are the ones you definitely have to remember for the test.

Installing these updates makes these operating systems compatible with Server Manager in Windows Server 2012. To configure the servers for remote management, run the Winrm Quickconfig command and (optionally) create the inbound firewall rules needed to support MMC traffic. As an alternative to running the Winrm Quickconfig command, you also can perform the following steps:

1. Open an elevated Windows PowerShell prompt.
2. Type **Set-ExecutionPolicy RemoteSigned**.
3. Type **Configure-SMRemoting.ps1 -force -enable**.

Using Group Policy to enable remote management

The most efficient way to configure remote management on multiple servers is to use Group Policy. Through Group Policy you can achieve two things: create WinRM listeners on IP address ranges of your choice and create inbound firewall rules allowing WinRM and DCOM traffic. These steps are described in the following procedure:

1. In a Group Policy object (GPO) editor, navigate to Computer Configuration \Administrative Templates\Windows Components\Windows Remote Management and then select WinRM Service. This location within a GPO is shown in Figure 2-8.

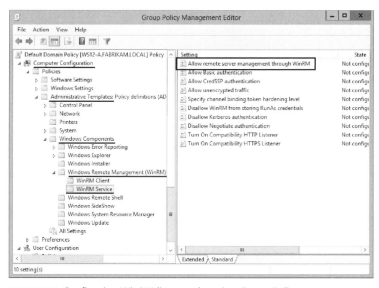

FIGURE 2-8 Configuring WinRM listeners by using Group Policy.

2. In the Details pane, double-click Allow Remote Server Management Through WinRM.

3. In the dialog box that opens (shown in Figure 2-9), select Enabled.

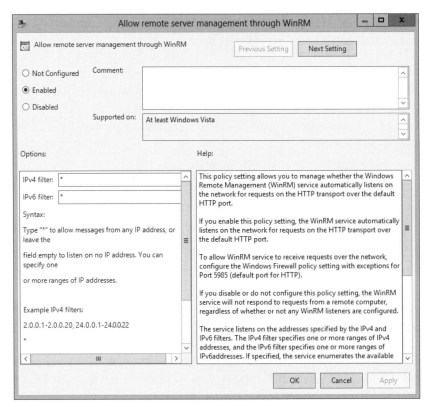

FIGURE 2-9 Configuring WinRM in Group Policy.

4. In the IPv4 Filter and IPv6 Filter text boxes, type the IP addresses on which you want to enable remote management through WinRM. If you want to enable remote management on all IP addresses, type *****.

5. Click OK.

6. In the GPO console tree, navigate to Computer Configuration\Windows Settings \Security Settings\Windows Firewall With Advanced Security\Windows Firewall With Advanced Security.

7. Right-click Inbound Rules and then click New Rule.

8. In the New Inbound Rule Wizard, on the Rule Type page, select Predefined.

9. On the Predefined drop-down menu, select Remote Event Log Management. Click Next.

10. On the Predefined Rules page, click Next to accept the new rules.

11. On the Action page, leave Allow The Connection as the default selection and then click Finish.

12. Repeat steps 7 through 11 to create new inbound rules for the following predefined rule types:

- Windows Remote Management
- COM+ Network Access
- Remote Volume Management
- Windows Firewall Remote Management

A GPO configured with these inbound firewall rules is shown in Figure 2-10.

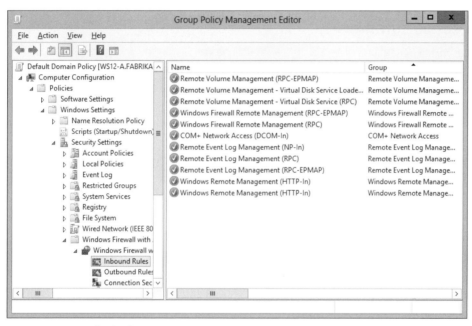

FIGURE 2-10 Firewall rules for remote management.

Remote Server Administration Tools for Windows 8

To support remote server management from client computers, you can download and install Remote Server Administration Tools for Windows 8. Remote Server Administration Tools for Windows 8 includes Server Manager, MMC snap-ins, consoles, Windows PowerShell, and some command-line tools for managing roles and features that run on Windows Server 2012.

Objective summary

- Remote management based on the WinRM service is enabled and configured by default in Windows Server 2012. This is a change from earlier versions of Windows Server.

- Server Manager in Windows Server 2012 enables you to manage multiple servers, including deploying roles to remove servers and opening a remote Windows PowerShell session.

- MMC consoles rely on DCOM as opposed to WinRM, so you need to enable different inbound firewall rules to use them for remote management. The number of inbound rules you need to enable has been greatly reduced in Windows Server 2012.

- Servers running previous versions of Windows Server can be managed remotely in Server Manager. To take full advantage of the administrative tasks and information available, you need to update these servers with .NET Framework 4 and Windows Management Framework 3.0.

- The best way to configure multiple servers for remote management is to use Group Policy. By using Group Policy, you can configure WinRM and create all the inbound firewall rules you need to support your remote management.

Objective review

Answer the following questions to test your knowledge of the information in this objective. You can find the answers to these questions and explanations of why each answer choice is correct or incorrect in the "Answers" section at the end of the chapter.

1. A server named SC2012 is running a Server Core installation of Windows Server 2012. You want to manage SC2012 remotely by using Server Manager.

   Which of the following will *not* help you achieve your goal?

   A. Configure-SMRemoting.exe

   B. Sconfig.exe

   C. Winrm Quickconfig

   D. Repadmin.exe

2. Your company network includes 25 servers running either Windows Server 2012 or Windows Server 2008 R2 in a single domain. The servers running Windows Server 2008 R2 have been updated with Windows Management Framework 3.0. You want to configure all these servers for remote management by using Windows PowerShell. What should you do? (Choose all that apply.)

   A. Enable the Allow Remote Server Management Through WinRM setting in Group Policy.

   B. Enable the Allow Remote Shell Access setting in Group Policy.

   C. Configure an inbound firewall policy rule for COM+ Remote Administration.

   D. Configure an inbound firewall policy rule for Windows Remote Management.

3. All your servers are running Windows Server 2012 and are enabled for remote management. You want to remotely manage three of these servers from a server named Admin01. However, when you attempt to manage remote servers through Computer Management on Admin01, you receive error messages.

   You create a GPO named Remote Computer Management Firewall Rules and link it to the domain. You now want to use the GPO to create predefined firewall rules in Windows Firewall with Advanced Security. You want to create only the predefined firewall rules that open the ports necessary for remote management through Computer Management. Which of the following predefined inbound rules should you enable? (Choose all that apply.)

   A. COM+ Network Access

   B. Remote Event Log Management

   C. Remote Volume Management

   D. WMI

Thought experiment

You are a network administrator at Fabrikam.com, which has a network that includes 20 servers and 250 clients, all of which belong to the Fabrikam.com domain. Ten of the servers are running Windows Server 2012, and ten are running Windows Server 2008 R2. All clients are running Windows 8.

The IT department is instituting a policy that removes IT personnel from the server room for most day-to-day administration. Most administration of all servers will now be conducted remotely by using Server Manager and various MMC consoles. Currently, administration is conducted locally in the server room or by using a Remote Desktop connection. The remote management settings on all servers remain at their original defaults.

1. All your servers are located in the server room. Which tool should you use to administer servers remotely from computers running Windows 8?

2. Which inbound rules do you need to create or enable on the servers running Windows Server 2012 to enable remote management by using Server Manager?

3. You want to be able to remotely manage the servers running Windows Server 2012 by using Computer Management, Disk Management, and Windows Firewall with Advanced Security. Which inbound rules should you enable in Group Policy?

4. You run the Winrm Quickconfig command on your servers running Windows Server 2008 R2. However, you find that you cannot manage these servers remotely by using Server Manager. In addition, some MMC administration tools don't work as they do on the servers running Windows Server 2012. How should you fix this problem?

Answers

This section contains the answers to the Objective Review and the Thought Experiment.

Objective 2.1: Review

1. **Correct Answer:** D

    A. **Incorrect:** This command, when used with the –enable parameter, enables remote management on Windows Server 2012.

    B. **Incorrect:** This command opens a utility in Server Core that allows you to enable remote management of the local server.

    C. **Incorrect:** This command enables remote management on Windows Server 2012.

    D. **Correct:** This tool helps administrators diagnose Active Directory replication problems between domain controllers. It doesn't help you enable remote management.

2. **Correct Answers:** A, D

    A. **Correct:** Remote management by using Windows PowerShell relies on the WinRM service. You can use this policy setting to configure WinRM listeners on your servers.

    B. **Incorrect:** This policy setting does not affect Windows PowerShell.

    C. **Incorrect:** This firewall rule does not open any of the ports needed by Windows PowerShell.

    D. **Correct:** This firewall rule opens the port needed for WinRM-based communication and is required for Windows PowerShell remote management.

3. **Correct Answers:** A, B, C

    A. **Correct:** This predefined rule enables you to connect to a remote computer by using Computer Management and use a few system tools such as Shared Folders and Local Users and Groups.

    B. **Correct:** This predefined rule group enables you to manage computers remotely in Computer Management by using the Event Viewer and Task Scheduler system tools.

    C. **Correct:** This predefined rule group enables you to use Disk Management remotely in Computer Management.

    D. **Incorrect:** This predefined rule doesn't enable you to use any tools in Computer Management.

Thought experiment

1. You should use Remote Server Administration Tools for Windows 8.

2. You don't need to create or enable any inbound rules. Servers running Windows Server 2012 have the required rules enabled by default.

3. You should enable COM+ Network Access (DCOM-In), Remote Event Log Management, Remote Volume Management, and Windows Firewall Remote Management.

4. Install .NET Framework 4, Windows Management Framework 3.0, and the update associated with KB article 2682011.

CHAPTER 3

Configure Hyper-V

I f you were to name the server role that has changed most between Microsoft Windows
Server 2008 R2 and Windows Server 2012, you'd have to say Hyper-V. First, Hyper-V now
has its own Windows PowerShell module, so the role is completely manageable at the
Windows PowerShell prompt. Beyond this new command-line manageability, there are
improvements in memory configuration, storage, Resource Metering, security, extensibility,
and other areas (such as fault tolerance) that aren't covered in this domain.

The good news is that none of these new features are particularly difficult to understand,
at least at the level on which they will be tested for the 70-417 exam. Studying this area
should therefore pay off well.

Objectives in this chapter:

- Objective 3.1: Create and configure virtual machine settings
- Objective 3.2: Create and configure virtual machine storage
- Objective 3.3: Create and configure virtual networks

Objective 3.1: Create and configure virtual machine settings

At the time of this writing, Microsoft mentions three specific features at least partially new
to Windows Server 2012 in the description of this exam objective: Dynamic Memory, Smart
Paging, and Resource Metering.

More broadly, it's important to know that all settings in Hyper-V can now be configured
at the Windows PowerShell prompt. From that perspective, every virtual machine setting is
new and every configuration option is fair game for the exam. You should be sure, therefore, to supplement your study of the new features in Windows Server 2012 Hyper-V with
a review of the new cmdlets related to virtual machine (VM) configuration in the Hyper-V
module.

This section covers the following topics:

- Hyper-V module in Windows PowerShell
- Dynamic Memory
- Smart Paging
- Resource Metering

Hyper-V Module in Windows PowerShell

As mentioned, Windows PowerShell in Windows Server 2012 includes a new module called Hyper-V that provides a command-line administration interface for almost all VM settings. It's uncertain how many of these cmdlets will show up on the 70-417 exam, and there are too many of them (over 150) to document them all here.

Instead, you can use Get-Command to review the names of these cmdlets so that you can at least recognize the most important ones. You can sort the output to group them by the cmdlet noun, the object of configuration. For example, to see a list of all cmdlets in the module, type the following:

```
Get-Command -Module Hyper-V | Sort Noun,Verb
```

If you want to see cmdlets that contain the string *VM* (and likely relate specifically to VM management and configuration), type the following:

```
Get-Command *VM* | Sort Noun,Verb
```

To further filter your results, you can use the wildcard character twice or more, as in the following example:

```
Get-Command *VM*adapter* | Sort Noun,Verb
```

You can then use Update-Help and Get-Help, with the –Examples or –Full option if you want, to get the latest documentation about any particular cmdlet that interests you.

Dynamic Memory

Dynamic Memory was introduced in Windows Server 2008 R2 Service Pack 1. Just one new configuration setting (Minimum RAM) has been added in Windows Server 2012, but you should be prepared to be tested on any or all of the feature's settings on the 70-417 exam.

If you haven't had the chance to learn about this feature yet, remember first of all the following point: Dynamic Memory pools the available RAM on a Hyper-V host for all running VMs for which Dynamic Memory is enabled. Using this pool, Dynamic Memory automatically modifies on the fly the amount of RAM assigned to each running VM as the need increases or decreases. The biggest benefit of Dynamic Memory is that it allows you to use your RAM resources highly efficiently, dramatically increasing the number of VMs you can run on that Hyper-V host. (Marketing materials talk about the benefit Dynamic Memory offers in "improving consolidation ratios" on your virtualization servers. It's good to know that phrase because exam question writers might use it.)

The second important concept you need to remember about Dynamic Memory is that starting a VM often requires more memory than does running the VM after it starts, and dynamic RAM assignment in Windows Server 2012 naturally mirrors these changing needs. If, for example, you have 6 GB of RAM on a server and try to start 10 VMs at once, you might get an error message regardless of whether Dynamic Memory is enabled. However, you must have Dynamic Memory enabled to make it possible to get them all up and running if you start them one at a time. The prototypical example that illustrates low memory usage after startup is virtual desktop infrastructure (VDI), where you might have a pool of unused virtual machines available in case several people happen to need a desktop all at once. (If you see a scenario about VDI and desktop pools, expect Dynamic Memory to somehow play a part in the solution.)

Now let's take a look at Dynamic Memory settings. They appear where you would expect, in the Memory section of a VM's settings in Hyper-V Manager, as shown in Figure 3-1. You also can enable and configure Dynamic Memory with Windows PowerShell by using the Set-VM cmdlet, which can be used to configure the various properties of a VM. Note that you can enable or disable Dynamic Memory only when the VM is in a stopped state. (Dynamic Memory does *not* mean you can manually adjust RAM settings while a VM is running.)

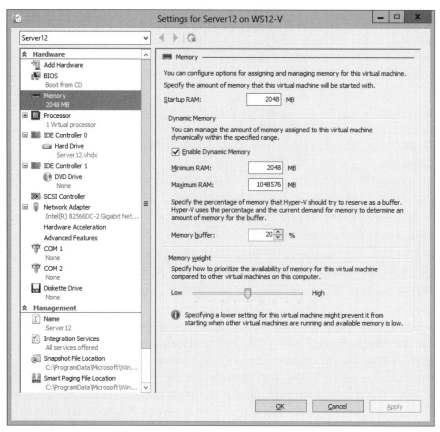

FIGURE 3-1 Dynamic Memory settings.

The settings here affect *how* memory is assigned dynamically. You need to understand the implications of these settings on behavior and performance:

- **Startup RAM** This value existed in Windows Server 2008 R2 SP1, but it had a slightly different meaning. On that operating system, the Startup RAM was both the amount of RAM used at startup and the minimum amount of RAM ever assigned to the VM.

  In Windows Server 2012, the Startup RAM setting is only the amount of RAM assigned at startup and is no longer the minimum RAM. If a running VM uses less RAM after startup, some of that RAM can now be reclaimed by other running VMs.

  Here is another important point to remember about Startup RAM: the more RAM you assign to a VM when it starts up, the faster it will be able to start up. But don't forget the flip side: if you set this level too high, you might temporarily (during startup) deprive other VMs of the RAM they need to perform at an acceptable level.

- **Minimum RAM** This is the only new setting that has been added since Windows Server 2008 R2 SP1, so make sure you understand it. If you have enabled Dynamic Memory on a VM running on a Windows Server 2012 host, by default this value is the same as the Startup RAM value. However, you can lower Minimum RAM to allow the amount of RAM allocated to the VM to decrease after startup.

Why would you want to manually lower the Minimum RAM level? On one hand, by allowing unused physical memory of a running VM to be reclaimed, you can make sure that physical memory is available to other VMs that might need it. On the other hand, by keeping the value higher, you can ensure that enough is available to the same VM when it restarts.

- **Maximum RAM**   This is the maximum amount of memory that can ever be dynamically assigned to the VM. Setting Maximum RAM is a balancing act. If you don't set this value high enough, the VM's performance could suffer. However, for a RAM-intensive workload, setting this value too high could deprive other VMs of needed RAM.

- **Memory Buffer**   This is the preferred amount of extra RAM (defined as a percentage) that is assigned to the system beyond what is necessary to run the active workload at any given point. The default is 20 percent. You don't normally have to change this setting, but if memory usage spikes intermittently on a VM, you might want to increase this percentage to help ensure that enough RAM is available when needed.

- **Memory Weight**   This parameter determines how available memory on the host is allocated among the different VMs running on the host. If you want to prioritize the performance and memory allocation of a given VM relative to other VMs, you would raise the Memory Weight setting on that VM.

NOTE   To review and configure Dynamic Memory settings in Windows PowerShell, use Get-VMMemory and Set-VMMemory.

Smart Paging

What if, with Dynamic Memory enabled, you have just enough RAM to start your VMs but not enough to restart a particular VM once they are all up and running? Maybe, for example, you used the last 256 MB of available RAM to start a VM running Microsoft Windows XP, and now you can't restart a VM running Windows 8, which requires 512 MB of RAM to start. To prevent this kind of scenario, Hyper-V in Windows Server 2012 introduces a new feature called Smart Paging. Smart Paging enables a VM that's being restarted to use disk resources temporarily on the host as a source for any additional memory needed to restart it. Once the VM has started successfully and its memory requirements decrease, Smart Paging releases the disk resources. The downside of Smart Paging, as you probably have guessed, is that performance is compromised. VMs restart, but slowly, with Smart Paging.

To minimize the performance impact of Smart Paging, Hyper-V uses it only when all of the following are true:

- The VM is being restarted.
- There is no available physical memory.
- No memory can be reclaimed from other VMs running on the host.

Smart Paging is *not* used in the following cases:

- A VM is being started from an "off state" (instead of a restart).
- Oversubscribing memory for a running VM is required.
- A VM is failing over in Hyper-V clusters.

Smart Paging is a new feature that is specifically mentioned in the objectives for the 70-417 exam, so don't be surprised if it appears as an important element in a test question. With this in mind, be aware that the only configuration option for Smart Paging relates to the storage location for the Smart Paging file. Why would the location of the Smart Paging file ever matter in a test question? Well, if the disk on which the Smart Paging file is stored becomes too full, there might not be enough disk space to allow a VM to restart. If this happens, the way to solve the problem would be to move the Smart Paging file to a disk with more space. (Assuming you can't add more RAM to the VM, of course.)

Resource Metering

Resource Metering is a new feature of Windows Server 2012 designed to make it easy to build tools that measure VM usage of CPU, memory, disk space, and network. This feature was primarily designed for hosting VMs for a customer. In such a scenario, you need to know how much of your computing resources are used so that you can charge the customer accordingly.

You can use Resource Metering in Windows Server 2012 to collect and report on historical resource usage of the following seven metrics:

- Average CPU usage by a VM
- Average physical memory usage by a VM
- Minimum physical memory usage by a VM
- Maximum physical memory usage by a VM
- Maximum amount of disk space allocated to a VM
- Total incoming network traffic for a virtual network adapter
- Total outgoing network traffic for a virtual network adapter

You can view this functionality in Windows PowerShell even though it is intended for use primarily with additional tools.

To enable Resource Metering on a VM, use the Enable-VMResourceMetering cmdlet. For example, to enable Resource Metering on a VM named VSrv1, type the following at a Windows PowerShell prompt:

```
Enable-VMResourceMetering -VMName VSrv1
```

At this point, the Resource Metering counters start running. To view all Resource Metering statistics on the VM since you ran the last command, use the Measure-VM cmdlet. For example, type the following to display the Resource Metering data on VSrv1 for all seven metrics:

```
Measure-VM -VMName VSrv1
```

Alternatively, you could save the usage statistics into a report by using this command:

```
$UtilizationReport = Get-VM VSrv1 | Measure-VM
```

You could then the display the contents of the report at a later time by using the following command:

```
Write-Output $UtilizationReport
```

To reset the counters to start counting usage from zero, you use the following command:

```
Reset-VMResourceMetering -VMName VSrv1
```

To stop the counters from running on VSrv1, type the following:

```
Disable-VMResourceMetering -VMName VSrv1
```

These metrics can be collected even when the VMs are moved between hosts by using Live Migration or when their storage is moved by using Storage Migration.

For the 70-417 exam, what's most important to remember about Resource Metering is that this feature allows you to measure CPU, memory, disk, and network usage on a particular VM. It's also a good idea to know the general steps required to configure Resource Metering, but don't worry about the specific syntax used in Windows PowerShell cmdlets.

> **NOTE**   If you want to measure Internet traffic as opposed to network traffic in general, you can use network metering port access control lists (ACLs), which are described later in this chapter.

> **MORE INFO**   For an overview of Resource Metering in Windows Server 2012, see the topic "Hyper-V Resource Metering Technical Preview" in the TechNet Library at *http://technet .microsoft.com/en-us/library/hh831661.aspx*. Also search for the specific Windows Power-Shell cmdlets on *http://technet .microsoft.com*.

Non-uniform memory access (NUMA) topology

NUMA is a new configuration node beneath the Processor node in a VM's settings. NUMA is a technology that improves system scalability by optimizing memory and memory bus usage in multiprocessor systems. In Windows Server 2012, VMs are NUMA-aware, which means that multiprocessor VMs can access memory resources in a more optimal and scalable way. Generally speaking, you don't need to change the default settings in the NUMA Topology configuration area because they are automatically configured correctly based on the host server's hardware. On rare occasions, however, it might be necessary to modify these settings if you have moved a VM between two physical hosts with different NUMA topologies. Configuring these settings is beyond the scope of the 70-417 exam, but you should know that the Use Hardware Topology button resets NUMA settings back to the defaults.

Objective summary

- In Windows Server 2012, almost all VM settings can be configured in Windows PowerShell.

- Dynamic Memory pools all the memory available on a host server for all VMs hosted on that server. Because computers tend to use more memory when they are starting than when they are running, Dynamic Memory enables you to use available RAM much more efficiently.

- Important Dynamic Memory settings include Startup RAM, Minimum RAM, and Maximum RAM.

- Smart Paging allows VMs to use virtual (paged) memory to complete a restart operation when insufficient physical memory is available.

- With the Resource Metering feature in Windows Server 2012, you can use the Enable-VMResourceMetering cmdlet to start metering the CPU, memory, disk, and network usage of a VM. To display usage statistics, use the Measure-VM cmdlet. To reset usage counters to zero, use Reset-VMResourceMetering. To disable Resource Metering, use Disable-VMResourceMetering.

Objective review

Answer the following questions to test your knowledge of the information in this objective. You can find the answers to these questions and explanations of why each answer choice is correct or incorrect in the "Answers" section at the end of the chapter.

1. A server named HYPV1 is running Windows Server 2012 and has been configured with the Hyper-V role. HYPV1 has 20 GB of RAM and is hosting 12 VMs. All VMs are running Windows Server 2012 and have Dynamic Memory enabled.

   One of the VMs hosted on HYPV1 is named VM1. VM1 is hosting a web application. VM1 averages five concurrent user connections to this web application, and users consider its performance acceptable.

   VM1 has the following memory settings:

   - Startup Memory: 1,024 MB
   - Minimum Memory: 384 MB

- Maximum Memory: 4,096 MB

- Memory Weight: Medium

You need to perform a scheduled restart of VM1 once per week. You have noticed during past scheduled restarts of VM1 that restarts have sometimes occurred only with the help of Smart Paging and have required several minutes to complete. You want to minimize downtime associated with restarting VM1 and reduce the likelihood that any restart operation will rely on Smart Paging. What should you do?

   A. Increase the Startup Memory on VM1.

   B. Increase the Minimum Memory setting on VM1.

   C. Decrease the Maximum Memory on other VMs.

   D. Change the Memory Weight setting on VM1 to High.

2. A server named HYPV2 is running Windows Server 2012 and has been configured with the Hyper-V role. HYPV2 has 16 GB of RAM and is hosting 10 VMs. All VMs are running Windows Server 2012 and have Dynamic Memory enabled.

   One of the VMs on HYPV2 is named VM2. VM2 hosts a little-used application that is used for testing only and is not used for any other purposes. You attempt to restart VM2 but receive an error message indicating that there is insufficient memory to perform the operation.

   You want to restart VM2 successfully. What should you do? (Choose all that apply.)

   A. Increase the Startup Memory setting on VM2.

   B. Decrease the Maximum Memory on other VMs.

   C. Increase the Memory Buffer % setting on VM2.

   D. Move the Smart Paging file to a disk with more space.

3. A server named HYPV3 is running Windows Server 2012 and has been configured with the Hyper-V role. HYPV3 hosts a VM named VM3. You have been measuring the CPU, memory, network, and disk space usage of VM3 for the past 24 hours. You would now like to display the collected usage data at the Windows PowerShell prompt.

   Which of the following commands should you type at an elevated Windows PowerShell prompt?

   A. Enable-VMResourceMetering -VMName VM3

   B. Disable-VMResourceMetering -VMName VM3

   C. Measure-VM -VMName VM3

   D. $UtilizationReport = Get-VM VSrv1 | Measure-VM

Objective 3.2: Create and configure virtual machine storage

There are only two new topics in this objective that are likely to be tested: VHDX and Virtual Fibre Channel. It's certain that VHDX questions are floating in the 70-417 question pool. This is an easy topic to understand, so studying this area should therefore pay off well.

> **This section covers the following topics:**
> - The benefits of the new VHDX format
> - The benefits of the new Virtual Fibre Channel adapter

New VHDX disk format

Virtual hard disk (VHD) files have a size limit of 2 TB, which can prevent you from virtualizing some workloads such as extra-large databases. To fix this problem, Windows Server 2012 introduces a new VHDX file format, which has a 64 TB limit.

Size is the biggest advantage of the VHDX, so if it appears in a test question, it will most likely be in the context of a scenario in which you need to support files that are larger than 2 TB. What is the disadvantage of VHDX? Backward compatibility. If you need to migrate storage to servers running Windows Server 2008 R2 or earlier, VHD is the way to go. Also note that the larger size of VHDX applies only to nonboot volumes. VHDX boot disks are also limited to 2 TB because of limitations found in the legacy AMI BIOS used in Hyper-V virtual machines.

Remember that VHDX is the default selection for a new VHD file, but you can opt to create a VHD just as easily, as shown in Figure 3-2.

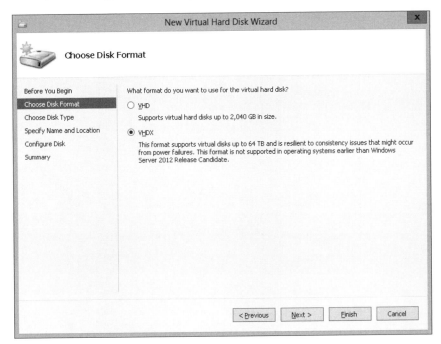

FIGURE 3-2 Creating a new VHDX.

You can also convert a disk from a VHDX to a VHD and vice versa as long as the disk isn't bigger than 2 TB. To do so, just select the virtual disk in the VM settings and click Edit, as shown in Figure 3-3.

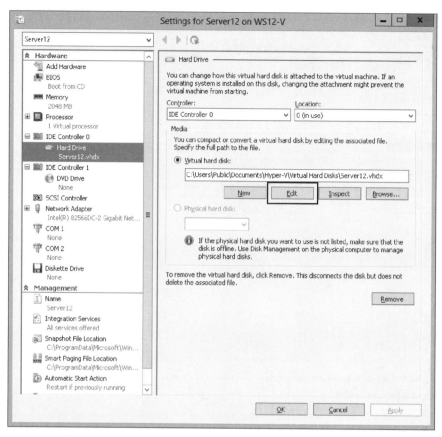

FIGURE 3-3 Converting a virtual hard disk to VHD or VHDX, step 1.

EXAM TIP

Remember the purpose of the Physical Hard Disk option shown in Figure 3-3. This option is often called a "pass-through disk" and has been available since Windows Server 2008. With a pass-through disk, you add a physical disk (as opposed to a VHD or VHDX) to a VM. As stated in the description of the feature in Figure 3-3, you need to take a physical disk offline before you can attach it to a VM as a pass-through disk.

Then, in the Edit Virtual Hard Disk Wizard, choose the Convert option, shown in Figure 3-4.

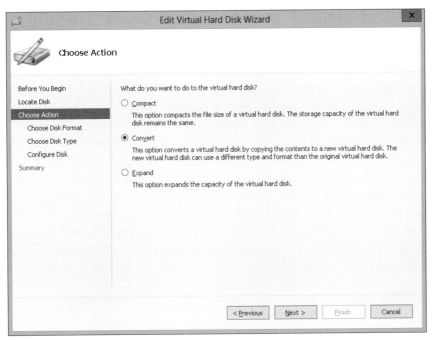

FIGURE 3-4 Converting a virtual hard disk to VHD or VHDX, step 2.

NOTE To convert a VHD to a VHDX file in Windows PowerShell, use the Convert-VHD cmdlet.

Although size is the biggest advantage of a VHDX, it isn't the only advantage. VHDX files also offer the following benefits:

- Improved resiliency from power failure thanks to a new disk log.
- Support for new low-cost storage options thanks to 4-KB sector disks.
- Better performance thanks to large block sizes.
- Support for user-defined file metadata. You could use metadata, for example, to include information about the service pack level of the guest operating system on the VM.

Any of these advantages could appear as requirements in a scenario question, so be sure to remember them.

MORE INFO For more information about the new VHDX format in Windows Server 2012, see the article titled "Hyper-V Virtual Hard Disk Format Technical Preview" in the TechNet Library at *http://technet.microsoft.com/en-us/library/hh831446.aspx*.

Virtual Fibre Channel adapter

Before Windows Server 2012, you could provision storage from a Fibre Channel storage area network (SAN) and then use it in a guest VM. However, you had to prepare everything in the host operating system so that the source of the storage was transparent to the guest.

What's new in Windows Server 2012 is that you can create a Fibre Channel adapter for your VM and then provision storage from your Fibre Channel SAN from within the guest operating system. This might be useful, for example, if you want to migrate to a virtual environment application that is already connected to specific logical unit numbers (LUNs) in your Fibre Channel SAN. Another advantage of the Fibre Channel adapter is that it allows you to cluster guest operating systems to provide high availability for VMs.

To configure virtual Fibre Channel, first use the Virtual SAN Manager option in the Actions pane of Hyper-V Manager to create a new virtual Fibre Channel SAN. Virtual Fibre Channel SANs are connected to one or more physical host bus adapters (HBAs). Then, add a new Fibre Channel adapter to the VM. To add a new Fibre Channel adapter to a VM, first open the settings of the VM and select Add Hardware from the menu on the left. Then select Fibre Channel Adapter and click Add, as shown in Figure 3-5.

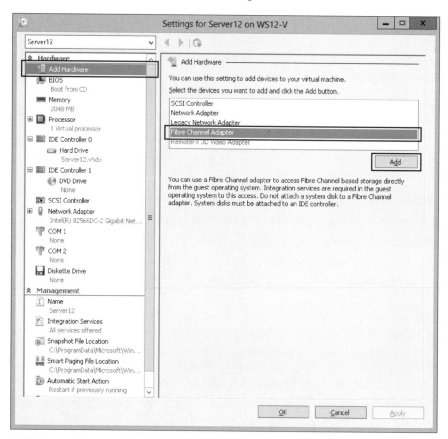

FIGURE 3-5 Adding a new virtual Fibre Channel adapter.

EXAM TIP

To configure a VM to connect to a Fibre Channel SAN, first create a virtual Fibre Channel SAN that connects to one or more physical HBAs.

You configure virtual Fibre Channel adapter settings by specifying a virtual SAN. Port addresses are supplied automatically, but you can edit them by clicking Edit Addresses. The port addresses include hexadecimal values representing the World Wide Node Name and World Wide Port Name, as shown in Figure 3-6.

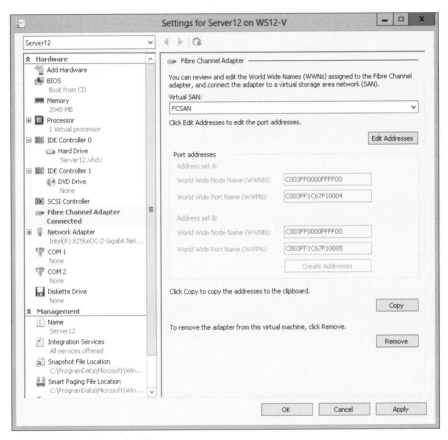

FIGURE 3-6 Fibre Channel settings.

The Fibre Channel adapter in Hyper-V includes a few limitations you need to know. First, the drivers for your host bus adapters (HBAs) have to support Virtual Fibre Channel. Some HBAs from Brocade and QLogic already include such updated drivers, and more vendors are expected to follow. Second, you can't use Virtual Fibre Channel to connect to boot media for your VMs. Finally, you can't use the Fibre Channel adapter with every guest operating system. The guest has to be running Windows Server 2008, Windows Server 2008 R2, or Windows Server 2012.

Objective summary

- Windows Server 2012 introduces a VHDX file, which has a 64 TB size limit. (VHD files have a 2 TB limit.) Other advantages of a VHDX are improved resiliency from power failures, user-defined metadata, and better performance.
- You can convert a VHD to a VHDX and vice versa.
- Hyper-V in Windows Server 2012 enables you to create virtual Fibre Channel adapters for virtual machines. If you have a Fibre Channel SAN and compatible HBA drivers, you can provision SAN storage from within a guest VM.

Objective review

Answer the following questions to test your knowledge of the information in this objective. You can find the answers to these questions and explanations of why each answer choice is correct or incorrect in the "Answers" section at the end of the chapter.

1. You have a VHD that is stored on a server running Windows Server 2012. The VHD is 1.5 TB in size and stores a rapidly growing database file that is 1.0 TB. You want to provide at least 4 TB of space for the database file. What should you do?

    A. Use the Edit Virtual Hard Disk Wizard and choose the Convert option.

    B. Use the Edit Virtual Hard Disk Wizard and choose the Expand option.

    C. Move the contents of the VHD to a new dynamically expanding disk.

    D. Move the contents of the VHD to a new differencing disk.

2. You work as a network administrator for Fabrikam.com. Fabrikam.com has a server room that includes 20 servers, 10 of which are virtualized on a server named HYPV4 running Windows Server 2012.

    The Fabrikam.com office recently experienced a power outage. After the power outage, the universal power supply connected to HYPV4 did not gracefully shut down HYPV4 or its 10 hosted virtual servers. Some VHDs were corrupted, which required you to restore the VHDs from backup, resulting in a loss of data.

You want to help ensure that future power outages do not corrupt data on your virtualized servers. What should you do?

    A. Configure NIC teaming for every VM.

    B. Convert the VHDs on your VMs to VHDX files.

    C. Create Fibre Channel adapters for each VM and move the VHDs to shared storage.

    D. Enable data deduplication on HYPV4.

3. You work as a network administrator for Fabrikam.com. One of your servers, named HYPV5, is running Windows Server 2012 and has been configured with the Hyper-V role. HYPV5 hosts five VMs running Windows Server 2008 R2.

You want to attach new VHDs to the VMs hosted on HYPV5 to increase storage space to these VMs. Until now, the VMs have relied on locally attached storage on HYPV5 to store VHDs attached to the VMs. However, adequate storage space is no longer available on HYPV5 for any new VHDs.

Your network includes a Fibre Channel SAN, from which HYPV5 can already provision storage. You want to provision new storage from the Fibre Channel SAN and use it for the new VMs, and you want to achieve this with the least amount of administrative effort. What should you do? (Choose all that apply.)

    A. Upgrade the VM operating systems to Windows Server 2012.

    B. From within the host operating system, provision new storage from the SAN.

    C. From within the guest operating system, provision new storage from the SAN.

    D. Convert the VHD files to VHDX files.

Objective 3.3: Create and configure virtual networks

This objective covers the bulk of the new features in Windows Server 2012 Hyper-V, but it's unclear which of these many features will actually appear on the 70-417 exam. Some, such as Network Virtualization and virtual switch extensions, are difficult to write questions about for an exam on Windows Server, as opposed to System Center Virtual Machine Manager or Windows development. Others are almost too easy; they can't be set up in a question without giving away the answer, like bandwidth management, DHCP guard, and router advertisement guard. Still others such as port ACLs are constrained by their lack of documentation at the time of this writing. SR-IOV stands out as a feature for which questions suitable to this exam can be written without too much trouble, but it is not currently mentioned by name as a topic in the objective description provided by Microsoft.

Where does that leave you? It's not easy to predict what questions from this objective will look like, so you can only learn the salient points about each of these features and expect to be surprised on the exam.

Virtual switch extensions

In Windows Server 2012, the "virtual networks" that appeared in the Windows Server 2008 and Windows Server 2008 R2 interface have been replaced by elements called virtual switches. From an administration point of view, it appears that virtual networks have just been renamed. Network adapters now connect to virtual switches instead of virtual networks, and just like the old virtual networks, virtual switches can be external, internal, or private.

But there is more to virtual switches than meets the eye, at least initially. One of the key innovations in Windows Server 2012 Hyper-V is that the functionality of these new virtual switches can be expanded through extensions provided by Microsoft or independent software vendors. You add these new extensions as you would install any new software.

Windows Server 2012 allows the following kinds of virtual switch extensions:

- Capturing extensions, which can capture packets to monitor network traffic but cannot modify or drop packets
- Filtering extensions, which are like capturing extensions but can also inspect and drop packets
- Forwarding extensions, which allow you to modify packet routing and enable integration with your physical network infrastructure

Once installed, extensions are made available to all switches but are enabled and disabled on a per-switch basis. To manage installed extensions for a virtual switch, from the Actions pane in Hyper-V Manager, select Virtual Switch Manager, as shown in Figure 3-7.

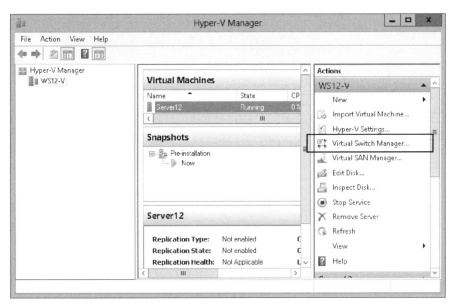

FIGURE 3-7 Opening the new Virtual Switch Manager.

Then, in the Virtual Switch Manager dialog box that opens, expand the desired switch and select Extensions, as shown in Figure 3-8. You can enable, disable, and rearrange the order of installed extensions in the Switch Extensions box.

By default, each switch has two extensions: Microsoft NDIS Capture, which is disabled, and Microsoft Windows Filtering Platform, which is enabled.

You can also use PowerShell to create, delete, and configure extensible switches on Hyper-V hosts. Use the Get-VMSwitchExtension cmdlet to display details about the extensions installed on a specific switch. To see the full list of cmdlets available to manage virtual switches in general, type **Get-Command *VMSwitch*** at a Windows PowerShell prompt.

If any questions about virtual switch extensions appear on the 70-417 exam, they will most likely involve fictional or hypothetical extensions. One possible scenario could involve two extensions that you need to enable but that don't work well together. If such a problem were to occur, and you wanted the functionality of both extensions, you could create two separate virtual switches, with one of these extensions enabled on each. Then you could connect chosen VMs to the appropriate switch as needed.

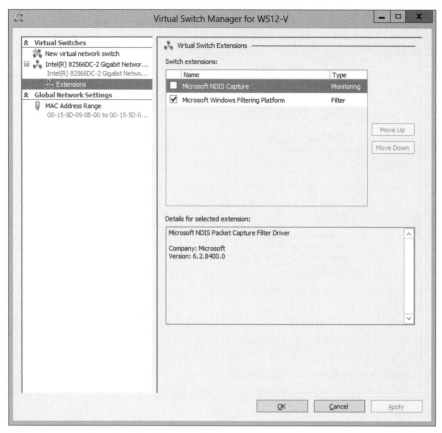

FIGURE 3-8 Managing virtual switch extensions.

> **NOTE** To manage virtual switch extensions in Windows PowerShell, you can use the cmdlets Enable-, Disable-, and Get-VMSwitchExtension. For a complete list, use Get-Command to search for the string *VMSwitchExtension*.

Network virtualization

Network virtualization is a new functionality that is built into Windows Server 2012 but is best configured and managed in System Center Virtual Machine Manager (SCVMM) 2012 SP1 or later. The feature is designed to be used primarily by hosting providers who manage a cloud infrastructure when the VMs of multiple customers share the same physical host servers and networks. The biggest benefit of network virtualization is that it enables these customers to migrate their existing server infrastructure into the hosting provider's cloud while keeping all their existing IP address settings. Network virtualization also gives these customers the freedom to assign to their VMs whichever IP addresses are optimal to them, regardless of potential IP address conflicts or any constraints related to the physical division of subnets in your infrastructure.

Network virtualization achieves this through either of two mechanisms:

- **IP rewrite** This mechanism modifies the customer addresses of packets while they are still on the VM and before they are transmitted onto the physical network.
- **IP encapsulation** In this mechanism, all the VM's packets are encapsulated with a new header before they are transmitted onto the physical network.

Although IP encapsulation offers better scalability, IP rewrite can provide better performance.

At the time of this writing, network virtualization is still mentioned explicitly in the domain objectives provided by Microsoft as a potential topic that could appear on the 70-417 exam. However, it is unclear how this feature might work its way into an exam question because configuring it in Windows Server 2012 without SCVMM 2012 SP1 requires elaborate Windows PowerShell scripting that is far more complex than what can feasibly appear in a Windows Server certification exam question. For now, just be aware of what the feature is so that if it is mentioned in a question scenario, you will recognize it. You can also view sample Windows PowerShell scripts that configure Network Virtualization by visiting the TechNet Script Center script repository at *http://gallery.technet.microsoft.com/ScriptCenter/* and searching for "network virtualization."

> **MORE INFO** For an overview of how network virtualization works, watch the video "Building secure, scalable multi-tenant clouds using Hyper-V Network Virtualization" from Microsoft's Build conference on Channel 9 at *http://channel9.msdn.com/Events/BUILD /BUILD2011/SAC-442T*. In addition, you can view two sample Windows PowerShell scripts for implementing network virtualization in the TechNet Script Center script repository at *http://gallery.technet.microsoft.com/scriptcenter/Simple-Hyper-V-Network-d3efb3b8* and *http://gallery.technet.microsoft.com/scriptcenter/Simple-Hyper-V-Network-6928e91b*.

Port ACLs (network isolation)

You can isolate VMs from unwanted network traffic by using the Add-VMNetworkAdapterAcl cmdlet in Windows PowerShell. At the time of this writing, the feature is most often called port ACLs in Microsoft documentation, but on the 70-417 exam it's possible you will see this feature mentioned only by its associated cmdlets.

Each port ACL is like a firewall rule that allows or denies traffic associated with a media access control (MAC) or IP address. If you configure the port ACL on a Hyper-V host running Windows Server 2012, it remains in effect even if you move the VM to another host server.

For example, to deny both inbound and outbound traffic between the remote address 192.168.9.111 and the VM named Server12, type the following at an elevated Windows PowerShell prompt on the Hyper-V host:

```
Add-VMNetworkAdapterAcl-VMName Server12 -RemoteIPAddress 192.168.9.111 -Direction Both
-Action Deny
```

You can then review the effects of this action by using the Get-VMNetworkAdapterAcl cmdlet. The specific command for this example and its associated output would be as follows:

```
Get-VMNetworkAdapterAcl -VMName Server12
VMName: Server12
VMId: eefb383d-5070-4a74-a16b-3e46a5d2b90c
AdapterName: Network Adapter
AdapterId: Microsoft:EEFB383D-5070-4A74-A16B-3E46A5D2B90C\C3F8188F-EF58-480E-A00F-
36F55F6CDA52


Direction    Address                                          Action
---------    -------                                          ------
Inbound      Remote 192.168.9.111                             Deny
Outbound     Remote 192.168.9.111                             Deny
```

To remove the port ACL and the associated traffic restriction, use the Remove-VMNetworkAdapterAcl cmdlet. For instance, following our example, you would type the following:

```
Remove-VMNetworkAdapterAcl -VMName Server12 -RemoteIPaddress 192.168.9.111 -Direction
Both -Action Deny
```

Resource Metering through port ACLs

You can use the same cmdlets to meter traffic to or from a specific address. To achieve this, use the Meter action instead of Allow or Deny, as in the following example:

```
Add-VMNetworkAdapterAcl-VMName Server12 -RemoteIPaddress 192.168.9.111 -Direction Both
-Action Meter
```

You would then use the Get-VMNetworkAdapterAcl cmdlet to view the metered usage. The following shows the command used with the same example and the associated output:

```
Get-VMNetworkAdapterAcl -VMName Server12
VMName: Server12
VMId: eefb383d-5070-4a74-a16b-3e46a5d2b90c
AdapterName: Network Adapter
AdapterId: Microsoft:EEFB383D-5070-4A74-A16B-3E46A5D2B90C\C3F8188F-EF58-480E-A00F-
36F55F6CDA52


Direction    Address                                          Action
---------    -------                                          ------
Inbound      Remote 192.168.9.111                             Meter (1 Mbytes)
Outbound     Remote 192.168.9.111                             Meter (0 Mbytes)
```

Metering usage through port ACLs might seem like an obscure feature, but don't be surprised if it shows up on an exam question. In a way, it's a showcase feature of Windows Server 2012 because it enables virtual hosting providers to specifically meter Internet usage (traffic to the default gateway) as opposed to network usage in general. Like the Resource Metering feature, this base functionality is intended to be leveraged through scripts and programs.

Single-root I/O virtualization

Single-root I/O virtualization (SR-IOV) is an extension to the PCI Express (PCIe) standard that can improve network performance. SR-IOV support in Hyper-V is new to Windows Server 2012. In Hyper-V, SR-IOV enables network traffic to bypass the software switch layer of the Hyper-V virtualization stack and reduce I/O overhead. If you assign only SR-IOV–enabled virtual network adapters and switches to a VM, the network performance of the VM can be nearly as good as that of a physical machine. In addition, the processing overhead on the host is reduced.

To enable SR-IOV, you first need to create a new virtual switch. (You cannot enable SR-IOV on any existing switch, such as the default virtual switch.) In Hyper-V Manager, from the Actions pane, select Virtual Switch Manager. In the Virtual Switch Manager window that opens, choose the option to create a new external virtual switch. Then, in the Virtual Switch Properties pane, in the Connection Type area (shown in Figure 3-9), select the Enable Single-Root I/O Virtualization (SR-IOV) check box. Supply a name and notes for the new virtual switch and then click OK.

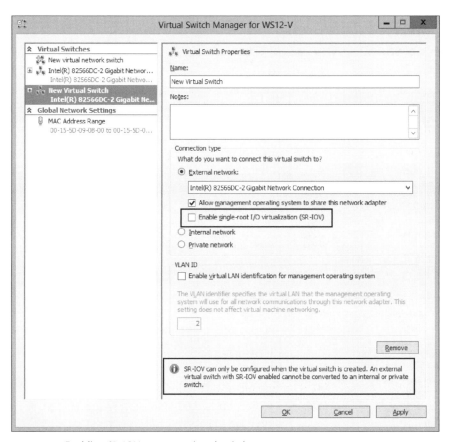

FIGURE 3-9 Enabling SR-IOV on a new virtual switch.

NOTE To create a new switch enabled for SR-IOV in Windows PowerShell, use the `New-VMSwitch` cmdlet with the `-EnableIOV $True` parameter.

After you create an SR-IOV–enabled virtual switch, open the settings of the VM for which you want to enable the adapter for SR-IOV and connect the network adapter to the new virtual switch you have just created. Then expand the Network Adapter settings in the Hardware pane, select Hardware Acceleration, and select the Enable SR-IOV check box, as shown in Figure 3-10.

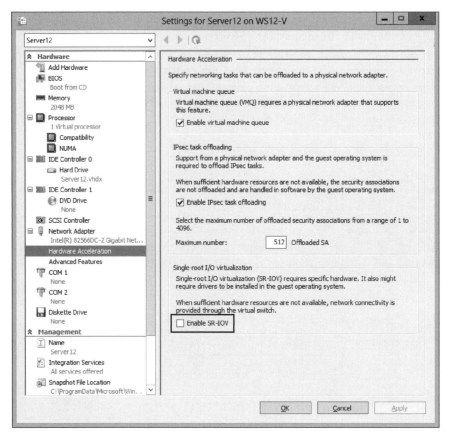

FIGURE 3-10 Enabling SR-IOV on a virtual network adapter.

Finally, depending on your hardware configuration, you might need to install drivers within the guest operating system to fully enable SR-IOV. You can check the status of SR-IOV by clicking the Networking tab for a particular VM in Hyper-V Manager. If SR-IOV is active, this information is displayed as shown in Figure 3-11.

FIGURE 3-11 A status message indicating the SR-IOV is active.

EXAM TIP

Remember that single-root I/O virtualization improves network performance on a VM by allowing a VM's network traffic to bypass virtual switches.

MORE INFO For more information about SR-IOV in Hyper-V, search for "Everything you wanted to know about SR-IOV in Hyper-V. Part 1" on *http://blogs.technet.com,* or visit *http://blogs.technet.com/b/jhoward/archive/2012/03/12/everything-you-wanted-to-know -about-sr-iov-in-hyper-v-part-1.aspx.*

Bandwidth management

Bandwidth management is a new feature in Windows Server 2012 Hyper-V that enables you to set both a minimum and maximum Mbps of throughput for any virtual network adapter. In Windows Server 2008 R2, you could configure a maximum bandwidth but not a minimum. Now you can configure both a minimum and a maximum for each virtual network adapter.

You enable and configure bandwidth management on a virtual network adapter in the settings of a VM, as shown in Figure 3-12. For either the Minimum Bandwidth or Maximum Bandwidth setting, configuring a value of 0 leaves that setting unrestricted.

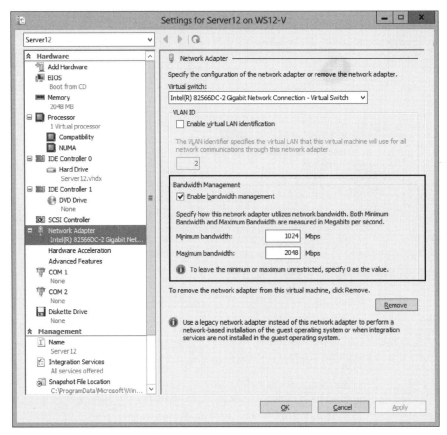

FIGURE 3-12 Enabling bandwidth management.

You can also use the Set-VMNetworkAdapter to configure minimum and maximum bandwidth on a virtual network adapter. As an alternative to specifying a value for Mbps, you can use this cmdlet to specify a relative bandwidth weight between 0 and 100 relative to other virtual network adapters. To ensure that all virtual network adapters are given an equal minimum or maximum bandwidth, you can assign the same bandwidth weight to all adapters. For example, by specifying a bandwidth weight of 1 to all network adapters on servers named Srv1, Srv2, and Srv3, the following command ensures that the same minimum bandwidth is assigned to those network adapters:

```
Get-VMNetworkAdapter -VMName Srv1,Srv2,Srv3 | Set-VMNetworkAdapter
-MinimumBandwidthWeight 1
```

EXAM TIP

Bandwidth management is not available as an option on legacy network adapters; it is available only on network adapters.

MORE INFO For more information about bandwidth management (also called Quality-of-Service for Hyper-V) in Windows Server 2012, visit *http://technet.microsoft.com /en-US/library/hh831511.*

Advanced features for virtual network adapters

A number of new features can be enabled for virtual network adapters in Hyper-V. These options appear when you select Advanced Features after you expand a Network Adapter in the Hardware menu, as shown in Figure 3-13. The new features in this area are defined next.

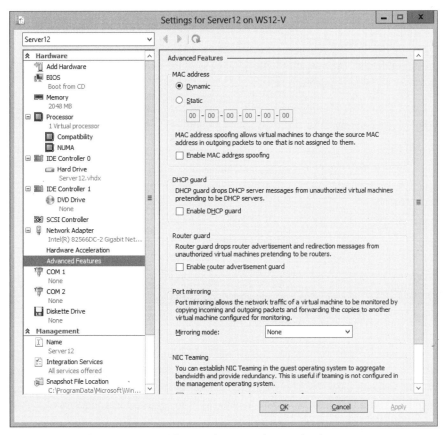

FIGURE 3-13 Configuring advanced features for a virtual network adapter.

- **DHCP Guard**   This feature helps safeguard against DHCP man-in-the-middle attacks by dropping DHCP server messages from unauthorized VMs pretending to be DHCP servers.

- **Router Guard**   This feature helps safeguard against unauthorized routers by dropping router advertisement and redirection messages from unauthorized VMs pretending to be routers.

- **Port Mirroring**   This feature enables monitoring of a VM's network traffic by forwarding copies of destination or source packets to another VM being used for monitoring purposes.
- **NIC Teaming**   In Windows Server 2012, the NIC teaming feature can be configured for virtual network adapters and for physical network adapters.

EXAM TIP

You need to remember the names and functions of these four features for the 70-417 exam.

NOTE   To configure settings for a virtual network adapter, including those for SR-IOV, bandwidth management, DHCP guard, router advertisement guard, port mirroring, and NIC teaming, use the Set-VMNetworkAdapter cmdlet. Use Get-Help to learn about the specific syntax used to configure each feature.

Objective summary

- The functionality of virtual networks in previous versions of Windows Server has been replaced by virtual switches in Windows Server 2012. Virtual switch features can be enhanced or expanded through extensions, which can be managed in the Hyper-V Manager interface.
- Network Virtualization is a low-level capability in Windows Server 2012 that is managed in System Center Virtual Machine Manager 2012 SP1. This feature gives VMs hosted in a cloud infrastructure the freedom to maintain IP addresses that ignore local logical constraints, physical constraints, or address conflicts.
- Port ACLs are like firewall rules that allow or deny traffic to a VM based on MAC or IP address. You can also use a port ACL to meter traffic between a VM and a specific address.
- SR-IOV is a way to optimize network performance between a Hyper-V guest and a physical network. To configure SR-IOV, you need to create a new virtual switch enabled for SR-IOV, connect a VM's network adapter to that switch, and enable SR-IOV on the adapter. You might also have to install drivers within the guest operating system.
- Windows Server 2012 includes many new configurable options for network adapters, such as bandwidth management, DHCP guard, router advertisement guard, port mirroring, and NIC teaming.

Objective review

Answer the following questions to test your knowledge of the information in this objective. You can find the answers to these questions and explanations of why each answer choice is correct or incorrect in the "Answers" section at the end of the chapter.

1. You work as a network administrator for Fabrikam.com. Fabrikam.com includes its own cloud infrastructure that is used to provide virtual hosting services to external customers. Customer servers are hosted as VMs on your servers running Windows Server. You want to block all traffic to and from the customer virtual servers except for communication with the default gateway.

   Which of the following cmdlets should you use on the host servers to isolate the guest VMs?

   A. Add-VMNetworkAdapterAcl

   B. Set-VMNetworkAdapterVLAN

   C. Set-VMSwitchExtensionPortFeature

   D. New-NetFirewallRule

2. You install the Hyper-V role on a server running Windows Server 2012 and then create a new VM. You now want to optimize network performance for the VM by enabling SR-IOV. What should you do? (Choose all that apply.)

   A. Create a new private switch.

   B. Enable SR-IOV on the virtual switch.

   C. Create a new external switch.

   D. Enable SR-IOV on the virtual network adapter.

3. You want to maximize security on a VM and help prevent man-in-the-middle attacks. Which of the following settings will help achieve this goal? (Choose all that apply.)

   A. Enable MAC Spoofing

   B. DHCP Guard

   C. Router Guard

   D. Port Mirroring

Thought experiment

You work as a network administrator for Fabrikam.com, a hosting provider that uses a private cloud infrastructure to provide virtual hosting services to external customers.

Your cloud infrastructure is composed of 20 physical servers running Windows Server 2012 with the Hyper-V role installed. Customer servers are hosted as VMs on these physical servers. Each physical server is equipped with 64 GB of RAM. Shared storage is provided by a Fibre Channel SAN. System Center Virtual Machine Manager 2012 with SP1 is used to manage the infrastructure.

Your goals are to use your physical resources as efficiently as possible and to provide a high level of security and performance for customers.

1. You are working with an in-house developer to create a tool that measures CPU, disk, and Internet usage for each customer VM. The developer wants to know how to access this raw information in Windows Server 2012 so that he can build a tool around it. Which method should you show the developer to retrieve the desired usage information?

2. Some customers want to have their servers hosted transparently so that the server appears as if it is hosted locally on the customers' premises. They want to use a VPN and assign to the server an IP address that is compatible with their local subnet. Which feature can you use to enable and configure this functionality?

3. A customer has a database application hosted in your cloud. The application is running in a VM that is running Windows Server 2008 R2 and SQL Server 2008. The database is stored on a VHD drive (stored on the host server) with a fixed size of 2 TB, but it will soon outgrow the space available. How can you provide more storage space for the database application in a way that minimizes the effort required for all stakeholders?

4. Your IT department has purchased two virtual switch extensions from independent software vendors. The first switch extension is a filtering extension that enables customers to search incoming packets for specific strings or patterns that are useful for security or market research. The second switch extension is a forwarding extension that forwards all incoming traffic received on a switch to any chosen IP address.

You want to be able to use these extensions to give customers the ability to search packets on the wire without significantly degrading network performance for services hosted on the customer VM. How can you achieve this goal?

Answers

This section contains the answers to the Objective Reviews and the Thought Experiment.

Objective 3.1: Review

1. **Correct Answer:** B

   A. **Incorrect:** Increasing the Startup Memory value will only increase the likelihood that Smart Paging will be used during startup.

   B. **Correct:** Increasing the Minimum Memory setting will help ensure that more physical memory remains allocated to VM1 when a restart begins.

   C. **Incorrect**: This isn't the best option because it could deprive other important applications of needed RAM.

   D. **Incorrect**: This setting would prioritize memory allocation to VM1 when needed. It wouldn't ensure that more memory is allocated to VM1 at the time of a restart operation.

2. **Correct Answer:** D

   A. **Incorrect:** Increasing the Startup Memory setting would decrease the possibility that VM2 will be able to start successfully because it will require HYPV2 to find more RAM to allocate to the startup operation. In addition, the fact that Smart Paging is not helping VM2 start most likely indicates that the drive that stores the Smart Paging file has run out of space.

   B. **Incorrect:** Decreasing the Maximum Memory on other VMs would have an unpredictable effect on the availability of RAM for VM2 during a restart operation. In addition, the other running VMs might host high-priority applications that need the memory. Finally, the fact that Smart Paging is not helping VM2 start most likely indicates that the drive that stores the Smart Paging file has run out of space.

   C. **Incorrect:** Increasing the Memory Buffer % setting would allocate more RAM to VM2 while it is running and would likely make more memory available at the time of a restart. However, VM2 hosts only low-priority applications that are rarely used. Allocating RAM to VM2 while it is running would deprive other VMs of the RAM they might need to support good performance in higher-priority applications. In addition, the fact that Smart Paging is not helping VM2 start most likely indicates that the drive that stores the Smart Paging file has run out of space.

   D. **Correct:** Both the host server and the guest VM are running Windows Server 2012, which supports Smart Paging. If insufficient RAM is available for a restart operation, the Smart Paging feature will normally rely on disk storage as virtual memory to help perform the restart. If a guest VM cannot restart in this scenario, it is most likely because not enough free space is available on the disk that currently stores the Smart Paging file.

3. **Correct Answer:** C

    A. **Incorrect:** This command would enable Resource Metering on the VM. However, according to the question, Resource Metering is already enabled.

    B. **Incorrect:** This command would stop the metering of resources on VM3 but would not display any usage statistics.

    C. **Correct**: This command would display usage statistics on VM3 because Resource Metering was enabled or reset.

    D. **Incorrect**: This command would save the resource data into a stored variable, not display it on the screen.

Objective 3.2: Review

1. **Correct Answer:** A

    A. **Correct:** VHDs have a size limit of 2 TB. The Convert option enables you to change the disk type to a VHDX, which has a size limit of 64 TB.

    B. **Incorrect:** VHDs have a size limit of 2 TB, and you need a VHD file that is larger than 4 TB. Choosing the Expand option would enable you to expand the size of the VHD from 1.5 TB to 2.0 TB.

    C. **Incorrect**: Creating a dynamically expanding VHD would not enable you to move beyond the 2 TB limit for VHD files. You need to convert the disk to a VHDX file.

    D. **Incorrect**: Creating a differencing VHD would not enable you to move beyond the 2 TB limit for VHD files. You need to convert the disk to a VHDX file.

2. **Correct Answer:** B

    A. **Incorrect:** NIC teaming will help ensure against network outages, but it will not help ensure against data corruption after a power failure.

    B. **Correct:** VHDX files, unlike VHD files, contain a log that helps these virtual disks avoid corruption resulting from a power outage.

    C. **Incorrect:** Moving the VHDs to shared storage will not make them more resilient to power outages.

    D. **Incorrect:** Data deduplication enables data to be stored more efficiently, but it doesn't help prevent corruption from power outages.

3. **Correct Answer:** B

    A. **Incorrect:** You don't need to upgrade to Windows Server 2012. You can currently provide new storage for the VMs just by provisioning new storage for the host server. You would need to upgrade to Windows Server 2012 only if you needed to provision storage directly from the guest operating system.

    B. **Correct:** You can provision storage from the SAN in the host operating system running Windows Server 2012. Then you can configure new volumes on the host server and store new VHDs for the VMs on those new volumes.

C. **Incorrect:** You don't need to provision new storage from the SAN from the guest operating system. Doing this would require you to upgrade the guest operating systems to Windows Server 2012. You would then need to create and configure virtual Fibre Channel ports. This set of actions would not help you achieve your goal with the least amount of administrative effort.

D. **Incorrect:** Converting the VHD files to VHDX files would require you to upgrade the guest operating systems to Windows Server 2012. In addition, converting to VHDX would not help you attach more available storage to your VMs.

Objective 3.3: Review

1. **Correct Answer:** A

   A. **Correct:** You can use Add-VMNetworkAdapterAcl to create a port ACL and allow or deny traffic between a VM and any specified addresses.

   B. **Incorrect:** This cmdlet enables you associate a VLAN ID with a network adapter. It does not isolate network traffic in a way that would be useful in this specific scenario.

   C. **Incorrect:** This cmdlet enables you to configure a feature on a virtual network adapter. It doesn't enable you to restrict network traffic in a way that would be helpful in this scenario.

   D. **Incorrect:** This cmdlet enables you to restrict traffic between any address and the host server, not the guest VMs.

2. **Correct Answers:** B, C, D

   A. **Incorrect:** You can only enable SR-IOV on an external switch.

   B. **Correct:** You need to enable SR-IOV on a new external virtual switch.

   C. **Correct:** You can only enable SR-IOV on a new switch. The switch must be external.

   D. **Correct:** You need to enable SR-IOV on the virtual network adapter connected to the new virtual switch.

3. **Correct Answers:** B, C

   A. **Incorrect:** MAC spoofing enables you to manually choose a MAC address. It doesn't prevent man-in-the-middle attacks.

   B. **Correct:** DHCP guard prevents man-in-the-middle attacks from unauthorized VMs pretending to be legitimate DHCP servers.

   C. **Correct:** Router guard prevents man-in-the-middle attacks from unauthorized VMs pretending to be legitimate routers.

   D. **Incorrect:** Port mirroring is used to forward traffic to a remote VM. It is not used to prevent man-in-the-middle attacks.

Thought experiment

1. To measure CPU and disk usage, use the Enable-VMResourceMetering, Measure-VM, and Reset-VMResourceMetering cmdlets. To measure Internet usage, create a port ACL that measures traffic specifically between a VM and the default gateway by using the Add-VMNetworkAdapterAcl cmdlet with the –Meter action.

2. Use the Network Virtualization feature, which you can configure in System Center Virtual Machine Manager 2012 SP1 or by using Windows PowerShell scripts.

3. Back up the VHD. Convert the VHD to a VHDX. Expand the new VHDX to a desired size up to 64 TB. (Only the host needs to be running Windows Server 2012 to support VHDX files. You don't need to upgrade the guest operating system to Windows Server 2012.)

4. Enable only the forwarding extension on the virtual switch currently used by the services hosted on the VM. Create a second virtual switch that enables only the filtering extension.

CHAPTER 4

Install and administer Active Directory

The important feature changes that have appeared since Windows Server 2008 R2 in the Install and Administer Active Directory domain all fall within a single objective, "Install domain controllers." Within this small area, however, the change could hardly be more significant: the very tool used in previous versions of Windows Server to install a domain controller, Dcpromo.exe, has been deprecated (which in Microsoft lingo means "officially set on a path to obsolescence"). More specifically, the use of Dcpromo is highly restricted in Windows Server 2012. You can use it for domain controller promotion *only with an answer file*. (Dcpromo also retains some specialized uses, such as the forced removal of Active Directory Domain Services with the /ForceRemoval option.)

What takes the place of Dcpromo in Windows Server 2012? A new Active Directory Domain Services Configuration Wizard, and a new set of Windows PowerShell cmdlets.

You need to understand these new installation tools well for the 70-417 exam.

Objectives in this chapter:

- Objective 4.1: Install domain controllers

Objective 4.1: Install domain controllers

In Windows Server 2008 and Windows Server 2008 R2, you had the option of installing the Active Directory Domain Services server role before promoting the server to a domain controller. In Windows Server 2012, that step is mandatory, and as a result, installing a domain controller is a two-step process. As an alternative, if you have a domain controller that is virtualized in Hyper-V, you can now quickly clone it if certain prerequisites are met.

> **This section covers the following topics:**
> - Installing domain controllers by using GUI
> - Installing domain controllers by using Windows PowerShell
> - Preparing for the Install From Media domain controller installation option without performing an offline defragmentation

Installing domain controllers by using the GUI

The first step in deploying a domain controller is to add the Active Directory Domain Services server role. If you use the Add Roles and Features Wizard to add the role, the next step is easy: you can just choose the option to promote the server to a domain controller on the final page of this wizard, as shown in Figure 4-1.

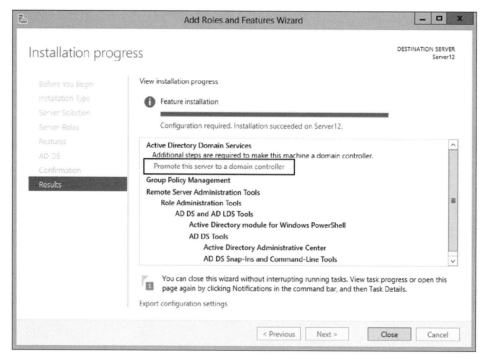

FIGURE 4-1 Installing a domain controller after installing the Active Directory Domain Services server role.

If you prefer to promote the server later, you can do so by using Server Manager. In Server Manager, expand the Notifications menu and choose the option to promote the server to a domain controller, as shown in Figure 4-2. (Note that this option appears only if you have added the Active Directory Domain Services server role.)

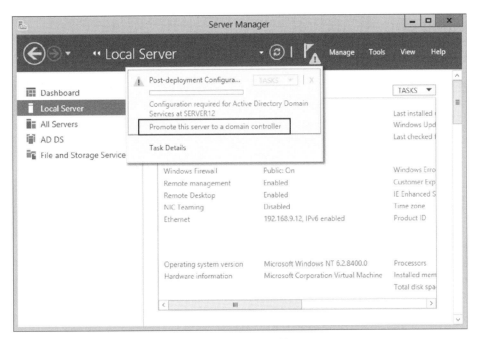

FIGURE 4-2 Installing a domain controller by using Server Manager.

 EXAM TIP

Make sure the PDC Emulator and RID Master are online and available whenever you add a new domain controller to an existing domain.

Whether you select the option immediately at the end of the Add Roles and Features Wizard or later on the Notification menu in Server Manager, the result is the same: the Active Directory Domain Services Configuration Wizard is started. This wizard is very similar to the Active Directory Domain Services Installation Wizard in Windows Server 2008 and Windows Server 2008 R2, even though the code behind it has been rewritten from scratch. The first page of this wizard is shown in Figure 4-3.

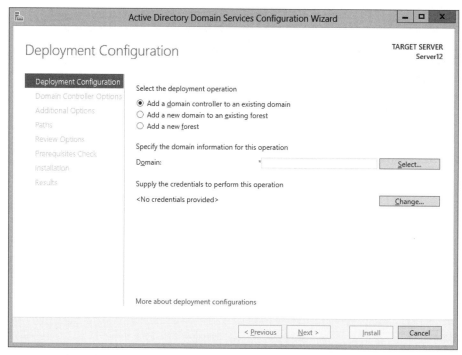

FIGURE 4-3 The Active Directory Domain Services Configuration Wizard is new to Windows Server 2012.

The options that appear in the wizard are so similar to those that appeared in the corresponding wizard in Windows Server 2008 and Windows Server 2008 R2 that it is not necessary to review them all. However, the Review Options page reveals an interesting change, shown in Figure 4-4. Remember how in Windows Server 2008 and Windows Server 2008 R2 you could export the settings you had selected in the wizard to an answer file to be used with Dcpromo? In Windows Server 2012, that has been replaced by a new option to export the settings you have selected to a *Windows PowerShell script*.

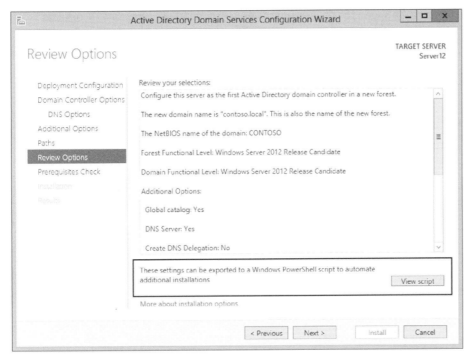

FIGURE 4-4 Exporting domain controller installation settings to a Windows PowerShell script.

The following code shows the contents of the exported Windows PowerShell script that results when you choose to add a new domain controller to an existing domain (fabrikam. local):

```
#
# Windows PowerShell script for AD DS Deployment
#
Import-Module ADDSDeployment
Install-ADDSDomainController '
-NoGlobalCatalog:$false '
-CreateDnsDelegation:$false '
-Credential (Get-Credential) '
-CriticalReplicationOnly:$false '
-DatabasePath "C:\Windows\NTDS" '
-DomainName "fabrikam.local" '
-InstallDns:$true '
-LogPath "C:\Windows\NTDS" '
-NoRebootOnCompletion:$false '
-SiteName "Default-First-Site-Name" '
-SysvolPath "C:\Windows\SYSVOL" '
-Force:$true
```

This next version shows the contents of the exported Windows PowerShell script that results when you choose to add a first domain controller to a new forest (contoso.local):

```
#
# Windows PowerShell script for AD DS Deployment
#
Import-Module ADDSDeployment
Install-ADDSForest '
-CreateDnsDelegation:$false '
-DatabasePath "C:\Windows\NTDS" '
-DomainMode "Win2012" '
-DomainName "contoso.local" '
-DomainNetbiosName "CONTOSO" '
-ForestMode "Win2012" '
-InstallDns:$true '
-LogPath "C:\Windows\NTDS" '
-NoRebootOnCompletion:$false '
-SysvolPath "C:\Windows\SYSVOL" '
-Force:$true
```

> **MORE INFO** For a detailed walkthrough of the Active Directory Domain Services Configuration Wizard, search for "Introducing the first Windows Server 2012 Domain Controller (Part 1 of 2)" or visit *http://blogs.technet.com/b/askpfeplat/archive/2012/09 /03/introducing-the-first-windows-server-2012-domain-controller.aspx*.

Adprep runs automatically

Another new development related to the Active Directory Domain Services Configuration Wizard is that this wizard automatically upgrades the forest and domain schema if necessary. In previous versions of Windows Server, if upgrading the schema was necessary to install a new domain controller, you needed to run Adprep first.

In Windows Server 2012, you still have the option of running Adprep to upgrade the schema, but if you haven't done so before completing the Active Directory Domain Services Configuration Wizard, the schema is upgraded automatically without prompting you first.

Installing domain controllers by using Windows PowerShell

The ability to install a domain controller by using Windows PowerShell is new to Windows Server 2012. As with using the GUI to perform the same task, promoting a domain controller is a two-step process when you use Windows PowerShell.

First, you need to add the Active Directory Domain Services server role by typing the following at an elevated Windows PowerShell prompt:

```
Install-WindowsFeature -Name AD-Domain-Services -IncludeManagementTools
```

Only after this role installation is complete can you get information about the available cmdlets in the ADDSDeployment module. To do so, type the following:

```
Get-Command -Module ADDSDeployment
```

Table 4-1 shows the 10 cmdlets available in the ADDSDeployment module.

Table 4-1 The cmdlets in the ADDSDeployment module

Cmdlet	Description
Add-ADDSReadOnlyDomainControllerAccount	Creates a read-only domain controller (RODC) account that can be used to install an RODC in Active Directory
Install-ADDSDomain	Installs a new Active Directory domain configuration
Install-ADDSDomainController	Installs a domain controller in Active Directory
Install-ADDSForest	Installs a new Active Directory forest configuration
Test-ADDSDomainControllerInstallation	Runs the prerequisites (only) for installing a domain controller in Active Directory
Test-ADDSDomainControllerUninstallation	Runs the prerequisites (only) for uninstalling a domain controller in Active Directory
Test-ADDSDomainInstallation	Runs the prerequisites (only) for installing a new Active Directory domain configuration
Test-ADDSForestInstallation	Runs the prerequisites (only) for installing a new forest in Active Directory
Test-ADDSReadOnlyDomainControllerAccountCreation	Runs the prerequisites (only) for adding an RODC account
Uninstall-ADDSDomainController	Uninstalls a domain controller in Active Directory

You need to understand the function of all of these cmdlets for the 70-417 exam.

Installing the first domain controller in a new forest

To install a domain controller in a new forest, use the Test-ADDSForestInstallation and Install-ADDSForest cmdlets.

TEST-ADDSFORESTINSTALLATION

Use Test-ADDSForestInstallation to verify that your environment meets the prerequisites to install the first domain controller in the new forest with the parameters specified. These same prerequisite tests are run if you use the Install-ADDSForest cmdlet.

For example, the following command runs the prerequisite tests for installing a new forest named corp.contoso.com. Because it doesn't specify a password by using the -SafeModeAdministratorPassword parameter, the user will be prompted to supply a Directory Services Restore Mode (DSRM) password. The *NoRebootOnCompletion* parameter specifies not to reboot after the new forest is created.

```
Test-ADDSForestInstallation -DomainName "corp.contoso.com" -NoRebootOnCompletion
```

The following command provides a more complex example. Here, the prerequisite tests are run for installing a new forest with the following specifications:

- Create a DNS delegation in the parent contoso.com domain (-*CreateDNSDelegation*).
- Set the domain functional level to Windows Server 2008 (-*DomainMode Win2008*).
- Set the forest functional level to Windows Server 2008 R2 (-*ForestMode Win2008R2*).
- Install the Active Directory database and SYSVOL on the D drive (-*DatabasePath "D:\NTDS"" -SysvolPath "D:\SYSVOL"*).
- Install the log files on the E drive (-*LogPath "E:\Logs"*).
- Have the server automatically restart after Active Directory Domain Services installation is complete (no -*NoRebootOnCompletion* parameter).
- Prompt the user to provide and confirm the DSRM password (no -*SafeModeAdministratorPassword* parameter).

```
Test-ADDSForestInstallation -DomainName corp.contoso.com -CreateDNSDelegation
-DomainMode Win2008 -ForestMode Win2008R2 -DatabasePath "D:\NTDS" -SysvolPath
"D:\SYSVOL" -LogPath "E:\Logs"
```

> **MORE INFO** For more information about the Test-ADDSForestInstallation cmdlet, visit
> *http://technet.microsoft.com/en-us/library/hh974717*.

INSTALL-ADDSFOREST

After you have tested the new forest creation with the Test-ADDSForestInstallation cmdlet, you are ready to use the Install-ADDSForest cmdlet to install the domain controller and create the new forest.

For example, the following command will create a new forest with the name corp.contoso.com, install a Domain Name System (DNS) server on the new local domain controller, and prompt the user to provide and confirm a DSRM password:

```
Install-ADDSForest -DomainName "corp.contoso.com" -InstallDNS
```

Note that in this next, more complex example, all the parameters used with the second Test-ADDSForestInstallation example are used again. Running the earlier test assures you that the following command will work:

```
Install-ADDSForest -DomainName corp.contoso.com -CreateDNSDelegation -DomainMode Win2008
-ForestMode Win2008R2 -DatabasePath "d:\NTDS" -SysvolPath "d:\SYSVOL" -LogPath "e:\Logs"
```

> **MORE INFO** For more information about the Install-ADDSForest cmdlet, visit
> *http://technet.microsoft.com/en-us/library/hh974720*.

Installing the first domain controller in a new domain in an existing forest

To install the first domain controller in a new domain in an existing forest, use the Test-ADDSDomainInstallation and Install-ADDSDomain cmdlets.

TEST-ADDSDOMAININSTALLATION

This cmdlet runs the prerequisite checks that are performed if you use the Install-ADDSDomain cmdlet to install a new domain controller in a new domain in an existing forest.

The following example runs prerequisite checks that verify the possibility of creating a new child domain named child.corp.contoso.com by using credentials of CORP\EnterpriseAdmin1. Because it doesn't specify a password by using the -SafeModeAdministratorPassword parameter, the user will be prompted to provide and confirm the DSRM password to complete the checks. This example also verifies the possibility of accomplishing the following:

- Installing a DNS server (-InstallDNS)
- Creating a DNS delegation in the corp.contoso.com domain (-CreateDNSDelegation)
- Setting the domain functional level to Windows Server 2003 (-DomainMode Win2003)
- Making the domain controller a global catalog server (no *-NoGlobalCatalog parameter*).
- Setting the site name to Houston (-SiteName Houston)
- Using DC1.corp.contoso.com as the replication source domain controller (-ReplicationSourceDC DC1.corp.contoso.com)
- Installing the Active Directory database and SYSVOL on the D drive (-DatabasePath "D:\NTDS" -SYSVOLPath "D:\SYSVOL")
- Installing the log files on the E drive (*-LogPath "E:\Logs"*)
- Avoiding an automatic restart after the domain installation is complete (*-NoRebootOnCompletion*)

```
Test-ADDSDomainInstallation -Credential (Get-Credential CORP\EnterpriseAdmin1)
-NewDomainName child -ParentDomainName corp.contoso.com -InstallDNS -CreateDNSDelegation
-DomainMode Win2003 -ReplicationSourceDC DC1.corp.contoso.com -SiteName Houston
-DatabasePath "D:\NTDS" -SYSVOLPath "D:\SYSVOL" -LogPath "E:\Logs" -NoRebootOnCompletion
```

> **MORE INFO**   For more information about the Test-ADDSDomainInstallation cmdlet, visit
> *http://technet.microsoft.com/en-us/library/hh974715.aspx.*

INSTALL-ADDSDOMAIN

After you have tested the possibility of creating a new domain by using the Test-ADDSDomainInstallation cmdlet, you are ready to use the Install-ADDSDomain to install the first domain controller in the new domain in an existing forest.

The following cmdlet creates the domain with the configuration verified in the test:

```
Install-ADDSDomain -Credential (Get-Credential CORP\EnterpriseAdmin1) -NewDomainName
child -ParentDomainName corp.contoso.com -InstallDNS -CreateDNSDelegation -DomainMode
Win2003 -ReplicationSourceDC DC1.corp.contoso.com -SiteName Houston -DatabasePath
"D:\NTDS" -SYSVOLPath "D:\SYSVOL" -LogPath "E:\Logs" -NoRebootOnCompletion
```

> **MORE INFO**   For more information about the Install-ADDSDomain cmdlet, visit
> *http://technet.microsoft.com/en-us/library/hh974722*.

Installing an additional domain controller in an existing domain

To install an additional domain controller in an existing domain, use the Test-
ADDSDomainControllerInstallation and Install-ADDSDomainController cmdlets.

TEST-ADDSDOMAINCONTROLLERINSTALLATION

This cmdlet runs prerequisite checks that verify that you can use the Install-
ADDSDomainController cmdlet to install a domain controller in Active Directory.

For example, the following command runs prerequisite checks to verify the possibility of
installing a domain controller in the existing corp.contoso.com domain (by using domain
administrator credentials). The domain controller will include a DNS server. The user will be
prompted to enter and confirm the DSRM password.

```
Test-ADDSDomainControllerInstallation -InstallDns -Credential (Get-Credential
CORP\Administrator) -DomainName "corp.contoso.com"
```

> **MORE INFO**   For more information about the Test-ADDSDomainControllerInstallation
> cmdlet, visit *http://technet.microsoft.com/en-us/library/hh974725*.

INSTALL-ADDSDOMAINCONTROLLER

If the test completes successfully, you can use the Install-ADDSDomainController cmdlet with
the same parameters to install the new domain controller in the existing corp.contoso.com
domain:

```
Install-ADDSDomainController -InstallDns -Credential (Get-Credential CORP\Administrator)
-DomainName "corp.contoso.com"
```

EXAM TIP

For the 70-417 exam, remember that you first need to use Install-WindowsFeature to
install the AD DS binaries. To then promote a server a domain controller, use either
Install-ADDSForest, Install-ADDSDomain, or Install-ADDSDomainController. Finally, to
demote a domain controller, use Uninstall-ADDSDomainController. (For a forced removal,
you can use Dcpromo.exe /ForceRemoval.)

MORE INFO For more information about the Install-ADDSDomainController cmdlet, visit *http://technet.microsoft.com/en-us/library/hh974723*.

Adding an RODC account

Use the Test-ADDSReadOnlyDomainControllerAccountCreation and Add-ADDSReadOnlyDomainControllerAccount cmdlets to create a computer account for an RODC. Once you have added the RODC account, you can use the Install-ADDSDomainController cmdlet with the -ReadOnlyReplica switch parameter to install an RODC.

For example, the following command adds a new RODC account to the corp.contoso.com domain by using the North America site as the source site for the replication source domain controller.

```
Add-ADDSReadOnlyDomainControllerAccount -DomainControllerAccountName RODC1 -DomainName
corp.contoso.com -SiteName NorthAmerica
```

MORE INFO For more information about the Test-ADDSReadOnlyDomainControllerAccountCreation and Add-ADDSReadOnlyDomainControllerAccount cmdlets, visit *http://technet.microsoft.com /en-us/library/hh974721* and *http://technet.microsoft.com/en-us/library/hh974718*.

Uninstalling a domain controller

Use the Test-ADDSDomainControllerUninstallation and Uninstall-ADDSDomainController cmdlets to uninstall a domain controller. Unlike the previous cmdlets, these cmdlets can be used without any parameters. If you do so, you will be prompted to supply a local Administrator password.

MORE INFO For more information about the Test-ADDSDomainControllerUninstallation and Uninstall-ADDSDomainController cmdlets, visit *http://technet.microsoft.com/en-us /library/hh974716* and *http://technet.microsoft.com/en-us/library/hh974714*.

Ntdsutil.exe Install from Media changes

Windows Server has included an Install from Media (IFM) option for deploying domain controllers since Windows Server 2003. By using this option, Active Directory Domain Services data is stored on a local drive, on removable media such as a DVD, or on a network shared folder. Using IFM enables you to avoid replicating all directory data over the network when you install the new domain controller.

The recommended method for creating Active Directory Domain Services installation media is to use the Ntdsutil.exe tool that is available when the Active Directory Domain Services server role is installed. Ntdsutil includes an IFM subcommand menu that creates the files necessary to install Active Directory Domain Services.

Windows Server 2012 adds two options to this IFM menu. These options enable you to create IFM stores without first performing an offline defrag of the exported NTDS.dit database file. An offline defrag, an operation that can be time-consuming, is performed by default. When disk space is not at a premium and you do not need to compact the Active Directory database, these new options save time creating the IFM.

Table 4-2 describes the two new menu items.

TABLE 4-2 Creating IFM media without defragmentation

Menu Item	Description
Create Full NoDefrag %s	Create IFM media without defragmenting for a full Active Directory domain controller or a Lightweight Directory Services (LDS) instance into folder %s
Create Sysvol Full NoDefrag %s	Create IFM media with SYSVOL and without defragmenting for a full Active Directory domain controller into folder %s

EXAM TIP

IFM does not work across different operating system versions. If you have a domain controller running Windows Server 2008 R2 and you want to promote a server running Windows Server 2012 by using IFM, you need to upgrade the domain controller first.

EXAM TIP

Windows Server 2008 R2 introduced a new feature called Offline Domain Join that relies on a utility called Djoin.exe. Djoin.exe allows you to join a computer to a domain even if there is no live connection to a domain controller. Because it's a new feature since Windows Server 2008, Offline Domain Join and Djoin.exe could easily appear on the 70-417 exam even though it doesn't fit within any of the indicated objectives for the exam. Note that for this exam, you don't need to understand the specifics of how to use Djoin. exe, you just should know what it is used for.

If you want specific information about how to use Offline Domain Join and Djoin.exe, search for "Offline Domain Join (Djoin.exe) Step-by-Step Guide" or visit *http://technet .microsoft.com/en-us/library/offline-domain-join-djoin-step-by-step(v=ws.10).aspx.*

Objective summary

- Windows Server 2012 has new procedures for installing a domain controller. To install a domain controller, first install the Active Directory Domain Services server role. You can accomplish this either by using the Add Roles and Features Wizard or by typing the following at an elevated Windows PowerShell prompt:

```
Install-WindowsFeature -Name AD-Domain-Services -IncludeManagementTools
```

- In the GUI, after you install the Active Directory Domain Services server role, you can choose the option to promote the server to a domain controller that appears both at the end of the Add Roles and Features Wizard and in the Notification menu in Server Manager.

- In Windows PowerShell, to install the first domain controller in a new forest, use the Install-ADDSForest cmdlet. To install the first domain controller in a new domain in an existing forest, use the Install-ADDSDomain cmdlet. To install a new domain controller in an existing domain, use the Install-ADDSDomainController cmdlet.

- Windows Server 2012 enables you to perform an IFM installation of a domain controller without first performing an offline defrag of the Active Directory database. To achieve this, in the IFM subcommand menu of the Ntdsutil utility, use either the Create Full NoDefrag or the Create Sysvol Full No Defrag option.

Objective review

Answer the following questions to test your knowledge of the information in this objective. You can find the answers to these questions and explanations of why each answer choice is correct or incorrect in the "Answers" section at the end of the chapter.

1. You are a network administrator for Fabrikam.com. You want to set up a new domain that is completely separate from the existing company network. The purpose of the domain is to test functionality and application compatibility in Windows Server 2012.

   You have installed Windows Server 2012 on the first server and now want to promote it to a domain controller. Which of the following commands do you need to run? (Choose two. Each answer is part of the solution.)

   A. Install-ADDSDomain

   B. Install-ADDSDomainController

   C. Install-ADDSForest

   D. Install-WindowsFeature

   E. Dcpromo.exe

2. You are a network administrator for Fabrikam.com. You want to add a new domain controller to the Fabrikam.com domain by using the Installation from Media (IFM) option.

   You select a storage device with 12 GB of space to store the NTDS database and the SYSVOL folder. The contents of the NTDS database total 100 MB, and the SYSVOL folder totals 30 MB.

   At an elevated command prompt on a Windows Server 2012 domain controller, you enter the Ntdsutil utility and activate the instance of NTDS. You then enter the IFM subcommand menu.

   Your goal is to write both the NTDS database and SYSVOL to your storage media and to achieve this as quickly as possible. Which option should you use?

   A. Create Full NoDefrag

   B. Create Sysvol Full NoDefrag

   C. Create Full

   D. Create Sysvol Full

3. You have installed Windows Server 2012 on a new server named RODC1. You now want to use Windows PowerShell to make RODC1 a read-only domain controller (RODC) in the Fabrikam.com domain.

   Which of the following Windows PowerShell cmdlets is NOT necessary to run to achieve your goal?

   A. Install-ADDSDomain

   B. Install-WindowsFeature

   C. Install-ADDSDomainController

   D. Add-ADDSReadOnlyDomainControllerAccount

Thought experiment

Your company, Contoso.com, is experiencing rapid growth.

To provide scalability to meet the IT demands of continued growth, the company is building a new virtual infrastructure. The IT department has purchased eight physical servers to host virtualized instances of your servers and of client machines. All eight servers are running Windows Server 2012 with the Hyper-V server role installed. All guest servers are currently running Windows Server 2008 R2.

A company goal is to move all Contoso's workloads to the virtual infrastructure.

Currently, the network includes a single domain named Contoso.com. Users have complained that logon times are slow, especially at the beginning of the workday. You can find the answers to these questions in the "Answers" section at the end of the chapter.

1. You create a new virtual machine and install Windows Server 2012. You name the server DC2012A. You now want to promote DC2012A to a new domain controller in the Contoso.com domain. What complete Windows PowerShell command should you run on DC2012A to install the server as an additional domain controller in the Contoso.com domain?

2. You install another domain controller named DC2012B, which is also running Windows Server 2012. What step can you take on DC2012B that will make DC2012A eligible for cloning?

3. The research department has requested that you create their own domain. You install Windows Server 2012 on a new virtual machine and name the computer ResDC. You now want to promote ResDC to be the first domain controller in a new domain named research.contoso.com. What complete Windows PowerShell command should you run on ResDC to achieve this goal?

Answers

This section contains the answers to the Objective Review and the Thought Experiment.

Objective 4.1: Review

1. **Correct Answers:** C, D

   A. **Incorrect:** You would use this cmdlet to install the first domain controller in a new domain, but only within an existing forest. You want the new domain to be completely separate from the existing company network.

   B. **Incorrect:** You would use this cmdlet to install an additional domain controller in an existing domain.

   C. **Correct**: You need to use the Install-ADDSDomainController cmdlet because you want to create a new domain that is completely separate from the company network. This cmdlet will automatically promote the server to a domain controller in the new domain.

   D. **Correct**: Before using the Install-ADDSForest cmdlet, you need to add the Active Directory Domain Services server role. This cmdlet helps you accomplish that goal. The full syntax of the command is the following:

   ```
   Install-WindowsFeature -Name AD-Domain-Services -IncludeManagementTools
   ```

   E. **Incorrect**: This command can be used only with an answer file in Windows Server 2012. There is no indication that an answer file is available, and if there were, it would most likely provide a configuration for the Fabrikam.com network, from which the new domain controller must be kept separate.

2. **Correct Answer:** B

   A. **Incorrect:** This option would copy the NTDS database but not the SYSVOL folder to the media.

   B. **Correct:** This option would write both the NTDS database and SYSVOL to the media. In addition, it would achieve the result as quickly as possible because it avoids the step of offline defragmentation of this data. You have ample storage space on your media, so offline defragmentation is not necessary.

   C. **Incorrect:** This option would copy the NTDS database but not the SYSVOL folder to the media.

   D. **Incorrect:** This option would write both the NTDS database and SYSVOL to the media. However, it would not achieve the result as quickly as possible because offline defragmentation would be performed.

3. **Correct Answer:** A

    A. **Correct:** This cmdlet would help you install the first domain controller in a new domain in an existing forest. You cannot use it to install an RODC because the first domain controller in a domain cannot be an RODC.

    B. **Incorrect:** You need to use this cmdlet to install Active Directory Domain Services before you install the domain controller.

    C. **Incorrect:** You need to use this cmdlet to install an additional domain controller in an existing domain. You would use the -ReadOnlyReplica option to make the new domain controller an RODC. Perform this step after you have created a computer account for the RODC.

    D. **Incorrect:** You would use this cmdlet to create a computer account for the RODC in the domain.

Thought experiment

1. Install-ADDSDomainController -DomainName " contoso.com "

2. Transfer the PDC emulator role in the Contoso.com domain to DC2012B.

3. Install-ADDSDomain -NewDomainName research -ParentDomainName contoso.com

CHAPTER 5

Deploy, manage, and maintain servers

This chapter contains a single objective: monitor servers. The vast majority of this topic is probably already familiar to you: Data Collector Sets, event forwarding and collection, alerts, performance counters, and network monitoring. None of these features has changed in any significant way since Windows Server 2008. That's not to say you shouldn't brush up on these topics if you don't feel confident about them. You absolutely should.

But if the question is *what's new* in server monitoring in Windows Server 2012, there's really just one development you need to know, and it relates to resource metering. We've already covered resource metering of virtual machines in Chapter 3, "Configure Hyper-V," and this chapter builds on that knowledge by introducing the related topic of virtual machine (VM) resource pools.

Objectives in this chapter:

- Objective 5.1: Monitor servers

Objective 5.1: Monitor servers

Windows Server 2012 introduces Windows PowerShell cmdlets to measure virtual machine resource pools, enabling you to monitor usage by all VMs of various resources on a Hyper-V host. The VM resource metering introduced in Chapter 3 is used to measure resource usage by individual VMs. VM resource pools, in contrast, are more useful for measuring usage of a host's resources by all guest VMs.

For the exam, you should learn how to configure and use this new feature.

> **This section covers the following topic:**
> - Monitoring virtual machines (VMs)

Virtual machine resource pools

Each Hyper-V host includes predefined VM resource pools that correspond to the individual host resource types—such as processor, Ethernet, memory, and disk (VHD)—that are available to the guest VMs on that host. You can use these resource pools to monitor aggregate usage of each resource by all VMs, or you can create new resource pools that measure some subset of a resource, such as a particular set of VHDs. To see the list of all VM resource pools, type **Get-VMResourcePool** at a Windows PowerShell prompt. The following shows a sample output:

```
Name                ResourcePoolType              ParentName  ResourceMeteringEnabled
----                ----------------              ----------  -----------------------
Primordial          FibreChannelPort                            False
Primordial          FibreChannelConnection                      False
Primordial          ISO                                         False
Primordial          VFD                                         False
Primordial          VHD                                         False
Primordial          Ethernet                                    False
Primordial          Memory                                      False
Primordial          Processor                                   False
```

Predefined resource pools are named Primordial because they represent the total amount of a resource available on the host machine, as opposed to a user-defined subset of that resource. The ResourceMeteringEnabled status of all the resource pools in the preceding example is labeled False because resource metering hasn't yet been enabled.

Metering virtual machine resource pools

As with VM resource metering, covered in Chapter 3, resource pool metering is intended only to provide raw data to be captured by applications developed either in-house or by third-party developers. However, you can use Windows PowerShell to test the functionality of VM resource pools and view usage data associated with them.

To begin metering usage of a resource pool, first use the Enable-VMResourceMetering cmdlet. Specify the resource pool by name with the -ResourcePoolName option and by type with the -ResourcePoolType option. For example, to enable metering of the primordial memory resource pool, type the following:

```
Enable-VMResourceMetering –ResourcePoolName Primordial –ResourcePoolType Memory
```

You can also use the wildcard "*" symbol in place of a specific name and ignore the -ResourcePoolType option if you want to enable all resource pools that can possibly be enabled:

```
Enable-VMResourceMetering –ResourcePoolName *
```

A predefined resource pool can only remain disabled after you run this command if no corresponding resource is found on the host computer. After you run the preceding command, the output of Get-VMResourcePool in this example changes to the following:

```
Name             ResourcePoolType          ParentName ResourceMeteringEnabled
----             ----------------          ---------- -----------------------
Primordial       Processor                            True
Primordial       FibreChannelConnection               False
Primordial       ISO                                  False
Primordial       VFD                                  False
Primordial       FibreChannelPort                     False
Primordial       VHD                                  True
Primordial       Ethernet                             True
Primordial       Memory                               True
```

You can measure the resource usage associated with a resource pool after metering is enabled on it. To enable metering, use the Measure-VMResourcePool cmdlet. For example, the following command provides usage for network data:

```
Measure-VMResourcePool -Name * -ResourcePoolType Ethernet
```

Sample output is shown here in an abbreviated format:

```
Name             ResourcePoolType      NetworkInbound(M)        NetworkOutbound(M)
----             ----------------      -----------------        ------------------
Primordial       {Ethernet}                  20                        4
```

Creating virtual machine resource pools

Instead of measuring primordial pool usage, you can use the New-VMResourcePool cmdlet to create resource pools for monitoring and reporting usage of a subset of resources.

For example, the following command creates a new VM resource pool associated with multiple VHD files:

```
PS C:\> New-VMResourcePool "New Resource Pool" VHD -Paths "D:\Hyper-V\Virtual Hard Disks"

Name                  ResourcePoolType ParentName    ResourceMeteringEnabled
----                  ---------------- ----------    -----------------------
New Resource Pool VHD {Primordial}                   False
```

As with the primordial resource pools, you can then enable resource metering on new VM resource pools and measure their usage.

Server monitoring through Windows PowerShell

The 70-417 exam is likely to test your knowledge of Windows PowerShell far more than did the exams you took to earn your earlier Windows Server certification. For this reason, it's a good idea to review the cmdlets related to monitoring.

Two of these cmdlets are new, and they both relate to *virtual machine eventing*, a minor new feature in Windows Server 2012 that is not well documented at the time of this writing.

According to Get-Help and Windows PowerShell documentation at *http://technet.microsoft .com/en-us/library/hh848462,* "[v]irtual machine eventing keeps Hyper-V PowerShell objects updated without polling the virtual machine host." You should be aware that it is enabled by default, and you can use the cmdlets Enable-VMEventing and Disable-VMEventing to reenable and disable the feature, respectively.

Use Table 5-1 to review some of the important Windows PowerShell cmdlets and other commands that relate to server monitoring. (More cmdlets are available to manage events. For a full list, type **get-command *event* | sort noun,verb** at a Windows PowerShell prompt.)

TABLE 5-1 Common command-line tools for server monitoring

CmDlet or command-line utility	description
Export-Counter	Exports data that is returned by the Get-Counter and Import-Counter cmdlets
Get-Counter	Gets performance counter data from local and remote computers
Import-Counter	Imports performance counter log files (.blg, .csv, .tsv) and creates the objects that represent each counter sample in the log
Get-Event	Gets events in the Windows PowerShell event queue for the current session
New-Event	Creates a new custom event
Clear-EventLog	Deletes all entries from specified event logs on the local or remote computers
Get-EventLog	Manages event logs and displays events contained within those event logs
Enable-VMEventing	Enables virtual machine eventing
Disable-VMEventing	Disables virtual machine eventing
Logman.exe	Manages and schedules performance counter and event trace log collections on local and remote systems

EXAM TIP

The Deploy, Manage, and Maintain Servers domain is taken from the 70-411 exam. In its original form, it includes two additional objectives, about Windows Deployment Services (WDS) and Windows Server Update Services (WSUS), respectively. Even though these objectives aren't officially indicated for the 70-417 exam, don't be surprised if you see a question about either of these topics on this test. For WDS, you can review its new features in Windows Server 2012 at *http://technet.microsoft.com/en-us/library/hh974416.aspx.* For WSUS, you can install the server role and browse the options available through the Options node. Pay special attention to the Update Files options described at the following address: *http://technet.microsoft.com/en-us/library/cc708431(v=ws.10).aspx.*

Reviewing older monitoring topics

More than with other objectives, you should expect the Monitor Servers objective on the 70-417 exam to be represented by questions about older topics that have not changed since Windows Server 2008. The topic of monitoring virtual machines (as distinct from resource metering in Hyper-V) is otherwise too narrow to account for a proportional representation of this objective on the exam. For this reason, make sure you brush up on the older topics also indicated for this objective on the official exam page on the Microsoft web site. (You can visit this page directly at *http://www.microsoft.com/learning/en/us/exam.aspx?ID=70-417#tab2*.) These topics include configuring Data Collector Sets, configuring alerts, monitoring real-time performance, monitoring events, configuring event subscriptions, and configuring network monitoring. These are all topics you have already learned well enough to achieve your current certification.

In this section, we'll point out two of these older topics that are particularly important for review.

Creating a Data Collector Set manually

When you create a new Data Collector Set in Performance Monitor in Windows Server 2012, as in Windows Server 2008, you are provided with two options: to create the new Data Collector Set from a template, or to create it manually.

If you choose to create the Data Collector Set manually, you are prompted to specify the type of data you want to include. You are provided with the following four options, which have not changed since Windows Server 2008:

- **Performance counter**. This option uses any set of performance counters you specify to gather and save data about the system's performance.

- **Event trace data**. This option provides information about activities and system events, as opposed to performance counters.

- **System configuration information**. This option allows you to record the value of specified registry keys as they change.

- **Performance counter alert.** This option allows you to configure an action to take place (such as running a program) when a selected performance counter crosses a threshold value you specify.

Make sure you remember the purpose of all four of these data collection types for the 70-417 exam.

> **MORE INFO** For additional information about creating a Data Collector Set manually, you can visit *http://technet.microsoft.com/en-us/library/cc766404.aspx*.

Data Manager settings on a Data Collector Set

After you create a new Data Collector Set, you can use the Data Manager settings to configure how data is stored for each Data Collector Set. These settings have not changed since Windows Server 2008. You access Data Manager settings by right-clicking a Data Collector Set and then selecting Data Manager on the shortcut menu.

Particularly important are the folder actions you can create on the Actions menu. You can use these settings, for example, to automatically delete the data collected by a Data Collector Set when that data reaches a certain age or folder size.

EXAM TIP

For the 70-417 exam, be sure to review these options, and remember that the Data Manager settings for a Data Collector Set allow you to set automatic actions such as data deletion based on age or size parameters.

> **MORE INFO** For more information about Data Manager settings, you can visit *http://technet.microsoft.com/en-us/library/cc765998.aspx.*

Objective summary

- In Windows Server 2012, you can meter usage of resource pools (such as memory, processor, or Ethernet) on a VM host.
- Use the Get-VMResourcePool cmdlet to display a list of all resource pools on a Hyper-V host running Windows Server 2012.
- Hyper-V hosts running Windows Server 2012 have preconfigured resource pools, each named Primordial, that correspond to the aggregate amount of a resource on the host. You can create new resource pools that correspond to a subset of these primordial resource pools.
- To configure resource metering of a resource pool, use the Enable-VMResourceMetering cmdlet and specify the name and type of the resource pool with the -ResourcePoolName and -ResourcePoolType options, respectively. Then, to view usage of the resource pool, use the Measure-VMResourcePool cmdlet.
- Use the Enable-VMEventing and Disable-VMEventing cmdlets to enable and disable the feature called virtual machine eventing. Virtual machine eventing keeps Hyper-V PowerShell objects updated without polling the VM host.
- More than with other objectives officially listed for the 70-417 exam, it is important to review the older features about monitoring servers (such as Data Collector Sets and Event Subscriptions) that you learned about for your Windows Server 2008 certification.

Objective review

Answer the following questions to test your knowledge of the information in this objective. You can find the answers to these questions and explanations of why each answer choice is correct or incorrect in the "Answers" section at the end of the chapter.

1. The Hyper-V server role has been installed on a server named HYPV01, which is hosting 10 VMs and has been configured with 32 GB of RAM. You want to determine average usage of the host server RAM over time by all your guest VMs. You have not yet configured resource metering of any resource pool or of any VMs.

    You want to view the usage of the primordial RAM resource pool on HYPV01, and you want to do so with the greatest amount of administrative efficiency. Which of the following Windows PowerShell cmdlets should you use to achieve your goal? (Choose all that apply.)

    A. Enable-VMResourceMetering

    B. New-VMResourcePool

    C. Measure-VM

    D. Measure-VMResourcePool

2. The Hyper-V server role has been installed on a server named HYPV02, which is hosting six VMs and has been configured with 16 GB of RAM. One of the guest VMs that is running on HYPV02 is named DBSrv1. DBSrv1 has been allocated 8 GB of RAM. You are concerned that more RAM than necessary has been allocated to DBSrv1.

    You want to measure average RAM usage by DBSrv1 during a period of high load, and you want to do so from a command-line interface on HYPV02. You have not yet configured resource metering of any resource pool or of any VMs.

    Which of the following Windows PowerShell commands or cmdlets can you use to measure RAM usage by DBSrv1? (Choose all that apply.)

    A. Enable-VMResourceMetering -ResourcePoolName DBSrv1 -ResourcePoolType Memory

    B. Enable-VMResourceMetering -VMName DBSrv1

    C. Measure-VM

    D. Measure-VMResourcePool

3. You want to ensure that Hyper-V PowerShell objects are updated without polling the VM host. Which Windows PowerShell cmdlet can you use to achieve this goal?

    A. Enable-VMEventing

    B. Register-EngineEvent

    C. Register-ObjectEvent

    D. Get-EventSubscriber

Thought experiment

You are a network administrator for Contoso.com. One of Contoso's application servers, named App1, is running a Server Core installation of Windows Server 2012. Company policy dictates that App1 be managed only remotely and only by using Windows PowerShell. None of the firewall exceptions have been enabled on App1 that would be required for remote management through graphical administration consoles. You can find the answers to these questions in the "Answers" section at the end of the chapter.

1. Which Windows PowerShell cmdlet should you use to review individual event logs such as the System log on App1?

2. Which command-line utility can you use to create daily counter collection queries on App1?

3. Which Windows PowerShell cmdlet should you use to delete all entries from a specified event log on App1?

4. Which Windows PowerShell cmdlet should you use to display current performance counter data from App1?

Answers

This section contains the answers to the Objective Review and the Thought Experiment.

Objective 5.1: Review

1. **Correct Answers:** A, D

    A. **Correct:** If resource metering has not yet been configured, you will need to enable it on the primordial RAM resource pool before you can measure its usage.

    B. **Incorrect:** You don't need to create a new resource pool because you want to measure the usage of a primordial resource pool, which is built in.

    C. **Incorrect**: You would use the Measure-VM cmdlet if you wanted to measure usage of a particular VM, not of a particular resource pool. You could use the command **Measure-VM *** to display average RAM usage by each individual VM, but this is not the most efficient solution because it would require you to add these values to derive the aggregate RAM usage.

    D. **Correct:** To view total usage of a resource pool by all VMs, use the Measure-VMResourcePool cmdlet.

2. **Correct Answers:** B, C

    A. **Incorrect:** This command enables resource metering of a memory resource pool named DBSrv1. The question does not state that a resource with such a name has been created. In addition, you cannot use this command to measure RAM usage by any one VM unless only one VM is running (which is not the case in this question).

    B. **Correct:** This command enables metering of all resources (including RAM) by the VM named DBSrv1.

    C. **Correct:** This cmdlet enables you to measure resource usage by a particular VM. In this case, you would enter the command **Measure-VM DBSrv1**.

    D. **Incorrect:** This cmdlet enables you to measure resource usage of a particular resource pool by all guest VMs. You cannot use it to measure resource usage by any one VM unless only one VM is running (which is not the case in this question).

3. **Correct Answer:** A

   A. **Correct:** The Enable-VMEventing cmdlet enables virtual machine eventing, which keeps Hyper-V PowerShell objects updated without polling the VM host. Virtual machine eventing is enabled by default, but running this command ensures that it is enabled.

   B. **Incorrect:** The Register-EngineEvent cmdlet enables you to subscribe to events that are generated by the Windows PowerShell engine and by the New-Event cmdlet. It doesn't enable you to keep Hyper-V PowerShell objects updated without polling the VM host.

   C. **Incorrect**: The Register-ObjectEvent cmdlet enables you to subscribe to the events that are generated by a Microsoft .NET Framework object. It doesn't enable you to keep Hyper-V PowerShell objects updated without polling the VM host.

   D. **Incorrect**: The Get-EventSubscriber cmdlet gets the event subscribers in the current session. It doesn't enable you to keep Hyper-V PowerShell objects updated without polling the VM host.

Thought experiment

1. Get-EventLog. (You would normally use options to limit the output. For example, the command **Get-EventLog System -Newest 25** retrieves only the most recent 25 events in the System event log.)

2. Logman.exe

3. Clear-EventLog

4. Get-Counter

CHAPTER 6

Configure network services and access

The Configure Network Services and Access domain is another with just one objective tested on the 70-417 exam: Configure DirectAccess. DirectAccess is an improved alternative to a VPN that was first introduced in Windows Server 2008 R2 and Windows 7. If you earned your last certification before the release of Windows Server 2008 R2, you might have missed this major new technology completely. Even if you are already familiar with DirectAccess in Windows Server 2008 R2, you should know that this feature has changed significantly in Windows Server 2012.

Objectives in this chapter:

- Objective 6.1: Configure DirectAccess

Objective 6.1: Configure DirectAccess

DirectAccess in Windows Server 2008 R2 and Windows 7 was a very promising technology, but it was difficult to configure. In Windows Server 2012 and Windows 8, the infrastructure requirements of DirectAccess have been simplified along with the configuration steps. At the same time, its feature set has expanded considerably.

For the 70-417 exam, you first need to understand basic DirectAccess concepts and components. You will also need to know how the infrastructure requirements to support DirectAccess clients differ to support various features. Finally, you will need to know how to configure DirectAccess.

> **This section covers the following topics:**
> - DirectAccess infrastructure options
> - Configuring DirectAccess clients
> - Configuring DirectAccess servers
> - Configuring DirectAccess infrastructure servers

What is DirectAccess?

DirectAccess is an always-on remote access technology based on IPv6 communication. Through DirectAccess, a user's computer automatically, transparently, and securely connects to a private corporate network from any location in the world as soon as the computer is connected to the Internet. When a DirectAccess connection is active, remote users connect to resources on the corporate network as if they were on the local premises.

DirectAccess overcomes the limitations of VPNs by providing the following benefits:

- **Always-on connectivity**   Unlike with a VPN, a DirectAccess connection is always on, even before the user logs on to his or her computer.

- **Seamless connectivity**   To the user, the DirectAccess connection to the corporate network is completely transparent. Aside from any delay that could be caused by a slow Internet connection, the user experience is the same as if the user's computer were connected directly to the corporate network.

- **Bidirectional access**   With DirectAccess, the user's remote computer has access to the corporate intranet and the intranet can see the user's computer. This means that the remote computer can be managed by using Group Policy and other management tools (such as System Center Configuration Manger [SCCM]) in the same way that computers located on the internal network are managed.

In addition, DirectAccess includes the following security features:

- DirectAccess uses IPsec to authenticate both the computer and user. If you want, you can require a smart card for user authentication.

- DirectAccess also uses IPsec to provide encryption for communications across the Internet.

IPv6 and DirectAccess

A DirectAccess connection from a remote client to an internal resource includes two legs. In the first half of the connection, the DirectAccess client always uses IPv6 to initiate contact with the DirectAccess server, typically found at the edge of the private network. IPv6 transition technologies are used to assist this connection when necessary. The second half of the connection occurs between the DirectAccess server and the internal network resource. This part of the connection can proceed either over IPv4 (only if the DirectAccess server is running Windows Server 2012 and acting as a NAT64/DNS64 device) or over IPv6.

Figure 6-1 shows the two legs of a DirectAccess connection between a remote client and an internal network resource.

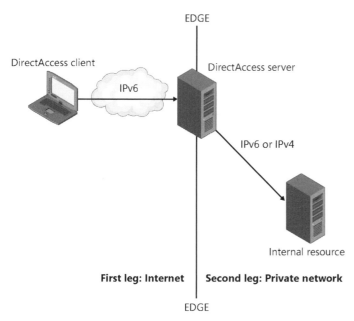

FIGURE 6-1 A DirectAccess connection to an internal resource.

First leg: External client to private network edge

If the DirectAccess client can obtain a global IPv6 address from its environment, then the connection to the DirectAccess server proceeds over the IPv6 Internet in a straightforward manner. However, IPv6 is not widely implemented yet on public networks, so three IPv6 transition technologies are used to assist in establishing the IPv6 connection to the DirectAccess server. If all three of the following transition technologies are enabled on the client through Group Policy, they are attempted in the following order of preference:

1. **6to4**   For DirectAccess clients that have a *public* IPv4 address, 6to4 can be used to connect to the DirectAccess server via IPv6 across the public IPv4 Internet. 6to4 achieves this by tunneling or encapsulating IPv6 data within an IPv4 header, in a technique known as IPv6-over-IPv4. 6to4 requires any intervening router or firewall to be configured so that outbound traffic for Protocol 41 is allowed. Note that 6to4 does not work if the client is behind a network address translation (NAT) device.

2. **Teredo**   For DirectAccess clients behind a NAT device and configured with a *private* IPv4 address, Teredo can be used to connect to the DirectAccess server via IPv6 across the public IPv4 Internet. Like 6to4, Teredo tunnels IPv6 traffic in IPv4. The intervening routers and firewalls must be configured to allow outbound traffic through User Datagram Protocol (UDP) port 3544.

3. **IP-HTTPS** For DirectAccess clients that cannot effectively establish IPv6 connectivity to the DirectAccess server through 6to4 or Teredo, IP-HTTPS is used. By using IP-HTTPS, DirectAccess clients encapsulate IPv6 traffic within HTTPS traffic. Virtually all routers allow outbound HTTPS traffic, so this option is almost always possible.

> **NOTE** In Windows Server 2012 and Windows 8, the performance of IP-HTTPS is close to that of Teredo because a "null encryption" option is used for HTTPS communication. However, in Windows Server 2008 R2 and Windows 7, IP-HTTPS uses Secure Sockets Layer (SSL) encryption on top of the IPsec encryption that is used to secure the connection between the DirectAccess client and server. This "double encryption" significantly degrades network performance.

Second leg: Private network edge to internal resource

Between the network edge and the internal network resource, the connection can proceed over either IPv6 or IPv4. You don't have to deploy global IPv6 on your internal network because Windows Server 2012 can act as a NAT64/DNS64 device when deployed as a DirectAccess server at the network edge. (A NAT64/DNS64 device translates between IPv6 and IPv4.) However, an all-IPv6 connection still provides the best performance and is the preferred scenario.

> **NOTE** Windows Server 2008 R2 doesn't provide NAT64/DNS64 functionality, but you could use Microsoft Forefront Unified Access Gateway 2010 or a third-party device to provide NAT64/DNS64 translation. Otherwise, to implement DirectAccess, you have to deploy global IPv6 on your internal network or use the IPv6 transition technology ISATAP. You can still use ISATAP in Windows Server 2012, but it is not recommended.

DirectAccess connection process

A DirectAccess connection to a target intranet resource is initiated when the DirectAccess client connects to the DirectAccess server through IPv6. IPsec is then negotiated between the client and the server. Finally, the connection is established between the DirectAccess client and the target resource.

This general process can be broken down into the following specific steps:

1. The DirectAccess client computer attempts to connect to an internal computer configured as the *network location server*. If the network location server is available, the DirectAccess client determines that it is already connected to the intranet, and the DirectAccess connection process stops. If the network location server is not available, the DirectAccess client determines that it is connected to the Internet, and the DirectAccess connection process continues.

2. The DirectAccess client computer connects to the DirectAccess server by using IPv6 and IPsec. If a native IPv6 network isn't available, the client establishes an IPv6-over-IPv4 tunnel by using 6to4, Teredo, or IP-HTTPS. The user does not have to be logged on for this step to complete.

3. As part of establishing the IPsec session, the DirectAccess client and server authenticate each other by using Kerberos or computer certificates.

4. By validating Active Directory Domain Services group memberships, the DirectAccess server verifies that the computer and user are authorized to connect using DirectAccess.

5. If Network Access Protection (NAP) is enabled and configured for health validation, the DirectAccess client obtains a health certificate from a Health Registration Authority (HRA) located on the Internet prior to connecting to the DirectAccess server. The HRA forwards the DirectAccess client's health status information to a NAP health policy server. The NAP health policy server processes the policies defined within the Network Policy Server (NPS) and determines whether the client is compliant with system health requirements. If so, the HRA obtains a health certificate for the DirectAccess client. When the DirectAccess client connects to the DirectAccess server, it submits its health certificate for authentication.

6. The DirectAccess server begins forwarding traffic from the DirectAccess client to the intranet resources to which the user has been granted access.

DirectAccess infrastructure options

You can deploy DirectAccess in a number of network scenarios, ranging from very simple to very complex. A few of these options are illustrated in the examples that follow.

Simple DirectAccess infrastructure

A simple DirectAccess infrastructure includes a DirectAccess server that is running Windows Server 2012 and is deployed at the network edge. This DirectAccess server is configured as a Kerberos proxy and NAT64/DNS64 translation device. The external interface is configured with a public IP address. (Two would be necessary to support Teredo.) The internal address is associated with the network location server.

Within the internal network is a domain controller/DNS server and at least one internal network resource, such as a file server or application server. Note that this simple infrastructure supports only Windows 8 clients because Windows 7 clients do not support Kerberos authentication for DirectAccess.

Figure 6-2 shows a simple DirectAccess infrastructure.

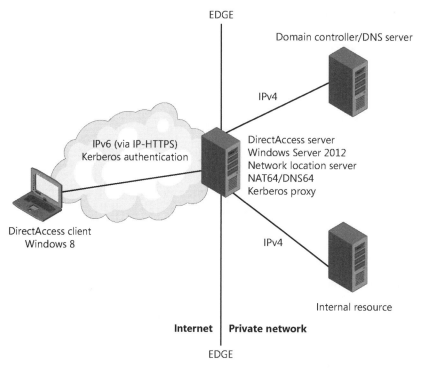

FIGURE 6-2 A simple DirectAccess infrastructure.

 EXAM TIP

Remember that only Windows Server 2012 and Windows 8 support Kerberos proxy, which greatly simplifies authentication for DirectAccess clients. In addition, only Windows Server 2012 includes built-in support for NAT64/DNS64 translation, which enables you to use DirectAccess with your existing internal IPv4 infrastructure.

DirectAccess server behind NAT

Both Windows Server 2008 R2 and Windows Server 2012 enable you to deploy a DirectAccess server behind the network edge in a perimeter network. However, only in Windows Server 2012 can you deploy the DirectAccess server behind a NAT device. In such a scenario, the DirectAccess server needs only a single network adapter and a single address. Connections from the DirectAccess clients through the NAT device to the DirectAccess server are established by using IP-HTTPS.

Figure 6-3 illustrates a DirectAccess network topology in which a DirectAccess server is deployed behind a NAT device.

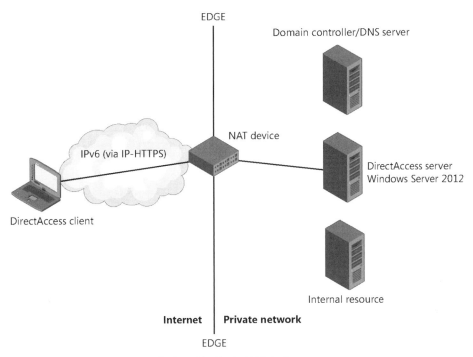

FIGURE 6-3 DirectAccess server deployed behind a NAT device.

Multisite/Multidomain DirectAccess infrastructure

Another infrastructure option new to Windows Server 2012 is the ability to deploy DirectAccess across multiple sites. A multisite deployment of DirectAccess requires a public key infrastructure (PKI) and computer authentication through certificates. In addition, in Windows Server 2012 multidomain support is a built-in feature of DirectAccess that requires no extra configuration.

When you configure a multisite deployment, the DirectAccess clients are provided with a list of the DirectAccess servers that act as entry points to the private network at each site. Before connecting, DirectAccess clients running Windows 8 ping each of these DirectAccess servers. Windows 8 clients then initiate contact with the server whose latency is determined to be the shortest. (Windows 7 clients in a multisite deployment just use a single, preconfigured DirectAccess server address.)

Figure 6-4 shows a multisite DirectAccess infrastructure.

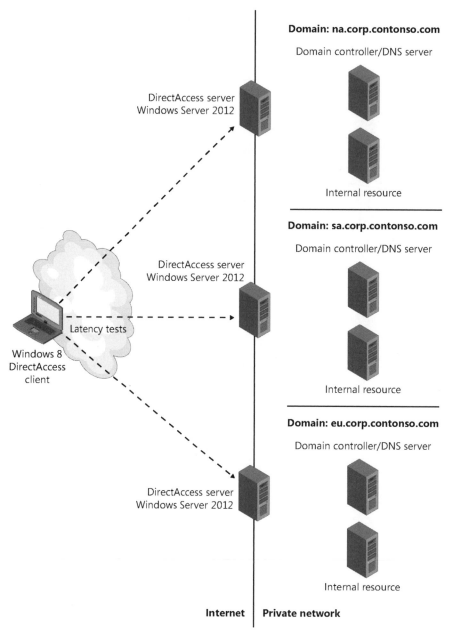

FIGURE 6-4 A multisite DirectAccess infrastructure.

Complex DirectAccess infrastructure

Although Windows Server 2012 greatly simplifies the basic infrastructure requirements for DirectAccess, the infrastructure can become complex if you need functionality that is not included by default in a basic setup. For example, one new feature in Windows Server 2012 is the ability to deploy DirectAccess servers in a Network Load Balancing (NLB) cluster. This functionality adds complexity to your infrastructure but is often necessary to support many remote clients. Another requirement that adds elements to your infrastructure is supporting Windows 7 clients. Windows 7 clients can authenticate DirectAccess connections only with computer certificates, so your DirectAccess infrastructure would require a PKI in such a scenario. In addition, DirectAccess can also be deployed with NAP, which is another factor that adds complexity but that your IT policies might require. Additional features such as two-factor authentication with one-time passwords (OTPs) would further raise the infrastructure requirements. Figure 6-5 illustrates a more complex DirectAccess infrastructure that supports all three IPv6 transition technologies, improves load capacity with an NLB cluster, supports Windows 7 clients with a PKI/certification authority, includes a NAP infrastructure, and has a network location server deployed apart from the DirectAccess server.

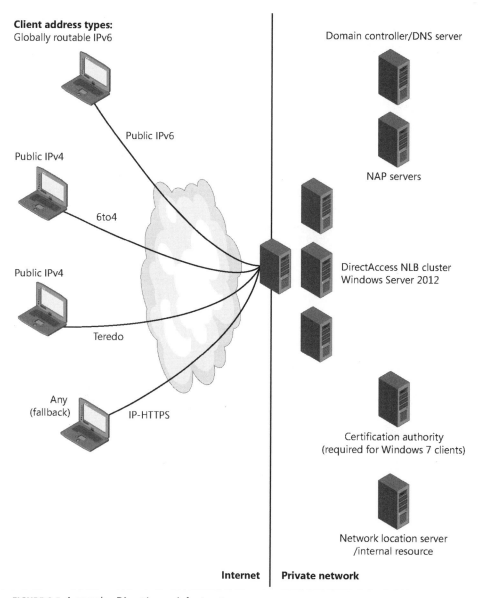

Client address types:
Globally routable IPv6

Public IPv6

Public IPv4

6to4

Public IPv4

Teredo

Any
(fallback)

IP-HTTPS

Domain controller/DNS server

NAP servers

DirectAccess NLB cluster
Windows Server 2012

Certification authority
(required for Windows 7 clients)

Network location server
/internal resource

Internet | **Private network**

FIGURE 6-5 A complex DirectAccess infrastructure.

Installing and configuring DirectAccess

Windows Server 2012 has greatly simplified the process of installing and configuring
DirectAccess. DirectAccess is now unified with traditional VPNs in a new Remote Access server
role and managed with the same tool, the Remote Access Management console. You can now
configure a Windows Server to act as both a DirectAccess server and a traditional VPN server
at the same time, an option that was not possible in Windows Server 2008 R2. Even more

significant than unified management are the new configuration wizards available in Windows Server 2012 that make the process of deploying and configuring DirectAccess and VPNs relatively easy.

Installing Remote Access

DirectAccess now belongs to the Remote Access server role. You can install the Remote Access role by using the Add Roles and Features Wizard or by typing the following at an elevated Windows PowerShell prompt:

```
Install-WindowsFeature RemoteAccess -IncludeManagementTools
```

You can then configure DirectAccess by using the Remote Access Management console, shown in Figure 6-6, or by using Windows PowerShell commands.

> **NOTE** To review the cmdlets used to configure DirectAccess, visit *http://technet.microsoft .com/en-us/library/hh918399* or type the following at a Windows PowerShell prompt:
>
> ```
> Get-Command -Module RemoteAccess *da*
> ```
>
> Note also that installing the Remote Access role and its role management tools installs the Windows PowerShell module named DirectAccessClientComponents, which provides the additional client cmdlets listed at the following address: *http://technet.microsoft.com /en-us/library/hh848426*.

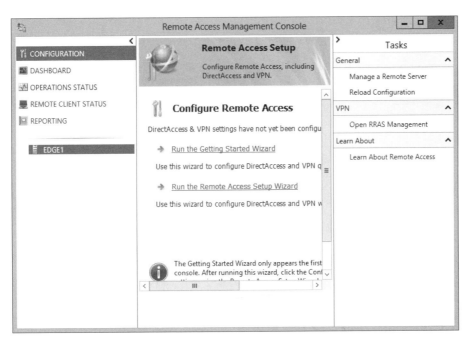

FIGURE 6-6 The Remote Access Management console provides a unified configuration and management tool for all remote access technologies.

Configuring DirectAccess

Figure 6-6 shows the Remote Access Management console before you take any configuration steps. The central pane shows two options for wizards: the Getting Started Wizard and the Remote Access Setup Wizard. Whichever wizard you choose to begin configuration, you are next presented with the option to configure just DirectAccess, just a VPN, or both, as shown in Figure 6-7.

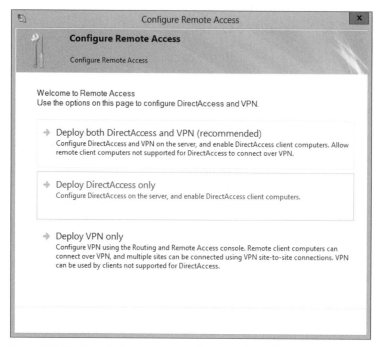

FIGURE 6-7 The Remote Access configuration wizards enable you to configure just DirectAccess, just a VPN, or both.

The Getting Started Wizard is an excellent new tool that helps you deploy a remote access solution quickly. However, it is not especially useful for exam preparation because it hides the configuration options you need to know and understand for the test. In addition, VPN configuration has not changed in Windows Server 2012 in any way that is significant for the 70-417 exam. For these reasons, to prepare for the Configure DirectAccess objective for the 70-417 exam, you should focus on configuration options that appear after you click Run The Remote Access Setup Wizard, as shown in Figure 6-6, and click Deploy DirectAccess Only, as shown in Figure 6-7.

After you click Deploy DirectAccess Only, the Remote Access Management console reappears with the center pane replaced by an image similar to the one shown in Figure 6-8. The four steps in the map are associated with four configuration wizards you must complete in order. The first is for configuring DirectAccess clients, the second is for configuring the DirectAccess server, the third is for configuring infrastructure servers, and the fourth is for configuring the application servers (if desired). These wizards create and configure group policy objects (GPOs) for DirectAccess servers and clients.

You won't be asked about any of these wizards by name on the 70-417 exam. However, you may be asked about *any configuration option* that appears in any of these four wizards. These four wizards provide a useful way to organize the new configuration options you need to learn and understand for the 70-417 exam, so we will look at them in order.

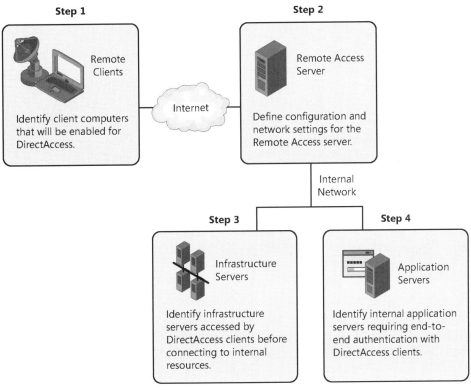

FIGURE 6-8 The four DirectAccess configuration wizards.

STEP 1: DIRECTACCESS CLIENT SETUP

The first page of the DirectAccess Client Setup wizard is shown in Figure 6-9. This Deployment Scenario page gives you the option to configure DirectAccess clients either for both remote access and remote management or for remote management only. The first, default option configures bidirectional communication for DirectAccess servers and clients. The second option allows administrators to manage remote DirectAccess clients by using tools such as SCCM, but prevents those clients from accessing the internal corporate network. Note that this second manage-only option is new to Windows Server 2012.

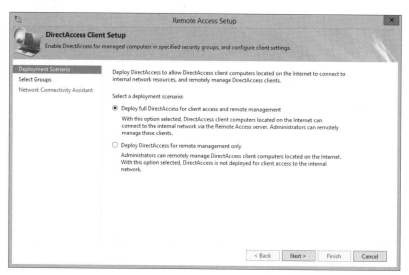

FIGURE 6-9 The Deployment Scenario page of the DirectAccess Client Setup wizard.

> **NOTE** To configure the deployment scenario in Windows PowerShell, use the Set-AServer cmdlet with the -DAInstall switch and either the FullInstall or ManageOut parameter. For example, to configure the DirectAccess deployment for remote management only, type the following at an elevated Windows PowerShell prompt on the DirectAccess server:

```
Set-DAServer -DAInstallType ManageOut
```

The second page of the DirectAccess Client Setup wizard is the Select Groups page, shown in Figure 6-10. The first option on this page enables you to specify the security groups that you want to enable for DirectAccess. This is an important step to remember: no DirectAccess client is allowed access to the internal network if you don't assign that client the right to do so. To perform this task in Windows PowerShell, use the Add-DAClient cmdlet with the -SecurityGroupNameList switch.

A second option on this page is to enable DirectAccess for mobile computers only. Interestingly, this option is selected by default if you run the Getting Started Wizard. Computers connecting remotely through DirectAccess are most likely mobile computers, but there are exceptions—and these exceptions could easily form the premise of an exam question. (Scenario: Some users working on domain-joined desktop computers from remote sites can't connect through DirectAccess. Why not? The option to enable DirectAccess for mobile computers only is selected.)

EXAM TIP

If only laptops are able to connect through DirectAccess, you can change this setting by modifying the the DirectAccess Client Settings GPO. Specifically, you need to remove the DirectAccess - Laptop Only WMI filter that is linked to this GPO in the Security Filtering settings.

The third option on this page is Use Force Tunneling. This option forces the DirectAccess client to tunnel *all* network traffic through the private network, regardless of that traffic's ultimate destination. This behavior, for example, could be used to ensure that all web traffic from DirectAccess clients passes through an internal web proxy server. In Windows PowerShell, this option is configured by using the Set-DAClient cmdlet with the -ForceTunnel parameter.

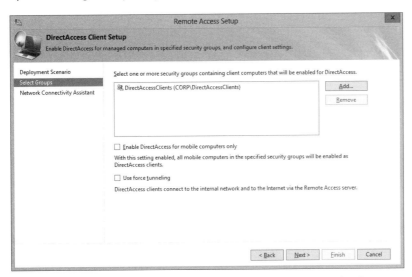

FIGURE 6-10 The Select Groups page of the DirectAccess Client Setup wizard.

The final page in the DirectAccess Client Setup wizard is the Network Connectivity Assistant page, shown in Figure 6-11.

The first setting on this page is the web probe host address. DirectAccess client computers use this web host to verify connectivity to the internal network. This setting is unlikely to appear on the 70-417 exam (except maybe as an incorrect answer choice), but if you need to enter this resource manually, you can use an address of *http://directaccess-webprobehost .yourdomain*. Your internal DNS should resolve this address to the internal IPv4 address of the Remote Access server or to the IPv6 address in an IPv6-only environment.

The most testable setting on this page is the option to allow DirectAccess clients to use local name resolution. Local name resolution in this case refers to the broadcast-based protocols of NetBIOS over TCP/IP and Link-Local Multicast Name Resolution (LLMNR). When this option is enabled, DirectAccess clients are allowed to resolve single label names such as App1 using local name resolution if they can't be resolved through DNS. Local name resolution must also be configured in the Infrastructure Server Setup wizard.

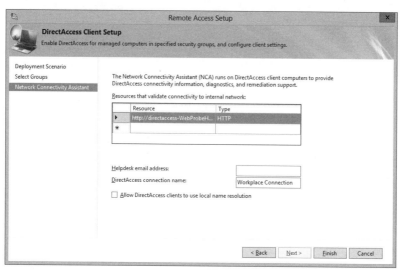

FIGURE 6-11 The Network Connectivity Assistant page of the DirectAccess Client Setup wizard.

STEP 2: REMOTE ACCESS SERVER SETUP

The first page of the Remote Access Server Setup wizard is the Network Topology page, shown in Figure 6-12. This page enables you to specify where in your network you are going to deploy your DirectAccess server.

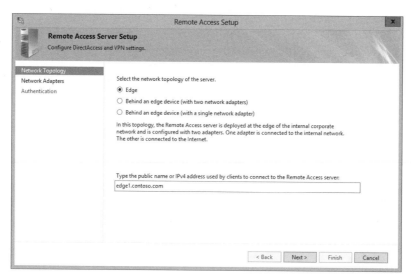

FIGURE 6-12 The Network Topology page of the Remote Access Server Setup wizard.

The first option is Edge. Choosing this option requires the DirectAccess server to be configured with two network adapters, one connected directly to the Internet and one connected to the internal network. The external interface needs to be assigned two consecutive public IPv4 addresses if you need to support Teredo.

The second option is Behind An Edge Device (With Two Network Adapters). Select this option if you want to deploy the DirectAccess server in a perimeter network behind a firewall or router. In this topology, the network adapter attached to the perimeter network is assigned one or two consecutive public IPv4 addresses, and the second adapter attached to the internal network can be assigned a private address.

The third option is Behind An Edge Device (With A Single Network Adapter). Choose this option if you want to deploy the DirectAccess server behind a NAT device. In this topology, the DirectAccess server is assigned a single private IP address.

The Network Topology page also requires you to specify the name or IPv4 address the DirectAccess clients will use to connect to the DirectAccess server. Be sure to specify a name that can be resolved through public DNS or an IPv4 address that is reachable from the public network.

The second page of the Remote Access Server Setup wizard is the Network Adapters page, shown in Figure 6-13. This page requires you to choose the network adapter or adapters that will be assigned to internal network and external network, as required by your specified topology.

This page also requires you to specify a certificate that the DirectAccess server will use to authenticate IP-HTTPS connections. If your organization has deployed a PKI, you can browse to a copy of the computer certificate for the local server. If you don't have a PKI, you need to choose the option to use a self-signed certificate instead. Note that this latter option is new to Windows Server 2012 and could easily serve as the basis for a test question.

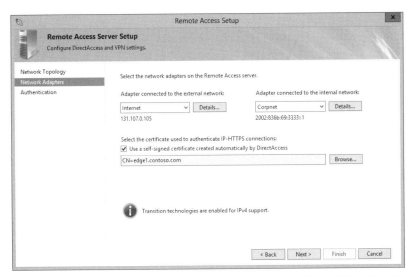

FIGURE 6-13 The Network Adapters page of the Remote Access Server Setup wizard.

The final page of the Remote Access Server Setup wizard is the Authentication page, shown in Figure 6-14. This page enables you to configure the following settings related to DirectAccess client authentication:

- **User authentication** By default, users authenticate only with Active Directory credentials. However, you can choose the option here to require two-factor authentication. Typically, two-factor authentication requires a user to insert a smart card in addition to typing his or her Active Directory credentials. Note that in Windows Server 2012, the Trusted Platform Module (TPM) of client computers can act as a virtual smart card for two-factor authentication.

  As an alternative, you can configure two-factor authentication so that users must enter an OTP such as one provided through RSA SecurID in addition to their Active Directory credentials. OTP requires a PKI and RADIUS server along with a number of configuration steps you don't need to understand for the 70-417 exam. For the 70-417 exam, you just need to know that OTP is an alternative to smart cards for two-factor authentication in DirectAccess.

- **Computer certificates** If you configure DirectAccess in the GUI, client computers are authenticated through Kerberos by default. However, you can select an option to require computer authentication through the use of certificates. Computer certificate authentication is required to support two-factor authentication, a multisite deployment of DirectAccess, and Windows 7 DirectAccess clients.

- **Windows 7 clients** By default, Windows 7 client computers cannot connect to a Windows Server 2012 Remote Access deployment. You need to enable that functionality here.

- **NAP** This page enables you to require a health check of client computers through NAP. To configure this setting in Windows PowerShell, use the Set-DAServer cmdlet with the -HealthCheck parameter.

> **MORE INFO** All the authentication settings displayed on this page can be configured through the Set-DAServer cmdlet. For more information, use Get-Help or visit *http://technet.microsoft.com/en-us/library/hh918371*.

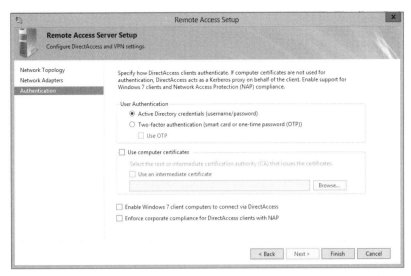

FIGURE 6-14 The Authentication page of the Remote Access Server Setup wizard.

STEP 3: INFRASTRUCTURE SERVER SETUP

The Infrastructure Server Setup wizard enables you to configure settings related to the network location server, the DNS server, and management servers such as update or antivirus servers.

The first page of this wizard is the Network Location Server page, shown in Figure 6-15. As explained earlier in this chapter, DirectAccess clients use this server to determine whether they are on the company network. It's recommended that you use an internal web server other than the DirectAccess (Remote Access) server for this purpose. (The DNS address and associated IP address in this case are naturally associated with the interface attached to the internal network.) If you do specify the DirectAccess server as the network location server, it must be authenticated by a computer certificate—a self-signed one if necessary. To configure the network location server using Windows PowerShell, use the Set-DANetworkLocationServer cmdlet.

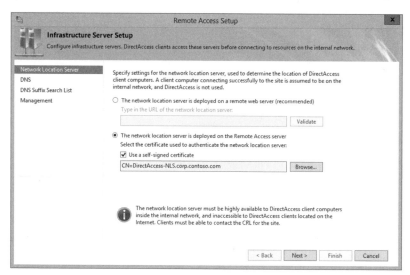

FIGURE 6-15 The Network Location Server page of the Infrastructure Server Setup wizard.

The second page of the Infrastructure Server Setup wizard is the DNS page, shown in Figure 6-16. The main function of this page is to enable you to configure the Name Resolution Policy Table (NRPT). The entries you create here are written to the GPO used to configure DirectAccess clients.

The NRPT is a feature that enables a DNS client to assign a DNS server address to particular namespaces rather than to particular interfaces. The NRPT essentially stores a list of name resolution rules that are applied to clients through Group Policy. Each rule defines a DNS namespace (a domain name or FQDN) and DNS client behavior for that namespace. Together, these name resolution rules are called a Name Resolution Policy. When a DirectAccess client is on the Internet, each name query request is compared with the namespace rules stored in the Name Resolution Policy. If a match is found, the request is processed according to the settings in the Name Resolution Policy rule. The settings determine the DNS servers to which each request is sent. If a name query request does not match a namespace listed in the NRPT, it is sent to the DNS servers configured in the TCP/IP settings for the specified network interface.

You might need to configure Name Resolution Policy entries if, for example, you need to enable DNS clients to resolve DNS suffixes found only within your intranet namespace. Another reason might be if you have a split public/private DNS environment based on the same domain name and you need to ensure that DirectAccess clients don't contact your company's public servers (such as a web server) through the DirectAccess connection.

EXAM TIP

You need to understand the function of a Name Resolution Policy and the NRPT for the 70-417 exam. Also know that you can view the NRPT by using the Get-DnsClientNrptPolicy cmdlet in Windows PowerShell.

The second configuration decision you need to make on the DNS page relates to the DirectAccess clients' use of local name resolution methods such as NetBIOS and LLMNR. Unlike the setting in the DirectAccess Client Setup wizard, which just allows (does not block) the use of local name resolution, the setting here determines how local name resolution will be used if allowed. You have three options. The most restrictive is to use local name resolution only if the name does not exist in DNS. This option is considered the most secure because if the intranet DNS servers cannot be reached, or if there are other types of DNS errors, the intranet server names are not leaked to the subnet through local name resolution. The second and recommended option is to use local name resolution if the name doesn't exist in DNS or if DNS servers are unreachable when the client computer is on a private network. The third and least restrictive option is to use local name resolution for any kind of DNS resolution error. This option is considered the least secure because the names of intranet network servers can be leaked to the local subnet through local name resolution.

To configure local name resolution for clients in Windows PowerShell, use the Set-DAClientDNSConfiguration cmdlet with the -Local parameter. The three choices available in the GUI are designated by the FallbackSecure, FallbackPrivate, or FallbackUnsecure options, respectively.

> **MORE INFO** For more information about the Set-DAClientDNSConfiguration cmdlet, use Get-Help or visit *http://technet.microsoft.com/en-us/library/hh918389.*

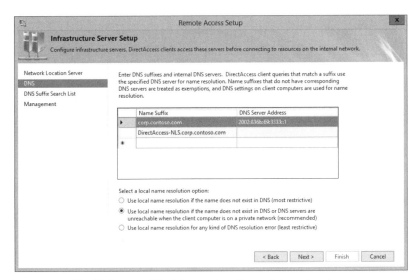

FIGURE 6-16 The DNS page of the Infrastructure Server Setup wizard.

The third page of the Infrastructure Server Setup wizard is the DNS Suffix Search List page, shown in Figure 6-17.

DirectAccess clients use the list you configure here to resolve single-label names, such as http://finance. DNS cannot resolve single-label names unless the DNS client first appends a suffix. By default, clients append the primary DNS suffix of the client computer.

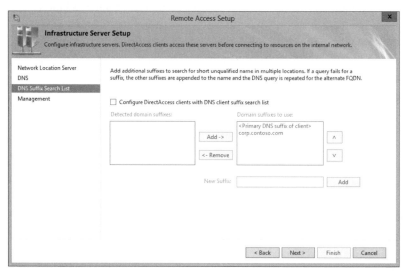

FIGURE 6-17 The DNS Suffix Search List page of the Infrastructure Server Setup wizard.

The fourth and final page of the Infrastructure Server Setup wizard is the Management page, shown in Figure 6-18.

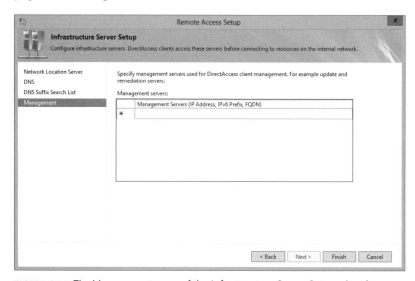

FIGURE 6-18 The Management page of the Infrastructure Server Setup wizard.

You don't need to enter any domain controllers or SCCM servers here because they are detected automatically the first time DirectAccess is configured. Instead, use this page to configure DNS clients with the names of management servers that cannot be detected automatically, such as Windows Server Update Services (WSUS) update servers and antivirus servers. Note that if the list of available domain controllers or SCCM servers is modified after you configure DirectAccess, you can just click Update Management Servers in the Remote Access Management console to refresh the management server list.

There is one other point to remember: management servers that initiate connections to DirectAccess clients must support IPv6 either natively or through ISATAP.

STEP 4: DIRECTACCESS APPLICATION SERVER SETUP

DirectAccess Application Server Setup is a single configuration page, shown in Figure 6-19. You can use this page to configure encryption between the application servers you specify here and the DirectAccess server. (By default, of course, traffic is already encrypted between the DirectAccess client and server.)

To configure the list of application servers using Windows PowerShell, use the Add-DAAppServer cmdlet.

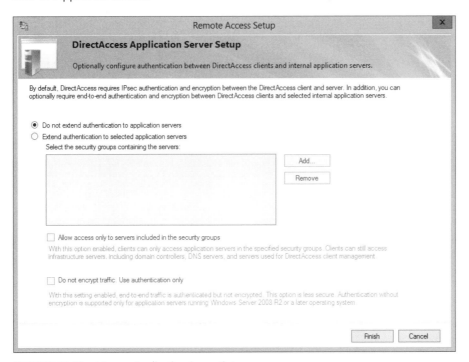

FIGURE 6-19 DirectAccess Application Server Setup.

STEP 5: ADVANCED CONFIGURATION OPTIONS

After you complete DirectAccess Application Server Setup, the Remote Access Management console appears as it does in Figure 6-20. At this point, you can start new wizards to configure advanced options such as a multisite deployment or load balancing by clicking the related options in the Tasks pane.

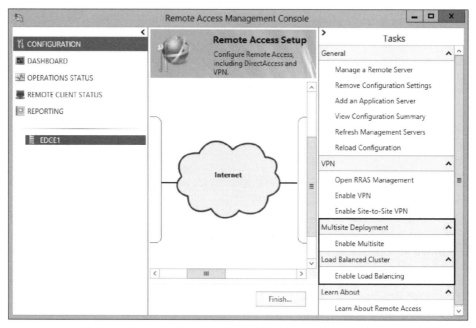

FIGURE 6-20 Configuring advanced DirectAccess options.

VERIFYING THE CONFIGURATION

After you have completed your configuration, you can use the Operations Status item in the left pane of the Remote Access Management console to verify that DirectAccess is ready to use. Remote clients can begin to connect to the network through DirectAccess after the operations status off all components is shown to be working, as shown in Figure 6-21. This process can take several minutes or longer after you complete the final configuration wizard.

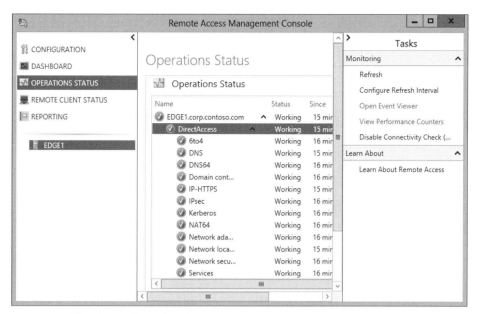

FIGURE 6-21 DirectAccess Operations Status.

After the server components are working, you can verify DirectAccess functionality from the client end. First, you can use the Get-DAConnectionStatus cmdlet to determine whether DirectAccess can properly determine the location of the client. Figure 6-22 shows a Windows PowerShell console session from a portable client that is initially plugged in to a corporate network. The first time the cmdlet is run, the client is shown to be connected locally. When the laptop is disconnected and an Internet broadband connection is enabled, the cmdlet is run again. This time, the client is determined to be connected remotely, and connectivity to the intranet is established through DirectAccess. Another way to verify DirectAccess functionality on the client end is to look at the connection status in the Networks bar. Figure 6-23 shows how a DirectAccess connection appears when it is available.

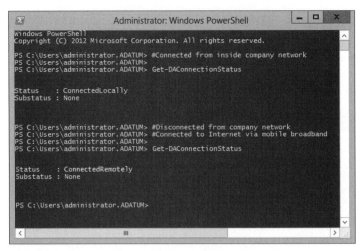

FIGURE 6-22 DirectAccess automatically determines when a client is connected locally or remotely.

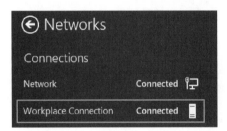

FIGURE 6-23 A DirectAccess connection as it appears in the Networks bar in Windows 8.

Notice that the icon representing a DirectAccess connection in Figure 6-23 resembles a server. Contrast this DirectAccess icon with the VPN icon shown in Figure 6-24. These icons are new in Windows Server 2012 and Windows 8. You need to be able to recognize both the DirectAccess and VPN icons for the 70-417 exam.

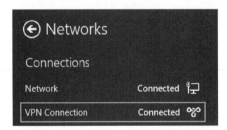

FIGURE 6-24 A VPN connection as it appears in the Networks bar in Windows 8.

Objective summary

- DirectAccess is a bidirectional, always-on alternative to a VPN that clients can use to connect to corporate resources while they are connected to the Internet. DirectAccess first appeared as a feature in Windows Server 2008 R2 and Windows 7, but in Windows Server 2012 and Windows 8, DirectAccess deployment has been simplified greatly.

- Windows Server 2012 and Windows 8 remove the requirement that DirectAccess clients authenticate themselves through computer certificates. Kerberos now is used as the default option.

- Windows Server 2012 introduces several new infrastructure and topology options for DirectAccess, including support for multiple domains, support for multiple sites, the ability to deploy the DirectAccess server behind a NAT device, and load balancing through an NLB cluster.

- In Windows Server 2012, DirectAccess and VPNs are unified in a new server role named Remote Access. To add this server role, type the following at an elevated Windows PowerShell prompt:

```
Install-WindowsFeature RemoteAccess -IncludeManagementTools
```

- You can configure DirectAccess by completing four wizards corresponding to DirectAccess clients, the DirectAccess server, infrastructure servers, and application servers. These wizards include a number of features and options that could appear in test questions on the 70-417 exam. For this reason, it is recommended that you learn all the options in these wizards to prepare for the exam.

Objective review

Answer the following questions to test your knowledge of the information in this objective. You can find the answers to these questions and explanations of why each answer choice is correct or incorrect in the "Answers" section at the end of the chapter.

1. Which of the following is required to establish a DirectAccess connection between a Windows 8 client and a DirectAccess server running Windows Server 2012?

    A. A computer certificate on the client

    B. A user certificate on the client

    C. An IPv6 address on the client

    D. An IPv4 address on the client

2. You are an administrator for a company with a network that includes 300 computers running Windows 8 and 20 servers running Windows Server 2012. The network consists of a single domain named Contoso.com.

   Your manager has asked you to begin testing DirectAccess with a group of 20 trial users in your organization. You deploy a single DirectAccess server on the company network edge and implement computer authentication through Kerberos. You later ask the trial users to attempt to connect to the corporate network from outside the company premises. All users attempt to connect on domain-joined computers running Windows 8. Although most users are able to connect remotely to the corporate network, certain users working on desktop computers or virtual machines report that they cannot establish a connection. You would like to enable these users to connect to the corporate network through DirectAccess.

   Which of the following Windows PowerShell commands is most likely to help you meet your goal?

   A. Set-DAClient -OnlyRemoteComputers "Enabled"

   B. Set-DAClient -OnlyRemoteComputers "Disabled"

   C. Set-DAClient -ForceTunnel "Enabled"

   D. Set-DAClient -ForceTunnel "Disabled"

3. You are an administrator for a company named Contoso.com, which has a network that includes 500 computers running Windows 8 and 30 servers running Windows Server 2012. The network consists of a single domain named Contoso.com.

   Many Contoso employees work on the road and rarely visit the company premises. They currently connect to the company network through a VPN. You want to deploy DirectAccess so you can apply software patches through System Center Configuration Manager. You don't want to enable computers to access resources on the company network through the DirectAccess connection.

   Which of the following Windows PowerShell commands will help you meet your goal?

   A. Set-DAServer -DAInstallType ManageOut

   B. Set-DAServer -DAInstallType FullInstall

   C. Set-DAServer -HealthCheck "Enabled"

   D. Set-DAServer -HealthCheck "Disabled"

Thought experiment

You work as a network administrator for Fabrikam.com, which is based in New York and has a branch office in London. The Fabrikam.com network includes three Active Directory domains. The Fabrikam.com domain includes resources in both the New York office and the London office. The Na.fabrikam.com domain includes resources that are situated mostly in the New York office, and Eu.fabrikam.com includes resources that are situated mostly in the London office. The domain name Fabrikam.com is also used for the company's public website.

The servers on the network are running a combination of Windows Server 2008 R2 and Windows Server 2012. The clients are running a combination of Windows 7 and Windows 8.

You are working with the rest of the IT department in planning a DirectAccess deployment. Currently, users connect to the network remotely through a VPN. The VPN servers in both offices are running Windows Server 2008 R2.

1. The New York and London offices each include two resources within the Fabrikam.com domain that some remote users might need to access through a DirectAccess connection. You want to ensure that DirectAccess clients connecting to resources within the Fabrikam.com domain perform DNS lookup of these resources by contacting internal DNS servers. You also want ensure that DirectAccess clients connect to public DNS servers when attempting to connect to the public website at www.fabrikam.com. What can you do to ensure that DirectAccess clients always contact the proper DNS servers when attempting to access resources with a domain suffix of fabrikam.com?

2. You want remote users to be able to automatically connect through a DirectAccess connection to the entry point nearest the company network, whether it is in London or New York. How can you achieve this, and what requirements must first be met?

3. You want to ensure that when remote users from the New York office are connected through a DirectAccess connection and enter an address such as http:// app1, the address for app1.na.contoso.com is queried first in DNS, followed by app1.eu.contoso.com. How can you achieve this?

4. Certain users connect to confidential resources when working remotely. For these users you want to configure two-factor authentication. However, you want to avoid the expense and administrative complexity of traditional smart cards. Which two alternative features can you consider in your environment to provide two-factor authentication?

Answers

This section contains the answers to the Objective Review and the Thought Experiment.

Objective 6.1: Review

1. **Correct Answer:** C

   A. **Incorrect:** In Windows Server 2012 and Windows 8, Kerberos can be used in place of a computer certificate.

   B. **Incorrect:** A user certificate is not required to establish a DirectAccess connection.

   C. **Correct**: DirectAccess connections are based on IPv6 communication. If the DirectAccess client cannot obtain a global IPv6 address from its environment, the client must obtain one with the aid of an IPv6 transition technology.

   D. **Incorrect**: IPv4 communication is not required for DirectAccess.

2. **Correct Answer:** B

   A. **Incorrect:** If only desktop computers and virtual machines are having trouble connecting through DirectAccess, this setting is most likely already enabled.

   B. **Correct:** This command would disable the setting that limits DirectAccess connectivity to mobile computers only.

   C. **Incorrect:** This setting would force all traffic from the client to pass through the DirectAccess connection. It would not help desktop and virtual computers establish a DirectAccess connection.

   D. **Incorrect:** This setting would remove the requirement that clients force all traffic to pass through the DirectAccess connection. It would not help desktop and virtual computers establish a DirectAccess connection.

3. **Correct Answer:** A

   A. **Correct:** This command would deploy DirectAccess for remote management only.

   B. **Incorrect:** This command would deploy full DirectAccess for client access and remote management.

   C. **Incorrect**: This command would require NAP health checks on DirectAccess clients. It would not configure DirectAccess clients for management only.

   D. **Incorrect**: This command would disable NAP health checks on DirectAccess clients. It would not configure DirectAccess clients for management only.

Thought experiment

1. You can configure the NPRT so the four internal Fabrikam.com resources are associated with internal DNS servers.

2. You can enable a multisite deployment. You first need to make sure that the DirectAccess servers are running Windows Server 2012, the clients are running Windows 8, and your company has deployed a PKI.

3. Configure a DNS suffix search list in the Infrastructure Server Setup for the DirectAccess deployment for the Na.fabrikam.com domain.

4. You can consider virtual smart cards or OTPs.

CHAPTER 7

Configure a network policy server infrastructure

Network Access Protection (NAP), as you know, is a Windows Server feature that enforces health requirements on client computers as they attempt to connect to a company network. These health requirements can relate to the status of software updates, of antivirus protection, of host firewall status, or of spyware protection. NAP was first introduced in Windows Server 2008.

Although NAP doesn't include any significant new features in Windows Server 2012, one important new feature, System Health Validator (SHV) Multi-configuration, appeared in Windows Server 2008 R2. This new feature falls within the one NAP objective listed for the 70-417 exam, Configure Network Access Protection.

Objectives in this chapter:

- Objective 7.1: Configure Network Access Protection

Objective 7.1: Configure Network Access Protection

NAP can be deployed in many different configurations, depending on whether it is enforced through DHCP, VPNs, IPsec, or Remote Desktop Services Gateway, or 802.1x. If your knowledge of NAP has become rusty since you earned your last certification, it's important to review how NAP enforcement is configured.

Most of NAP has remained the same since Windows Server 2008, but there is one new feature in NAP that falls within the Configure Network Access Protection objective: SHV Multi-configuration. For the 70-417 exam, you definitely need to know about this new feature, but one small feature might not be sufficient to represent the entire Configure Network Access Protection objective on the exam. For this reason, you might encounter one or more questions about NAP configuration that are similar to the ones you saw when you earned your Windows Server 2008 certification.

How NAP works

First, let's review some basic NAP concepts. When a client computer first attempts to connect to a network, its first point of contact could be a DHCP server, a VPN server, or another type of device. In a NAP infrastructure, this first point of contact is configured as a NAP enforcement point, and the NAP client is configured to report its system status (called a statement of health or SoH) to this NAP enforcement point.

The NAP enforcement point uses the RADIUS protocol to forward the SoH and connection request to a Network Policy Server (NPS). The NPS server uses connection request policies to determine whether the client connection request will be processed by NAP. If evaluated by NAP, the client request is next processed by network policies, which provide potential instructions about whether to allow the connection, block the connection, or allow restricted access only to a remediation server or set of servers. The instructions of only the first network policy that matches the conditions of the connection request are followed.

Figure 7-1 shows an example of a simple NAP infrastructure.

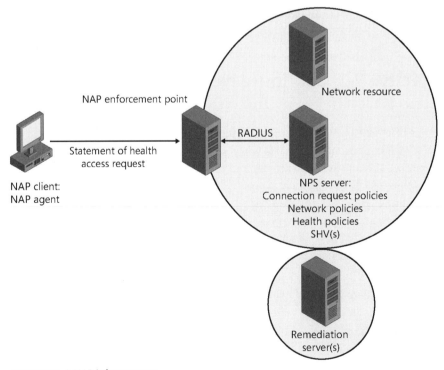

FIGURE 7-1 A NAP infrastructure.

Network policies usually include health policies as matching conditions. Health policies determine whether a NAP client matches an indicated state of failing or passing a health check according to an SHV. Windows Server includes one built-in SHV, Windows Security Health Validator.

Besides the network policies that assess the health compliance of NAP clients, an additional network policy is normally included to match clients that are not NAP-capable. These network policies include a condition named "NAP-Capable" whose value is configured as "Computer is non NAP-capable." (NAP-capable computers are ones that send an SoH.) Network policies created to match non-NAP-capable clients may be configured either to allow or block the connection request.

The following list further describes these components involved in NAP processing:

- **Connection request policies** Rules that determine whether a connection request will be processed by network policies
- **Network policies** Rules that compare the health of connection requests to health policy statements and accordingly allow access, block access, or allow remediated access to those requests. Network policies include conditions and condition values configured to match different types of clients. The Health Policy condition uses a health policy check to match a client. The NAP-Capable condition matches clients based on whether they have sent an SoH. The MS-Service class condition is used to match particular DHCP scopes.
- **Health policy** A statement of health compliance or noncompliance according to a particular SHV
- **SHV** A software component that performs a particular set of tests about the safety of a client connection
- **Windows SHV** The default SHV and only SHV built into Windows Server 2012

EXAM TIP

Make sure you understand network policies and conditions well for the 70-417 exam.

Figure 7-2 illustrates how these components could work together in a particular example of NAP processing.

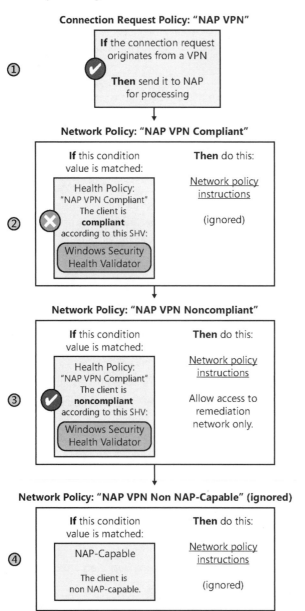

FIGURE 7-2 The first network policy that accurately describes a stated health policy condition about a NAP client provides the instructions about how to handle the NAP client request.

The procedures for configuring the various NAP enforcement types all differ from each other, but they do share common steps. In general, you first configure the NAP server by using the NAP Configuration Wizard. You use this wizard to specify the NAP enforcement type you want to implement and to create the required connection request policies, network policies, and health policies. After running the wizard, you create security groups for NAP and configure Group Policy. For more information about implementing the various NAP enforcement types, visit *http://technet.microsoft.com/en-us/library/dd314175(v=ws.10).aspx.*

EXAM TIP

In particular, configuring NAP with IPsec enforcement requires extra steps beyond those stated above. Although the configuration steps haven't changed since Windows Server 2008, it's recommended that you review IPsec-specific NAP topics such as HRAs and HRA automatic discovery as they are described at the following address: *http://technet .microsoft.com/en-us/library/dd125312(v=ws.10).aspx.*

SHV Multi-configuration

Windows Server 2008 allowed you to configure just one set of health tests for each SHV. As a result, an NPS server couldn't typically adjust its health checks to suit different NAP client types.

This limitation could sometimes present a problem. In some scenarios, you might prefer to apply different health checks to different enforcement methods, computers, or users. For example, you might want to require all VPN-connected computers to have their antivirus software both enabled and up to date but require local DHCP-based connections to have their antivirus software enabled only. To meet such a requirement in Windows Server 2008, you usually needed to use two NPS servers.

In Windows Server 2008 R2 and Windows Server 2012, however, you can create multiple configurations for each SHV. After you create configurations in addition to the default configuration, you can specify which SHV configuration you want to use for a particular health policy. Figure 7-3 shows an example of multiple configurations created for the built-in SHV, Windows Security Health Validator.

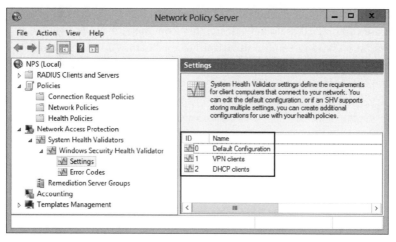

FIGURE 7-3 An SHV with three configured sets of health requirements.

Default configuration

In Windows Server 2008 R2 and Windows Server 2012, a Settings node appears in the Network Policy Server console beneath the default Windows Security Health Validator (and beneath any additional SHVs you have installed that are also compatible with multiple configurations). When you select the Settings node, only the Default Configuration appears by default. This configuration can't be deleted or renamed.

Creating additional SHV configurations

To create an additional configuration for an SHV, perform the following steps. (These steps demonstrate the procedure using the built-in Windows Security Health Validator as the SHV.)

1. In the Network Policy Server console tree, navigate to Network Access Protection \System Health Validators\Windows Security Health Validator\Settings.

2. Right-click Settings and then click New, as shown in Figure 7-4.

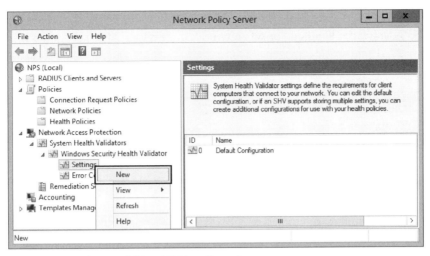

FIGURE 7-4 Creating an additional SHV configuration.

3. In the Configuration Friendly Name dialog box, type a name for the new configuration, and then click OK.

4. In the Windows Security Health Validator window, shown in Figure 7-5, specify the desired system health requirements for the configuration.

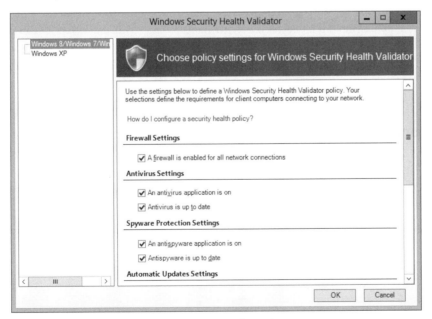

FIGURE 7-5 Specifying settings for a new SHV configuration.

You can enable any of the following health checks:

- **A Firewall Is Enabled For All Network Connections** If this check box is selected, the client computer must have a firewall that is registered with Windows Security Center and enabled for all network connections.

- **An Antivirus Application Is On** If this check box is selected, the client computer must have an antivirus application installed, registered with Windows Security Center, and turned on.

- **Antivirus Is Up To Date** If this check box is selected, the client computer can also be checked to ensure that the antivirus signature file is up to date.

- **An Antispyware Application Is On** If this check box is selected, the client computer must have an antispyware application installed, registered with Windows Security Center, and turned on.

- **Antispyware Is Up To Date** If this check box is selected, the client computer can also be checked to ensure that the antispyware signature file is up to date.

- **Automatic Updating Is Enabled** If this check box is selected, the client computer must be configured to check for updates from Windows Update. You can choose whether to download and install them.

- **Security Update Settings** Use this section to define health checks related to security updates. If you select the option to restrict access for clients that do not have all available security updates installed, clients will be designated as noncompliant if they do not meet this requirement according to the criteria you specify. You can specify the minimum severity level required for the updates and the minimum number of hours allowed since the client has checked for security updates. You can also require clients to use Windows Server Update Services (WSUS), Windows Update, or both sources.

Assigning an SHV configuration to a health policy

To assign different health checks to different NAP client types, you can assign different SHV configurations to the health policies created for these different client types. For example, you might want to assign one SHV configuration to your VPN client health policies and another to your DHCP client health policies.

It's best to use the Configure NAP Wizard to generate your health policies automatically. You start the Configure NAP Wizard by clicking Configure NAP in the Details pane of the Network Policy Server console when the main NPS node is selected, as shown in Figure 7-6.

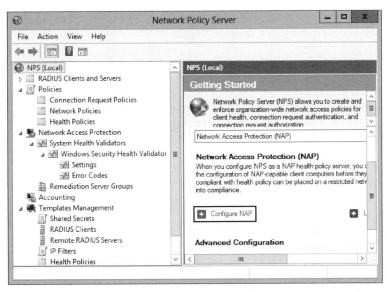

FIGURE 7-6 It's best to use the Configure NAP Wizard to generate health policies.

The health policies created by the Configure NAP Wizard will be assigned appropriate names and be set as conditions in new, correctly configured network policies. Usually there will be two health policies for each client type: one compliant and one noncompliant. For example, if you run the Configure NAP Wizard twice and specify first VPN and then DHCP as the network connection methods, the wizard will generate the four health policies shown in Figure 7-7. For each client type, the noncompliant health policy serves as a matching condition for clients that do not pass one of the health checks.

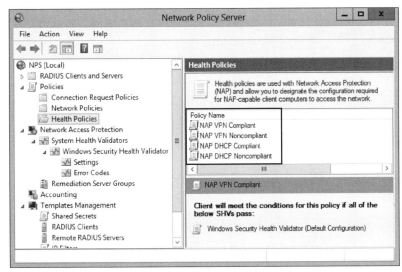

FIGURE 7-7 The Configure NAP Wizard creates a compliant and noncompliant health policy for each network connection method.

If you want to assign a custom SHV configuration to a certain type of client, the only thing you have to do after running the Configure NAP Wizard is to modify the properties of the newly created health policies. You want to specify the same SHV configuration for both the compliant and noncompliant versions of the same NAP client type (for example, VPN or DHCP).

By default, when a new health policy is created, the Default Configuration of the SHV is used to define the health checks for that health policy. To assign a nondefault SHV configuration instead, perform the following steps:

1. In the Network Policy Server console, navigate to Policies\Health Policies, and then double-click the name of the health policy you want to modify.

2. On the Settings tab, in the SHVs Used In This Health Policy list, click the drop-down arrow in the Setting column for the Windows Security Health Validator SHV to see a list of available configurations. (Figure 7-8 shows an example.)

3. Select the desired configuration in the Setting drop-down list and click OK.

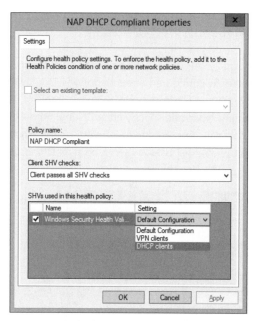

FIGURE 7-8 Assigning an SHV configuration to a health policy.

Objective summary

- NAP is a feature that enforces health requirements on client computers as they attempt to connect to a network.

- The NAP feature most likely to be tested is SHV Multi-configuration. This feature first appeared in Windows Server 2008 R2. By using SHV Multi-configuration, you can define different sets of health checks for a single SHV. You might use this feature to assign a higher health standard for certain types of NAP clients, such as VPN clients.

- After you create a new configuration for an SHV, you can assign that configuration to health policies. The configuration is applied to a particular NAP client type if you modify the health policies created for that client type.

- NAP has not changed much since Windows Server 2008, so you should be prepared to answer some of the same types of questions about this feature that you saw when you last earned your certification.

Objective review

Answer the following questions to test your knowledge of the information in this objective. You can find the answers to these questions and explanations of why each answer choice is correct or incorrect in the "Answers" section at the end of the chapter.

1. You have deployed NAP in your network with VPN enforcement. You have deployed a single NPS on a computer running Windows Server 2012 and are using Windows Security Health Validator as the only SHV.

    Through your NAP policies, VPN clients that are evaluated as noncompliant are allowed access only to a set of remediation servers.

    You now want to implement NAP with DHCP enforcement. However, you only want to log noncompliant DHCP clients. You don't want to block noncompliant DHCP clients from accessing any part of the network.

    What should you do?

    A. Create a new configuration for the SHV for the DHCP clients.

    B. Install an additional SHV and configure it for the DHCP clients.

    C. Modify the default NAP DHCP connection request policy.

    D. Modify the default NAP DHCP Noncompliant network policy.

2. You have deployed NAP in your network with VPN enforcement. You have deployed a single NPS on a computer running Windows Server 2012 and are using Windows Security Health Validator as the only SHV. Your VPN clients are allowed only restricted access to the network if either security updates or virus definitions are not up to date.

    You now want to implement NAP with DHCP enforcement. However, you want to use NAP to ensure only that automatic updates and antivirus software are enabled on the DHCP client.

    What should you do?

    A. Create a new configuration for the SHV for the DHCP clients.

    B. Install an additional SHV and configure it for the DHCP clients.

    C. Modify the default NAP DHCP connection request policy.

    D. Modify the default NAP DHCP Noncompliant network policy.

3. You have been testing a new deployment of NAP in your network. NAP is currently configured so that VPN clients with antivirus software that is not up to date log their status with the NPS. These clients are currently not blocked from network access.

You now want to change your NAP configuration so that the access of the same VPN clients is now restricted to a set of remediation servers on the company network.

How can you achieve this goal?

A. Modify the NAP VPN Compliant network policy.

B. Modify the NAP VPN Noncompliant network policy.

C. Modify the NAP VPN Compliant health policy.

D. Modify the NAP VPN Noncompliant health policy.

 Thought experiment

You work as a network administrator for Fabrikam.com. A month ago, you began testing NAP on VPN clients. You configured the Windows Security Health Validator to determine whether VPN clients had antivirus software enabled. In your current configuration, clients that are determined to be noncompliant just report their status. They are not denied access to the network.

In the month since you implemented NAP, you have successfully remediated the client computers that have reported their antivirus application as disabled. You now are ready to move beyond the testing and want to modify your configuration to enforce a stricter NAP policy. You can find the answers to these questions in the "Answers" section at the end of the chapter.

1. Currently, your NAP policies determine only whether an antivirus application is enabled on the client. You now want to add a second health check to ensure that a firewall is enabled on the client. You also want to ensure that the client firewall is enabled automatically if it is determined to be in a disabled state. How can you achieve this?

2. You want to block access completely to VPN clients that are determined to be infected. How can you achieve this without blocking other clients?

3. You want to assign additional security update health checks to users who are members of the Finance group who connect through a VPN. How can you achieve this?

Answers

This section contains the answers to the Objective Review and the Thought Experiment.

Objective 7.1: Review

1. **Correct Answer:** D

   A. **Incorrect:** An SHV configuration does not affect how a client request is handled. It is used only to perform health checks on a client.

   B. **Incorrect:** A new SHV would not determine whether a client connection is allowed or blocked. That behavior is determined by network policies.

   C. **Incorrect**: Connection request policies do not determine how noncompliant client requests are handled. They determine whether connection requests are evaluated by NAP.

   D. **Correct**: The Configure NAP Wizard creates a NAP DHCP Noncompliant policy that determines how noncompliant DHCP client requests are handled. To allow noncompliant DHCP clients to access the network and just log the noncompliance, you need to modify the properties of this policy.

2. **Correct Answer:** A

   A. **Correct:** You can create an additional configuration for the SHV that performs only the desired checks on DHCP clients. You then need to assign this configuration to the health policies created for DHCP clients.

   B. **Incorrect:** You don't need to install an additional SHV. The built-in SHV includes the health checks you need. You need only to create a second configuration of the built-in SHV.

   C. **Incorrect:** A connection request policy doesn't determine which health checks are performed. It determines whether a connection request is evaluated by NAP.

   D. **Incorrect:** A network policy doesn't allow you to specify the health checks to be performed. It specifies a health policy that in turn specifies a SHV configuration. To modify which health checks are performed, you need to change the SHV configuration.

3. **Correct Answer:** B

   A. **Incorrect:** You don't want to change how compliant VPN clients are handled. You want to change how noncompliant VPN clients are handled.

   B. **Correct:** A network policy determines how compliant or noncompliant connection requests are handled. In this case, you want to change how noncompliant VPN clients are handled. To achieve your goal, modify the NAP Enforcement setting on the Settings tab of the NAP VPN Noncompliant network policy. Change the setting from Allow Full Network Access to Allow Limited Access.

C. **Incorrect**: A health policy doesn't change how the connection requests from compliant or noncompliant clients are handled. It changes only how connection requests are evaluated.

D. **Incorrect**: A health policy doesn't change how the connection requests from compliant or noncompliant clients are handled. It changes only how connection requests are evaluated.

Thought experiment

1. Modify the Windows Security Health Validator policy so that it verifies that a firewall is enabled for all network connections. Next, in the network policy that matches the VPN clients that are noncompliant, select the option on the Settings tab to enable autoremediation of client computers.

2. Create a new health policy that specifies the client SHV check as Client Reported As Infected By One Or More SHVs. Create a new network policy that specifies the new health policy as a condition, and configure the new network policy to deny access. Move the new network policy to the top of the list of network policies.

3. First, run the Configure NAP Wizard and specify VPN as the connection method and the Finance group as the user group to which the policy should apply. Next, create a second configuration for the Windows Security Health Validator that performs a check of security updates in the manner you wish. Finally, attach the new configuration of the Windows Security Health Validator to the new health policies just created by the Configure NAP Wizard.

CHAPTER 8

Configure and manage Active Directory

This domain is inherited from Exam 70-411: Administering Windows Server 2012. Two of the four original objectives from that domain are officially listed for the 70-417 exam: Configure Domain Controllers and Maintain Active Directory. More important for our upgrade exam purposes, these objectives together include just two new features that have appeared since Windows Server 2008: domain controller cloning and the Active Directory Recycle Bin.

Objectives in this chapter:

- Objective 8.1: Configure domain controllers.
- Objective 8.2: Maintain Active Directory.

Objective 8.1: Configure domain controllers

Our interest in "configuring domain controllers" is quite narrow here. Although you might see a question or two on the 70-417 exam that tests only what you needed to know in this area for your Windows Server 2008 certification (how to configure read-only domain controllers, for example), the focus within this objective will be on domain controller cloning. Domain controller cloning is a genuinely new feature in Windows Server 2012, and you will almost certainly see questions about this topic on the 70-417 exam.

Here's the first thing you need to know: The cloning capability applies only to *virtualized* domain controllers, which is itself a newly supported capability in Windows Server 2012.

> **This section covers the following topic:**
> - Configure domain controller cloning

Cloning domain controllers

Beginning with Windows Server 2012, you can now deploy additional domain controllers in a domain by safely copying an existing virtual domain controller. In earlier versions of Windows Server, the fastest way to deploy a new domain controller, physical or virtual, was to start a fresh sysprepped image, promote the new server based on that image to a domain controller, and then complete additional configuration requirements as necessary. Cloning is much faster.

Cloning a domain controller has certain environmental requirements. In addition, cloning a domain controller is a special, specific procedure that includes adding the source virtual machine (VM) to a built-in group account and running certain Windows PowerShell cmdlets prior to exporting and importing.

It's also worth noting that cloning seems tailor-made for questions on the 70-417 exam. Not only is this feature new in Windows Server 2012, but the cloning prerequisites and the cloning procedure also are made up of details that are just specific enough for the exam. For this reason, be sure to learn these details well, such as the specific names of cmdlets and XML files.

> **MORE INFO**   For more information about virtualized domain controllers, see "Test Lab Guide: Demonstrate Virtualized Domain Controller (VDC) in Windows Server '8' Beta" at *http://www.microsoft.com/en-us/download/details.aspx?id=29027.*

Prerequisites for cloning

To clone a domain controller, three different servers need to be running Windows Server 2012:

- The host server with the Hyper-V server role installed, on which the source VM is running as a guest
- A second server, physical or virtual, that is itself a domain controller in the same domain as the VM to be cloned, and that is hosting the PDC Emulator operations master role
- The source VM to be cloned that is a domain controller, and that cannot be hosting the PDC Emulator operations master role

Note also that the clone domain controller that results from the cloning procedure will be located in the same site as the source domain controller.

Add the source domain controller to the Cloneable Domain Controllers group

If your environment meets the prerequisites, you are ready to begin the cloning procedure. The first step in this procedure is to add the source VM that is a domain controller to the Cloneable Domain Controllers global security group. This built-in group account is new to Windows Server 2012 and is found in the Users container within a domain, as shown in Figure 8-1.

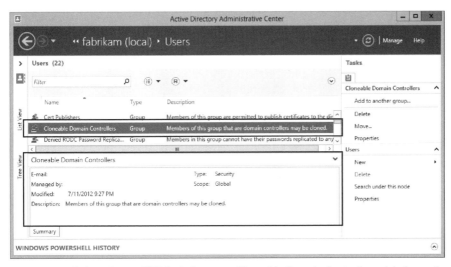

FIGURE 8-1 Windows Server 2012 includes a new Cloneable Domain Controllers global security group.

> **MORE INFO** To add a user or computer account to a new security group, you can use the Add-ADGroupMember cmdlet. For more information about this cmdlet, visit *http://technet.microsoft.com/en-us/library/ee617210.aspx.*

Review applications with the Get-ADDCCloningExcludedApplicationList cmdlet

The next step in cloning a virtual domain controller is to run the Get-ADDCCloningExclude dApplicationList cmdlet on the source VM. The purpose of this cmdlet is to present a list of applications or services that are not evaluated for cloning and that are installed on the source VM. If no such applications are found, the cmdlet provides the output shown in Figure 8-2. If an unevaluated application is found, an output similar to the one in Figure 8-3 is displayed.

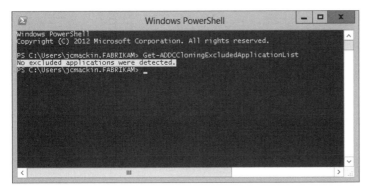

FIGURE 8-2 Output of Get-ADDCCloningExcludedApplicationList revealing no unsafe applications.

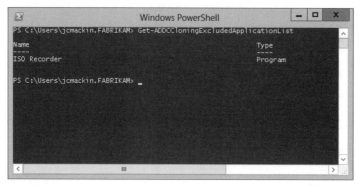

FIGURE 8-3 Output of Get-ADDCCloningExcludedApplicationList revealing a potentially unsafe application.

If the cmdlet returns a list of services and installed programs, review the list. Consult the software vendor of each application to determine whether it can be safely cloned. If any applications or services in the list cannot be safely cloned, you must uninstall them from the source domain controller at this point.

Next, if you determine that the services or applications returned by the Get-ADDCCloningExcludedApplicationList cmdlet are safe for cloning, you can add them to an inclusion list called CustomDCCloneAllowList.xml. To do so, use the -GenerateXml option with the same cmdlet. For example, the following command generates the excluded application list as a file named CustomDCCloneAllowList.xml at the specified folder path (C:\Windows\NTDS) and forces overwrite if a file by that name is found to already exist at that path location:

```
Get-ADDCCloningExcludedApplicationList -GenerateXml -Path C:\Windows\NTDS -Force
```

The output of this command is shown in Figure 8-4, and the contents of the CustomDCCloneAllowList.xml file are shown in Figure 8-5.

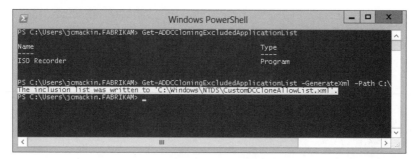

FIGURE 8-4 Adding detected applications to the inclusion list.

```
<?xml version="1.0" encoding="UTF-8"?>
<dc:CustomDCCloneAllowList xmlns:dc="uri:microsoft.com:schemas:CustomDCCloneAllowList">
    <Allow>
        <Name>ISO Recorder</Name>
        <Type>Program</Type>
    </Allow>
</dc:CustomDCCloneAllowList>
```

FIGURE 8-5 The CustomDCCloneAllowList.xml file.

After you perform this step, the Get-ADDCCloningExcludedApplicationList cmdlet will provide the output shown in Figure 8-6.

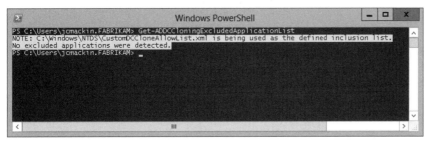

FIGURE 8-6 The output of Get-ADDCCloningExcludedApplicationList after adding a detected application to the inclusion list.

Note that if any programs originally returned by the Get-ADDCCloningExcludedApplicationList cmdlet are not added to the inclusion list (CustomDCCloneAllowList.xml), the next step will fail.

> **MORE INFO**   For more information about the Get-ADDCCloningExcludedApplicationList cmdlet, visit *http://technet.microsoft.com/en-us/library/hh852291*.

Run the New-ADDCCloneConfigFile cmdlet on the source VM

The New-ADDCCloneConfigFile cmdlet runs a list of prerequisite checks on the source VM and generates a clone configuration file, DCCloneConfig.xml, if all the checks succeed. The clone configuration file includes settings that you have specified for the new clone VM, such as an IP address configuration and computer name, by using parameters with the cmdlet. If the command runs successfully, the DCCloneConfig.xml file is saved in a location (C:\Windows\NTDS) that will automatically configure the clone with these settings when you later start the clone for the first time, so you don't need to look for the file or move it from its default location. (If you don't specify a name for the clone, one will be chosen automatically. If you don't specify a static IP configuration, it will be set dynamically.)

The checks succeed if the answers to the following three questions are all "yes":

- Is the PDC Emulator operations master role hosted on a domain controller running Windows Server 2012?

- Is this computer a member of the Cloneable Domain Controllers group?

- Are all programs and services originally listed in the output of the Get-ADDCCloningExcludedApplicationList cmdlet now captured in CustomDCCloneAllowList.xml?

A successful check of a source domain controller is shown in Figure 8-7.

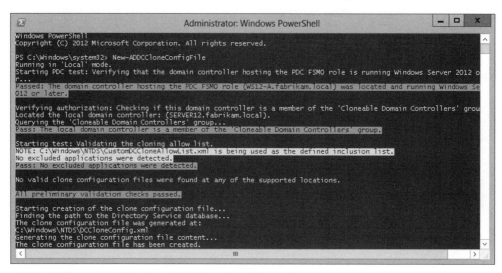

FIGURE 8-7 The output of the New-ADDCCloneConfigFile cmdlet.

EXAM TIP

You need to remember the function of both the CustomDCCloneAllowList.xml file and the DCCloneConfig.xml file, and that these files are saved in %Systemroot%\NTDS.

MORE INFO   For more information about the New-ADDCCloneConfigFile cmdlet, visit *http://technet.microsoft.com/en-us/library/jj158947.*

Export and then import the VM of the source domain controller

To clone the VM, first shut it down. Then, you can use the Export command in Hyper-V Manager to copy the VM files to a location you choose. To export the VM using Windows PowerShell instead, use the Export-VM cmdlet as in the following example:

```
Export-VM -Name Test -Path D:\
```

At this point, you must delete all the snapshots in the Snapshots subdirectory of the exported VM. If desired, you can then copy the exported VM and its associated files to another computer running Windows Server 2012 that has the Hyper-V role installed.

Next, you can use the Import command in Hyper-V Manager to import the exported VM. Use the Copy The Virtual Machine (Create A New Unique ID) option when importing the VM, as shown in Figure 8-8. To perform this step in Windows PowerShell, use the Import-VM cmdlet as in the following example:

```
Import-VM -Path 'D:\Test2\Virtual Machines\8F148B6D-C674-413E-9FCC-4FBED185C52D.XML' -
Copy -GenerateNewId
```

Finally, after importing the copy of the source VM, you can restart the source VM and start the new clone VM.

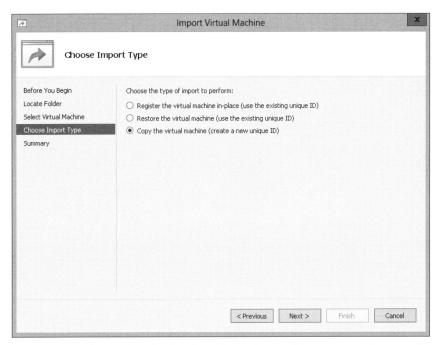

FIGURE 8-8 Creating a unique ID when importing an image allows you to use the source image again.

EXAM TIP

The topic of read-only domain controllers (RODCs) falls within the Configure Domain Controllers domain. Although this feature has not changed since Windows Server 2008, it's worth mentioning that the Dcpromo utility, which has been deprecated in Windows Server 2012, retains a specialized usage with RODCs: You can use Dcpromo with the /CreateDCAccount option to create an RODC account in Active Directory. For more information about the options still used with Dcpromo in Windows Server 2012, type **Dcpromo /?** at a command prompt.

Objective summary

- Windows Server 2012 allows you to clone a virtualized domain controller for rapid deployment of a new domain controller.
- The source VM must be a member of the Cloneable Domain Controllers global security group.
- Three computers must be running Windows Server 2012: the host server running Hyper-V, the guest VM that is the domain controller to be cloned, and a third domain controller that owns the PDC Emulator operations master role for the domain.
- You need to use the Get-ADDCCloningExcludedApplicationList cmdlet to determine whether any applications on the source domain controller have not yet been determined to be safe for cloning. You must either uninstall such applications or add them to the inclusion list by running the same cmdlet again with the -GenerateXml switch.
- Next, run the New-ADDCCloneConfigFile cmdlet to run prerequisite checks to determine whether the domain controller is ready to be cloned.
- When the domain controller passes the prerequisite checks, use Hyper-V Manager or the Export-VM and Import-VM cmdlets to copy the VM. Be sure to delete the snapshots of the exported VM before you import. When importing, choose the option to copy the VM and create a new unique ID.

Objective review

Answer the following questions to test your knowledge of the information in this objective. You can find the answers to these questions and explanations of why each answer choice is correct or incorrect in the "Answers" section at the end of the chapter.

1. You are a network administrator for Fabrikam.com. The Fabrikam.com network includes a private cloud built on six physical servers with the Hyper-V role installed, three of which are running Windows Server 2012 and three of which are running Windows Server 2008 R2. These physical servers host a total of 24 virtualized guest servers, including domain controllers, infrastructure servers, database servers, and application servers. All VMs are members of the Fabrikam.com domain.

   One of the virtualized domain controllers is named DC1. DC1 is hosted on a physical server named HYPV1. You want to clone DC1 to add another domain controller to the Fabrikam.com domain.

   Which of the following is NOT a requirement for cloning DC1?

   A. DC1 must own the PDC emulator role.

   B. HYPV1 must be running Windows Server 2012.

   C. DC1 must be running Windows Server 2012.

   D. All programs and services originally listed in the output of the Get-ADDCCloningExcludedApplicationList cmdlet when it is run on DC1 must be added to the Allow list in CustomDCCloneAllowList.xml.

2. You want to clone a domain controller named VDC1 that is running Windows Server 2012 within a VM. VDC1 is hosted on a server named Host01, which is also running Windows Server 2012.

   VDC1 belongs to the Contoso.local domain and owns both the PDC Emulator and Infrastructure Master operations master roles for that domain. Contoso.local currently includes just one other domain controller, named VDC2. VDC2 is running Windows Server 2008 R2 and is the only global catalog server in Contoso.local.

   You want to create a new domain controller named DC3 that is based on a clone of VDC1. Which steps do you need to take before you can achieve this? (Choose all that apply.)

   A. Move the Infrastructure Master operations master role to VDC2.

   B. Make VDC1 a global catalog server.

   C. Upgrade VDC2 to Windows Server 2012.

   D. Make Host01 a member of the Cloneable Domain Controllers global security group.

   E. Make VDC1 a member of the Cloneable Domain Controllers global security group.

3. You want to clone a domain controller named DCA.fabrikam.local that is running Windows Server 2012 in a VM. DCA is hosted on a server named HV01, which is also running Windows Server 2012.

   When you run the cmdlet Get-ADDCCloningExcludedApplicationList on DCA, the output displays the name of a single application, App1. You want to ensure that App1 is made available on all future domain controllers that result from cloning DCA. You have verified that App1 is safe for cloning.

   What should you do next?

   A. Export the DCA VM.

   B. Add App1 to the CustomDCCloneAllowList.xml file.

   C. Run the New-ADDCCloneConfigFile cmdlet.

   D. Run the New-VirtualDiskClone cmdlet.

Objective 8.2: Maintain Active Directory

Windows Server 2008 R2 introduced Active Directory Recycle Bin, a Windows PowerShell–based feature that allowed you to restore objects deleted from the Active Directory Domain Services database. Windows Server 2012 brings this functionality of Active Directory Recycle Bin to Active Directory Administrative Center, the graphical tool for managing Active Directory Domain Services that also first appeared in Windows Server 2008 R2.

> **This section covers the following topics:**
> - Enable Active Directory Recycle Bin
> - Use Active Directory Recycle Bin to restore deleted objects
> - Set the deleted object lifetime in a domain

Restoring deleted objects in Active Directory

Before Windows Server 2008 R2, there were just two methods you could use to restore an object that had accidentally been deleted from Active Directory Domain Services: you could perform an authoritative restore with the Ntdsutil command-line utility, or you could use the LDP utility to perform a procedure called tombstone reanimation. Both of these methods, however, had significant drawbacks. With Ntdsutil, the drawbacks were that you first had to boot the domain controller into Directory Services Restore Mode (making the domain controller temporarily unavailable to clients on the network) and that you could only restore deleted objects that you had previously backed up. With tombstone reanimation, the drawbacks were that it was a complicated procedure and that it couldn't be relied on to restore an object's group memberships.

EXAM TIP

Remember that you use Ntdsutil to perform an authoritative restore and LDP to perform tombstone reanimation.

> *MORE INFO* For more information about performing an authoritative restore with Ntdsutil, visit *http://technet.microsoft.com/en-us/library/cc755296(v=WS.10).aspx*. For more information about reanimating tombstoned objects, visit *http://technet.microsoft .com/en-us/magazine/2007.09.tombstones.aspx*.

Active Directory Recycle Bin

Windows Server 2008 R2 and Windows Server 2012 have removed these drawbacks with Active Directory Recycle Bin. With Active Directory Recycle Bin, you don't have to take the domain controller offline to restore a deleted object, and the original group memberships of the deleted objects are preserved when you restore them.

Windows Server 2008 R2 introduced Active Directory Recycle Bin in a Windows PowerShell–only mode. Windows Server 2012 makes this new feature more accessible by bringing its functionality to the graphical Active Directory Administrative Center tool. For the exam, you need to know how to enable and use Active Directory Recycle Bin in both Windows PowerShell and Active Directory Administrative Center.

ENABLING ACTIVE DIRECTORY RECYCLE BIN

For the exam and the real world, remember that the Active Directory Recycle Bin is not enabled by default. You can use Active Directory Recycle Bin to restore only those objects that have been deleted after the feature is enabled. Objects you deleted before that point can be restored only through authoritative restore or tombstone reanimation.

To enable Active Directory Recycle Bin in Windows PowerShell, first make sure that all domain controllers in the domain are running Windows Server 2008 R2 or Windows Server 2012. In addition, the functional level of your forest must be set to Windows Server 2008 R2 or higher. You can use the Get-ADForest cmdlet to check the functional level of your forest:

```
Get-ADForest ForestName
```

If you need to raise the functional level of the forest, you can use the Set-ADForestMode cmdlet with the following syntax:

```
Set-ADForestMode -Identity ForestName -ForestMode Windows2008R2Forest
```

Once your environment meets the prerequisites of Active Directory Recycle Bin, you can enable the feature by using the following Windows PowerShell command:

```
Enable-ADOptionalFeature 'Recycle Bin Feature' -scope ForestOrConfigurationSet -target
DomainName -server DomainControllerName
```

To enable Active Directory Recycle Bin in the graphical user interface (GUI) in Windows Server 2012, open Active Directory Administrative Center from the Tools menu in Server Manager. Then, in Active Directory Administrative Center, right-click the domain icon in the console tree and select Enable Recycle Bin from the shortcut menu, as shown in Figure 8-9.

EXAM TIP

Remember that Active Directory Recycle Bin requires all domain controllers to be running Windows Server 2008 R2 or later, and similarly, that the forest functional level must be set to Windows Server 2008 R2 or higher.

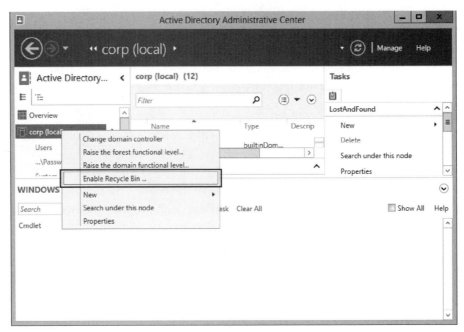

FIGURE 8-9 Enabling Active Directory Recycle Bin in Windows Server 2012.

Enabling Active Directory Recycle Bin is irreversible. In some environments, allowing administrators to see previously deleted objects might be undesirable. Consequently, you should make sure that Active Directory Recycle Bin is compatible with your organization's security policy before enabling the feature.

RESTORING DELETED OBJECTS IN ACTIVE DIRECTORY ADMINISTRATIVE CENTER

A new Deleted Objects container appears in Active Directory Administrative Center at the root of the domain container after you enable Active Directory Recycle Bin, as shown in Figure 8-10. Objects that you delete appear in this container for a period of time called the deleted object lifetime, which is 180 days by default.

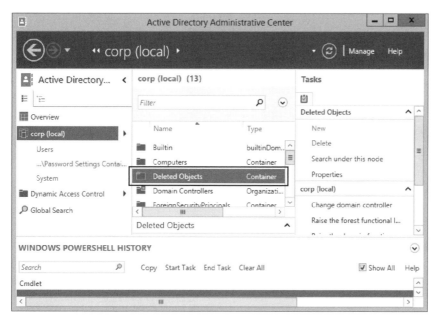

FIGURE 8-10 A Deleted Objects container appears after you enable Active Directory Recycle Bin.

Restoring an object in the GUI is simple—so simple, in fact, that it might be challenging for the exam writers to think up hard enough questions about restoring objects from the GUI. To restore the object to its last known parent container, just right-click the object and select Restore from the shortcut menu, as shown in Figure 8-11.

To restore an object to a different container, select Restore To and select the new container in which you want the object to appear. The Locate Parent option opens the former parent container in the console.

One potential complication in restoring an object might occur if you have deleted both the container and the object. In this case, you need to restore the parent before the child object, or choose to restore the object to another container.

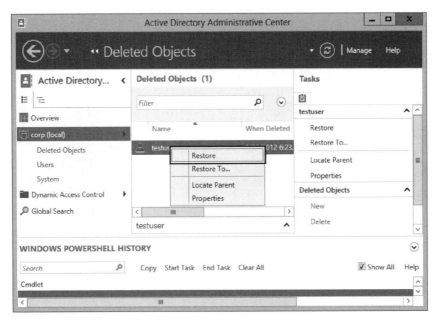

FIGURE 8-11 Restoring a deleted object in Active Directory.

EXAM TIP

In preparing for the Maintain Active Directory objective, make sure you review the functions and features of the Ntdsutil utility. Even though this utility has not changed since Windows Server 2008, it's an essential Active Directory maintenance tool. A good way to review the capabilities of Ntdsutil is to type **ntdsutil help** at a command prompt on a domain controller. Alternatively, you can search for the utility online at the TechNet web site. Be sure to review all of the Ntdsutil contexts, such as Snapshot, which allows you to create and manage snapshots of the Active Directory database, and Files, which allows you to move the Active Directory database (Ntds.dit) to a new location.

RESTORING DELETED OBJECTS IN WINDOWS POWERSHELL

To restore a deleted object in Windows PowerShell, first use the Get-ADObject cmdlet with the -Filter and -IncludeDeletedObjects switches, and then pipe the result to the Restore-ADObject cmdlet. For example, to restore a deleted user with the display name "Mary," type the following command at an elevated Windows PowerShell prompt:

```
Get-ADObject -Filter {DisplayName -eq "Mary"} -IncludeDeletedObjects | Restore-ADObject
```

Here's another example: to restore a user whose canonical name (CN) is like "Jorge," type the following:

```
Get-ADObject -Filter {CN -like "Jorge"} -IncludeDeletedObjects | Restore-ADObject
```

In the real world, it doesn't make much sense to restore a deleted object by using Windows PowerShell if you don't have to. However, don't be surprised if the Windows PowerShell method of Active Directory Recycle Bin still appears on the exam.

EXAM TIP

Don't forget about the Dsamain tool, which was introduced in Windows Server 2008. Dsamain allows you to mount a shadow copy-enabled backup or Ntdsutil snapshot of the Active Directory database. After using Dsamain to mount an Active Directory backup or Ntdsutil snapshot, you can use Ldp.exe to view the historical contents of the database, including object attributes. When you use Dsamain, be sure to mount the backup or snapshot in a *port other than port 389*, which is the reserved LDAP port used by the currently running instance of the Active Directory database. For more information about Dsamain, search for "Active Directory Domain Services Database Mounting Tool (Snapshot Viewer or Snapshot Browser) Step-by-Step Guide," or visit *http://technet.microsoft.com/en-us/library /cc753609(v=ws.10).aspx*.

MORE INFO For more information about how to use Get-ADObject, visit *http://technet .microsoft.com/en-us/library/ee617198.aspx*.

DELETED OBJECT LIFETIME
By default, you have only 180 days to restore an object after it is deleted. This period is known as the deleted object lifetime and is governed by the msDS-DeletedObjectLifetime attribute assigned to the domain. To change the value of this attribute, use the Set-ADObject cmdlet in the following manner:

```
Set-ADObject -Identity "CN=Directory Service,CN=Windows NT,CN=Services,CN=Configuration,
DC=<mydomain>,DC=<com>" -Partition "CN=Configuration,DC=<mydomain>,DC=<com>" -Replace:@
{"msDS-DeletedObjectLifetime" = <value>}
```

Replace *DC=<mydomain>,DC=<com>* with the appropriate forest root domain name of your Active Directory environment, and replace *<value>* with the new value of the deleted object lifetime.

For example, to set the deleted object lifetime to 365 days, run the following command:

```
Set-ADObject -Identity "CN=Directory Service,CN=Windows NT,CN=Services,CN=Configuratio
n,DC=contoso,DC=com" -Partition "CN=Configuration,DC=contoso,DC=com" -Replace:@{"msDS-
DeletedObjectLifetime" = 365}
```

Objective summary

- Windows Server 2008 R2 introduced Active Directory Recycle Bin, a Windows PowerShell–based tool that allowed you to restore a deleted object such as a user without taking the domain controller offline and without risk of losing the object's group memberships.

- Windows Server 2012 brings the functionality of Active Directory Recycle Bin to the GUI, in the Active Directory Administrative Center.

- Active Directory Recycle Bin must first be enabled. Once enabled, it can't be disabled.

- Once Active Directory Recycle Bin is enabled, a Deleted Object container appears at the root of the domain in Active Directory Administrative Center. You can easily find and restore objects from this location.

- Deleted objects have a default lifetime of 180 days. This period is a configurable attribute of a domain, called the deleted object lifetime. To change the deleted object lifetime, use the Set-ADObject cmdlet.

Objective review

Answer the following questions to test your knowledge of the information in this objective. You can find the answers to these questions and explanations of why each answer choice is correct or incorrect in the "Answers" section at the end of the chapter.

1. You are a network administrator for Contoso.com. You have learned that a user account was accidentally deleted from the Contoso.com Active Directory domain. The domain controllers in your network are all running Windows Server 2012. Active Directory Recycle Bin is not yet enabled.

   You want to restore the deleted user account without taking any domain controller offline. What should you do?

   A. Perform an authoritative restore of the deleted user account with the Ntdsutil utility.

   B. Reanimate the tombstone of the deleted object.

C. Enable Active Directory Recycle Bin and use Active Directory Administrative Center to restore the object.

D. Enable Active Directory Recycle Bin and use Windows PowerShell to restore the object.

2. You are a network administrator for Contoso.com. You have learned that a user account for a user named Dan Park was accidentally deleted from the Contoso.com Active Directory domain. The domain controllers in your network are all running Windows Server 2012. Active Directory Recycle Bin was enabled at the time the object was deleted.

You want to restore the deleted user account without taking any domain controller offline. What should you do?

A. Restore the object from the Deleted Objects container in Active Directory Administrative Center.

B. Perform an authoritative restore using the Ntdsutil utility.

C. Reanimate the tombstone of the deleted object.

D. Run the following command:

```
Get-ADObject -Filter {displayName -eq "Dan Park"} | Restore-ADObject
```

3. You are a network administrator for Adatum.com. You have learned that all 10 user accounts in the Finance department were accidentally deleted from the Adatum.com Active Directory domain. The domain controllers in your network are all running Windows Server 2012. Active Directory Recycle Bin was enabled at the time the user accounts were deleted.

You attempt to restore the deleted user accounts in Active Directory Administrative Center, but you receive errors indicating that the objects' parent is deleted.

You want to restore the deleted user accounts. What should you do?

A. Use the Set-ADObject cmdlet to extend the deleted object lifetime in the domain.

B. Re-create the parent organizational unit of the user accounts and then restore the user accounts.

C. Restore the parent organizational unit of the user accounts and then restore the user accounts.

D. Restart a domain controller in Directory Services Restore Mode and perform an authoritative restore of the deleted user accounts.

Thought experiment

You are a network administrator for Proseware.com. The Proseware.com network consists of a single Active Directory domain, including two domain controllers. One domain controller named DC1 is running Windows Server 2012, and the other named DC2 is running Windows Server 2008 R2. Both domain controllers are running in GUI mode in VMs, on host servers running Windows Server 2012.

One of your goals as a network administrator is to help improve both the resiliency and scalability of the network. Proseware.com has been experiencing rapid growth, and you want the network to handle increasingly heavy workloads in the coming months and years. You also want to be able to improve fault tolerance so that configuration errors such as accidental deletions can be quickly reversed.

With this information in mind, answer the following questions. You can find the answers to these questions in the "Answers" section at the end of the chapter.

1. Is DC1 is eligible for cloning? Why or why not?

2. You install a third domain controller named DC3. DC3 is running a fresh installation of Windows Server 2012, with no additional software or applications. Which step(s) must you take before DC3 can be cloned?

3. You export the DC3 VM. Which step(s) must you take before importing the exported VM?

4. How would you find out if Active Directory Recycle Bin is enabled on the Proseware.com domain?

5. If Active Directory Recycle Bin is not enabled, how would you determine whether this feature can be enabled in the domain?

Answers

This section contains the answers to the Objective Reviews and the Thought Experiment.

Objective 8.1: Review

1. **Correct Answer:** A

    A. **Correct:** DC1 must not own the PDC Emulator operations master role.

    B. **Incorrect:** The host server must be running Windows Server 2012.

    C. **Incorrect**: The source virtualized domain controller must be running Windows Server 2012.

    D. **Incorrect**: Cloning cannot occur unless every program listed in the output of the Get-ADDCCloningExcludedApplicationList cmdlet also appears on the inclusion list, CustomDCCloneAllowList.xml.

2. **Correct Answers:** C, E

    A. **Incorrect:** The cloned domain controller can be the Infrastructure Master. It cannot be the PDC Emulator. Also, the Infrastructure Master role should not be placed on a global catalog server.

    B. **Incorrect:** It is not necessary to make VDC1 a global catalog server to clone it.

    C. **Correct:** The PDC Emulator in the domain needs to be running Windows Server 2012.

    D. **Incorrect:** The host computer doesn't need to be in any global security group.

    E. **Correct:** The domain controller you want to clone must be a member of the Cloneable Domain Controllers global security group.

3. **Correct Answer:** B

    A. **Incorrect:** You shouldn't export the VM until you add App1 to the Allow list and run the New-ADDCCloneConfigFile cmdlet.

    B. **Correct:** The next step is to add App1 to the Allow list, called CustomDCCloneAllowList.xml, by running the Get-ADDCCloningExcludedApplicationList with the -GenerateXml switch.

    C. **Incorrect**: You should run the New-ADDCCloneConfigFile cmdlet only after you add App1 to the inclusion list. This cmdlet runs a list of prerequisite checks on the source VM.

    D. **Incorrect**: You don't use this cmdlet to clone a domain controller. You would use the cmdlet to clone a virtual disk.

Objective 8.2: Review

1. **Correct Answer:** B

    A. **Incorrect:** The solution requires that no domain controller should be taken offline. To perform an authoritative restore with the Ntdsutil utility, you first need to take a domain controller offline by booting it in Directory Services Restore Mode.

    B. **Correct:** You cannot restore the object by using Active Directory Recycle Bin because this feature was not enabled when the object was deleted. To restore the object without taking a domain controller offline, you will have to reanimate the tombstone of the object.

    C. **Incorrect**: You cannot restore the object by using Active Directory Recycle Bin because this feature was not enabled when the object was deleted.

    D. **Incorrect**: You cannot restore the object by using Active Directory Recycle Bin because this feature was not enabled when the object was deleted.

2. **Correct Answer:** A

    A. **Correct:** Restoring the deleted object in the GUI is by far the simplest option. You can restore the object in Active Directory Administrative Center because Active Directory Recycle Bin was enabled when the object was deleted and at least one of your domain controllers is running Windows Server 2012.

    B. **Incorrect:** You should not perform an authoritative restore because this procedure requires you to take a domain controller offline.

    C. **Incorrect:** Although you can perform this procedure, it is unnecessarily complicated. In addition, through this procedure the object you restore might be stripped of its group memberships, so it is not the best option.

    D. **Incorrect:** This command will not work without the -IncludeDeletedObjects switch.

3. **Correct Answer:** C

    A. **Incorrect:** The errors indicate that the objects' parent is deleted. Extending the deleted object lifetime will have no effect on the state of the parent container.

    B. **Incorrect:** You need to restore the original parent container, not re-create one with the same name.

    C. **Correct:** If the parent container is deleted, you are able to restore it from the Deleted Objects container. After it is restored, you are able to restore its child objects.

    D. **Incorrect:** This step would not help. Restoring the deleted objects in Directory Services Restore Mode would not affect the underlying problem that the parent container is missing.

Thought experiment

1. No, it is not. Although DC1 and the host computer both meet the requirements of running Windows Server 2012, the network environment does not meet the requirement of a second domain controller running Windows Server 2012 with the PDC Emulator role.

2. You need to ensure that DC1 holds the PDC Emulator role and transfer the role to that computer if necessary. In addition, you need to add DC3 to the Cloneable Domain Controllers global security group.

3. You need to delete the snapshots in the Snapshots subdirectory.

4. You can look in Active Directory Administrative Center and determine whether a Deleted Objects container exists at the root of the domain.

5. Use the Get-Forest cmdlet to determine the functional level of the forest. The forest needs to be running at the Windows Server 2008 R2 functional level or higher.

CHAPTER 9

Configure and manage Group Policy

Windows Server 2012 includes an assortment of enhancements to Group Policy, but only the narrow topic of configuring Group Policy processing has been singled out for the 70-417 exam. As it turns out, the most important new Group Policy feature is the only one to fall within this "processing" objective: remote Group Policy updating. This chapter introduces you to this useful new functionality in Windows Server 2012.

In addition, Windows Server 2008 R2 introduced a new GroupPolicy module to Windows PowerShell. The module includes 26 cmdlets, some of which are likely to appear on the exam. This chapter introduces these cmdlets as a reference for your exam preparation.

Objectives in this chapter:

- Objective 9.1: Configure Group Policy processing

Objective 9.1: Configure Group Policy processing

Remote Group Policy updating is the most important new Group Policy feature you need to learn for the 70-417 exam. It appears in two guises: GUI and Windows PowerShell. The GUI feature alone might be too straightforward to serve as the basis for exam questions, so be sure to learn the extra details explained next, such as how the feature actually works and which service and open ports are required for the feature to function. In Windows PowerShell, the feature is perfectly suited for exam-level questions, so it's more likely you will see questions based on this version of the feature on the 70-417 exam. Therefore, make sure you understand the syntax and the options that can accompany the Invoke-GpUpdate cmdlet.

You don't need to understand the syntax of other Windows PowerShell cmdlets in the GroupPolicy module. You just need to be able to recognize their purpose.

This section covers the following topics:
- Remote Group Policy update
- Group Policy cmdlets in Windows PowerShell

Remote Group Policy update

Windows Server 2012 and Windows PowerShell 3.0 introduce a handy feature that is sure to please network administrators: the ability to perform a Group Policy update on many remote computers at once. You can accomplish this task by using either the Group Policy Management console or Windows PowerShell. Previously, you had to use the GPUpdate command on a local computer to refresh policy for just that computer and the locally logged-on user. If you wanted to update many computers at once, you had to use a script or a third-party tool.

Updating Group Policy in an organizational unit with Group Policy Management console

To remotely refresh Group Policy in the Group Policy Management console, just right-click an organizational unit (OU) container in the console tree and select Group Policy Update from the shortcut menu, as shown in Figure 9-1. This step schedules GPUpdate.exe to be run within 10 minutes on all clients running Windows Vista or later and on all servers running Windows Server 2008 or later in that OU.

Note that this feature has limitations. You can force a Group Policy refresh on all computers *within a single OU and all subcontainers only.* You cannot single out computers or update Group Policy on computers that are not located in an OU. (This restriction applies only to the Group Policy Management console, not to Windows PowerShell.) Also, you cannot use this feature to update computers running operating systems earlier than Windows Vista and Windows Server 2008, whether through Group Policy Management or through Windows PowerShell.

After you select the Group Policy Update option, a message box appears indicating the number of computers that will be affected and asking you to confirm the update, as shown in Figure 9-2.

When you give your consent, a window appears (as shown in Figure 9-3), indicating the success or failure of the *scheduling* of the update. The update itself is not immediate. As shown in Figure 9-3, the message indicates that a Group Policy update will be forced on all computers in the OU and all subcontainers within 10 minutes. This slight delay is a good thing when there are many computers in the OU because the computers will not all update at the same time and strain the resources of domain controllers.

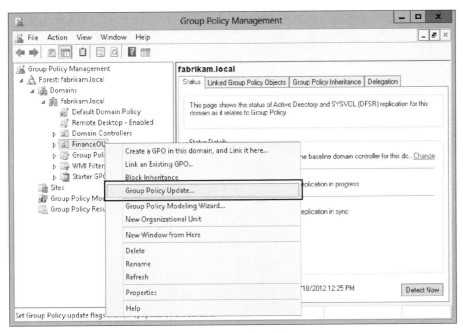

FIGURE 9-1 Updating Group Policy on all computers in an OU.

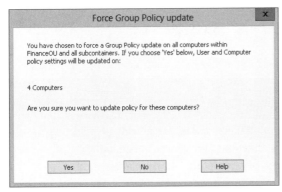

FIGURE 9-2 A remote update in Group Policy Management forces the update for all computers in an OU.

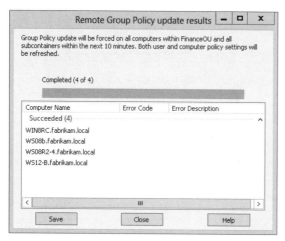

Group Policy update will be forced on all computers within FinanceOU and all subcontainers within the next 10 minutes. Both user and computer policy settings will be refreshed.

Completed (4 of 4)

Computer Name	Error Code	Error Description
Succeeded (4)		
WIN8RC.fabrikam.local		
WS08b.fabrikam.local		
WS08R2-4.fabrikam.local		
WS12-B.fabrikam.local		

FIGURE 9-3 Updating Group Policy on all computers in an OU.

Updating Group Policy by using Invoke-GpUpdate

You can update Group Policy on computers in a much more flexible way if you use the Invoke-GpUpdate cmdlet in Windows PowerShell.

Used without any parameters, the cmdlet is similar to GPUpdate.exe; it updates Group Policy on the local computer only. It is different from GPUpdate.exe because, like the Group Policy Management console, the task is not performed immediately but is scheduled to be completed within 10 minutes by default.

Used with the -Computer option, however, the Invoke-GpUpdate cmdlet enables you to update a remote computer, as in the following example:

```
Invoke-GpUpdate -Computer WS12-B
```

Other options you can use with Invoke-GpUpdate include -Force and -RandomDelayInMinutes. The -Force option resembles the /Force option with GPUpdate .exe: it reapplies all policy settings regardless of whether they have changed. The -RandomDelayInMinutes option enables you to specify a random interval in minutes, up to the number of minutes specified, before the Group Policy update will be run. The purpose of this option is typically to reduce the network load on domain controllers when many remote computers are updated with a scripted command, but it can also be used with a single computer to reduce or remove the default delay of 10 minutes. A value of 0 will cause the Group Policy refresh to run immediately. The following example therefore causes all Group Policy settings to be updated immediately on a computer named WS12-B:

```
Invoke-GpUpdate -Computer WS12-B -RandomDelayInMinutes 0 -Force
```

As mentioned, you can also leverage Windows PowerShell to execute the Invoke-GpUpdate cmdlet on more than one computer. You can begin with the Get-ADComputer cmdlet to retrieve any group of computer objects and then pipeline the results to a ForEach construction that includes Invoke-GpUpdate.

For example, the following command displays all the computers in the container named Computers, in the Fabrikam.local domain:

```
Get-ADComputer -Filter * -Searchbase "CN=Computers,DC=Fabrikam,DC=local"
```

If you pipe the results of this command to a ForEach statement, you can execute the Invoke-GpUpdate cmdlet on each computer returned by the command. The net result of the following command, for example, is to schedule GPUpdate.exe to run on every computer in the Computers container within 10 minutes:

```
Get-ADComputer -Filter * -Searchbase "CN=Computers,DC=Fabrikam,DC=local" | ForEach
{Invoke-GpUpdate -Computer $_.name}
```

You don't need to target computers in any specific container or OU. The following example attempts to schedule GPUpdate.exe to run on every computer in the domain within 10 minutes:

```
Get-ADComputer -Filter * | ForEach {Invoke-GpUpdate -Computer $_.name}
```

This next example schedules GPUpdate.exe to run immediately on every computer in the domain with a description that includes the term "finance."

```
Get-ADComputer -Filter 'Description -like "*finance*"' | ForEach {Invoke-GpUpdate
-Computer $_.name -RandomDelayInMinutes 0}
```

One final example: the following schedules GPUpdate.exe to run immediately on all computers in the domain with an operating system name that includes the string "Vista":

```
Get-ADComputer -Filter 'OperatingSystem -like "*Vista*"' | ForEach {Invoke-GpUpdate
-Computer $_.name -RandomDelayInMinutes 0}
```

> **NOTE** For a full list of property types for which you can search, such as Description, OperatingSystem, LastLogonDate, and Name, run the following command at a Windows PowerShell prompt, specifying the name of any computer in the domain in place of "ComputerName":
>
> ```
> Get-ADComputer ComputerName -Properties *
> ```

Remote Group Policy update and Task Scheduler

Remote Group Policy update works by remotely creating scheduled tasks for GPUpdate.exe. You can see these scheduled tasks for GPUpdate if you open Task Scheduler on the target computer and navigate in the console tree to Task Scheduler (Local)\Task Scheduler Library \Microsoft\Windows\Group Policy, as shown in Figure 9-4.

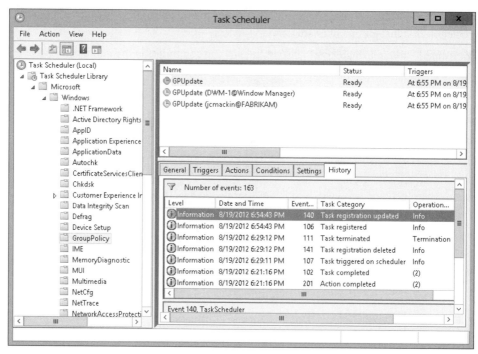

FIGURE 9-4 GPUpdate configured as a scheduled task.

The connection between remote Group Policy update and Task Scheduler has implications for troubleshooting. If you are unable to successfully schedule a remote Group Policy update on a remote computer, you should verify that the Task Scheduler service is running on that remote machine. More important, for some computers, a remote Group Policy update requires you to enable firewall rules related to remote scheduled tasks, as described in the next section.

Firewall rules for remote Group Policy update

Remote Group Policy update relies on remote management, which is enabled by default in Windows Server 2012 in a domain environment. Although remote Group Policy update works by default on domain-joined computers that are started and running Windows Server 2012, you might have to enable firewall rules for scheduled tasks on other operating system types, such as Windows clients or earlier versions of Windows Server that do not have Windows Management Framework 3.0 installed.

Fortunately, there's a new starter group policy object (GPO) for remote Group Policy updates that makes the process of enabling the required firewall rules easy. The starter GPO, called Group Policy Remote Update Firewall Ports, is shown in Figure 9-5.

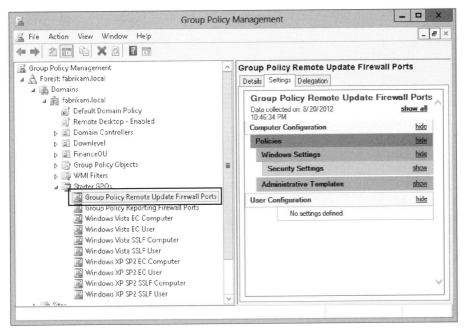

FIGURE 9-5 A starter GPO for remote Group Policy updates.

After you create a GPO from the starter GPO and link the new GPO to the domain, you can view the three firewall rules enabled by this GPO, as shown in Figure 9-6:

- Both rules in the Remote Scheduled Tasks Management rule group:
    - Remote Scheduled Tasks Management (RPC)
    - Remote Scheduled Tasks Management (RPC-EPMAP)
- Windows Management Instrumentation (WMI-In)

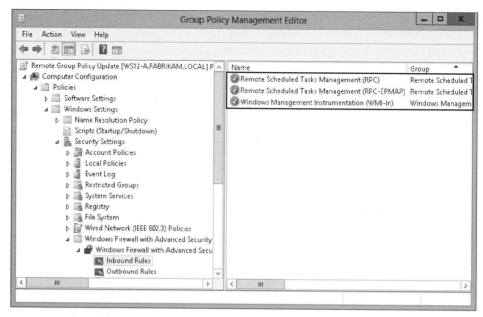

FIGURE 9-6 Inbound firewall rules for remote Group Policy update.

TABLE 9-1 Group Policy cmdlets in Windows Server 2012

Group Policy Cmdlet	Function
Backup-GPO	Backs up one GPO or all GPOs in a domain
Copy-GPO	Copies a GPO
Get-GPInheritance	Retrieves Group Policy inheritance information for a specified domain or OU
Get-GPO	Gets one GPO or all GPOs in a domain
Get-GPOReport	Generates a report in either XML or HTML format for a specified GPO or for all GPOs in a domain

Get-GPPermission	Gets the permission level for one or more security principals on a specified GPO
Get-GPPrefRegistryValue	Retrieves one or more registry preference items under either Computer Configuration or User Configuration in a GPO
Get-GPRegistryValue	Retrieves one or more registry-based policy settings under either Computer Configuration or User Configuration in a GPO
Get-GPResultantSetOfPolicy	Outputs the Resultant Set of Policy (RSoP) information to a file for a user, a computer, or both
Get-GPStarterGPO	Gets one Starter GPO or all Starter GPOs in a domain
Import-GPO	Imports the Group Policy settings from a backed-up GPO into a specified GPO
Invoke-GPUpdate	Updates Group Policy on a local computer or remote computer
New-GPLink	Links a GPO to a site, domain, or OU
New-GPO	Creates a new GPO
New-GPStarterGPO	Creates a new Starter GPO
Remove-GPLink	Removes a GPO link from a site, domain, or OU
Remove-GPO	Deletes a GPO
Remove-GPPrefRegistryValue	Removes one or more registry preference items from either Computer Configuration or User Configuration in a GPO
Remove-GPRegistryValue	Removes one or more registry-based policy settings from either Computer Configuration or User Configuration in a GPO
Rename-GPO	Assigns a new display name to a GPO
Restore-GPO	Restores one GPO or all GPOs in a domain from one or more GPO backup files
Set-GPInheritance	Blocks or unblocks inheritance for a specified domain or OU
Set-GPLink	Sets the properties of the specified GPO link, including -Order (precedence), -LinkEnabled, and -Enforced
Set-GPPermission	Grants a level of permissions to a security principal for one GPO or for all GPOs in a domain
Set-GPPrefRegistryValue	Configures a registry preference item under either Computer Configuration or User Configuration in a GPO
Set-GPRegistryValue	Configures one or more registry-based policy settings under either Computer Configuration or User Configuration in a GPO

EXAM TIP

Even though they aren't new to Windows Server 2012, make sure you know the commands Dcgpofix and Gpfixup and how to use them. You can use Dcgpofix to re-create or restore the original version of either the Default Domain Policy GPO, or the Default Domain Controllers Policy GPO, or both GPOs at once. Gpfixup, for its part, fixes domain links after a domain rename operation. Search for these commands on TechNet to learn about their syntax.

MORE INFO   For more information about new features related to Group Policy in Windows Server 2012, visit *http://technet.microsoft.com/en-us/library/jj574108*.

Objective summary

- In Windows Server 2012, you can use the Group Policy Management console to schedule Group Policy to be updated on all computers in a single OU at a random point within 10 minutes. To perform this task, just right-click an OU and select the Group Policy Update option.

- Windows PowerShell 3.0 introduces the Invoke-GpUpdate cmdlet, which enables you to update Group Policy on remote computers in a flexible way.

- In both Group Policy Management and Windows PowerShell, remote Group Policy updates work through remote task scheduling. The feature schedules GPUpdate to run on remote computers.

- To receive scheduled tasks from remote computers, domain-joined computers running an operating system other than Windows Server 2012 might need to have certain inbound firewall rules enabled in the Remote Scheduled Task Management group and Windows Management Instrumentation (WMI-In).

- You can easily enforce the inbound rules required by using the starter GPO named Group Policy Remote Update Firewall Ports. Use the starter GPO to create a new GPO that enables the required firewall rules, and then link the new GPO to the domain.

- Windows Server 2012 includes a GroupPolicy module for Windows PowerShell that includes 26 cmdlets. You need to be able to recognize the function of these cmdlets by name.

Objective review

Answer the following questions to test your knowledge of the information in this objective. You can find the answers to these questions and explanations of why each answer choice is correct or incorrect in the "Answers" section at the end of the chapter.

1. You are a network administrator for Cpandl.com. The Cpandl.com network consists of 25 servers running Windows Server 2012 and 300 clients running Windows 8. You are administering the network by using Remote Server Administration Tools on a computer running Windows 8.

   You have recently implemented a change to Group Policy that affects only the servers and computers in the Marketing OU. The Marketing OU includes three servers and 40 clients. You now want to update Group Policy on all computers in the Marketing OU within the next 10 minutes.

All computers in the Marketing OU are capable of having Group Policy updated remotely. Which of the following tools should you use to accomplish this task most efficiently?

A. Group Policy Management

B. Invoke-GpUpdate

C. GPUpdate.exe

D. Server Manager

2. You are a network administrator for Adatum.com. The Adatum.com network consists of 20 servers running either Windows Server 2012 or Windows Server 2008 R2, and 250 clients running either Windows 8 or Windows 7. You are administering the network by using Remote Server Administration Tools on a computer running Windows 8.

You have recently implemented a change to Group Policy that affects only the computers running Windows Server 2012 or Windows 8. You now want to update Group Policy on all these computers over the next hour.

All computers running Windows Server 2012 and Windows 8 in the domain are capable of having Group Policy updated remotely. You want to update Group Policy on these computers without triggering a Group Policy update on computers running Windows Server 2008 R2 or Windows 7. Which of the following tools should you use to accomplish this task most efficiently?

A. Update Group Policy with Group Policy Management

B. Windows PowerShell

C. GPUpdate.exe

D. Server Manager

3. You are a network administrator for Proseware.com. The Proseware.com network consists of 20 servers running either Windows Server 2012 or Windows Server 2008 R2, and 300 clients running either Windows 8 or Windows 7. You are administering the network by using Remote Server Administration Tools on a computer running Windows 8.

You have recently implemented a change to Group Policy that affects only computers in the Finance OU. When you choose to update Group Policy on all computers in the Finance OU, you receive a message indicating that the update is not successful on a number of computers that you know to be running.

You want to be able to update Group Policy on all running computers in the Finance OU without receiving an error. Which of the following actions should you take? (Choose all that apply.)

A. Enable the inbound firewall rules for Remote Scheduled Tasks Management on all computers in the OU.

B. Enable an inbound firewall rule for Windows Management Instrumentation (WMI) on all computers in the OU.

C. Enable the Remote Registry service on all computers in the OU.

D. Enable the Windows Event Collector service on all computers in the OU.

 Thought experiment

You are a network administrator for Woodgrove Bank. The woodgrovebank.com private network spans seven branch offices in seven cities throughout New York state. The network includes 50 servers running Windows Server 2012, Windows Server 2008 R2, or Windows Server 2008, and 700 clients running Windows 8, Windows 7, or Windows Vista. Each of the seven offices is assigned its own OU in Active Directory and at least two domain controllers, all of which are running Windows Server 2012.

Your manager has asked you to investigate the requirements for remote updates to Group Policy. He wants to implement this capability within the next few weeks.

With this background information in mind, answer the following questions. You can find the answers to these questions in the "Answers" section at the end of the chapter.

1. How can you most efficiently create the firewall rules required to allow all your servers and clients to receive remote Group Policy updates?

2. Besides firewall settings, which other setting could you enforce through Group Policy to ensure that your servers and clients will be able to receive remote Group Policy updates?

3. How can you most efficiently update Group Policy on all computers in one of the seven branch offices?

4. Your manager wants to be able to force all running computers in the domain to update Group Policy at random points over the course of four hours. He wants you to write a Windows PowerShell command for this purpose. Which Windows PowerShell command would achieve this goal when executed?

5. Your manager wants to be able to force all computers in the domain that are started and running Windows 8 to update Group Policy within 10 minutes. He wants you to write a Windows PowerShell command for this purpose. Which Windows PowerShell command would achieve this goal when executed?

Answers

This section contains the answers to the Objective Review and the Thought Experiment.

Objective 9.1: Review

1. **Correct Answer:** A

    A.   Correct: The Group Policy Management console allows you to schedule an update Group Policy on all computers in an OU. To do so, right-click the OU and select Group Policy Update. The update occurs on all computers in the OU within 10 minutes of choosing this option.

    B.   Incorrect: The Invoke-GpUpdate cmdlet by itself does not allow you to perform a Group Policy update on all computers in an OU. You can create a scripted command in Windows PowerShell that combines Get-AdComputer and Invoke-GpUpdate to achieve this result, but it is not the most efficient solution if you are managing the network by using Remote Server Administration Tools.

    C.   Incorrect: GPUpdate.exe refreshes Group Policy on one computer only. To update Group Policy on all computers in the Marketing OU, you would need to run this command 43 times. This solution is much less efficient than using the Group Policy Management console.

    D.   Incorrect: Server Manager does not provide an option to refresh Group Policy on multiple computers at once.

2. **Correct Answer:** B

    A.   Incorrect: You can use Group Policy Management to remotely update Group Policy only in a particular OU. The update applies to all computers in the OU and occurs within 10 minutes. You cannot use Group Policy Management to remotely update Group Policy on computers running any particular operating systems, and you cannot use this tool to specify that these updates should occur over the next hour.

    B.   Correct: You can use a single scripted command in Windows PowerShell that will invoke a remote Group Policy update over the next hour only on computers running either Windows Server 2012 or Windows 8. The following command is one way to accomplish this task:

    ```
    Get-ADComputer -Filter {(OperatingSystem -like "*Windows 8*") -or
    (OperatingSystem -like "*Windows Server 2012*")} | ForEach {Invoke-GpUpdate
    -Computer $_.name -RandomDelayInMinutes 60}
    ```

C. **Incorrect:** GPUpdate.exe refreshes Group Policy on one computer only. To update Group Policy on all computers running Windows Server 2012 and Windows 8, you would need to run this command many times either locally on each computer or through a Remote Desktop connection. This solution is much less efficient than using Windows PowerShell.

D. **Incorrect:** Server Manager does not provide an option to refresh Group Policy on multiple computers at once.

3. **Correct Answers:** A, B

A. **Correct:** Certain operating systems, such as clients and older versions of Windows Server without Windows Management Framework 3.0, do not allow you to remotely update Group Policy by default. To allow remote Group Policy updates, you need to enable inbound ports for Remote Scheduled Tasks Management and WMI.

B. **Correct:** An inbound rule allowing WMI is one of the three firewall rules needed to allow various clients to receive remote Group Policy updates.

C. **Incorrect**: This service enables remote users to modify registry settings on the local computer. It is not needed to allow a remote computer to schedule GPUpdate.exe to run locally.

D. **Incorrect**: This service manages persistent subscriptions to events from certain remote sources. It is not needed to allow a remote computer to schedule GPUpdate.exe to run locally.

Thought experiment

1. Use the Group Policy Remote Update Firewall Ports starter GPO to create a new GPO. Link the new GPO to the domain.

2. You could use Group Policy to ensure that the Task Scheduler service is set to Automatic on all computers in the domain.

3. Use the Group Policy Management console to update Group Policy on the OU corresponding to the branch office.

4. `Get-ADComputer -Filter * | ForEach {Invoke-GpUpdate -Computer $_.name -RandomDelayInMinutes 240}`

5. `Get-ADComputer -Filter 'OperatingSystem -like "*Windows 8*"' | ForEach {Invoke-GpUpdate -Computer $_.name}`

CHAPTER 10

Configure and manage high availability

The Configure and Manage High Availability domain relates to failover clustering and the live migration of virtual machines.

A failover cluster, as you know, is a group of two or more computers that work together to help ensure the availability of a service or application. (In Windows Server 2012, these clustered services and applications are now known as roles.) There are a number of improvements in failover clustering in Windows Server 2012, beginning with scalability: failover clusters now support up to 64 nodes (as opposed to 16 in Windows Server 2008 R2). Failover clusters in Windows Server 2012 also support many new enhancements, such as Cluster-Aware Updating, role priority, VM monitoring, and node drain.

Live migration of virtual machines (VMs) used to be restricted to failover clusters, but this feature has been expanded to provide uninterrupted availability in all domain contexts.

To learn about the new developments in failover clustering and live migration for the 70-417 exam, it's best (as always) to implement these features in a test environment. For failover clustering, the good news is that you can now perform all of this testing on a single server with VMs running in Hyper-V and using the new built-in iSCSI Target feature for shared storage. For live migration, you will need two physical servers.

Objectives in this chapter:

- Objective 10.1: Configure failover clustering
- Objective 10.2: Manage failover clustering roles
- Objective 10.3: Manage virtual machine (VM) movement

Objective 10.1: Configure failover clustering

Failover clustering in Windows Server 2012 introduces many improvements. The topics covered here are the ones most likely to appear on the 70-417 exam.

Cluster storage pools

In Windows Server 2012, you can draw from data storage provided by a Serial Attached SCSI (SAS) disk array to create one or more storage pools for a failover cluster. These storage pools are similar to the ones you can create for an individual server by using Storage Spaces. As with the Storage Spaces feature, you can use storage pools in a failover cluster as a source from which you can create virtual disks and then volumes.

To create a new storage pool, open Failover Cluster Manager and navigate to Failover Cluster Manager\[*Cluster Name*]\Storage\Pools, right-click Pools, and then select New Storage Pool from the shortcut menu, as shown in Figure 10-1. This step starts the same New Storage Pool Wizard used with Storage Spaces. (If you have a shared SAS disk array, you can use Server Manager to create the pool and use the Add Storage Pool option to add it to the machine.) After you create the pool, you need to create virtual disks from the new pool and virtual volumes from the new disks before you can use the clustered storage space for hosting your clustered workloads.

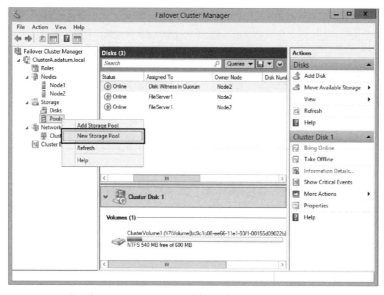

FIGURE 10-1 Creating a new storage pool for a cluster.

The availability of storage pools for failover clusters has implications for the 70-417 exam, especially because these storage pools have a number of requirements and restrictions that could easily serve as the basis of a test question. Note the following requirements for failover cluster storage pools:

- A minimum of three physical drives with at least 4 GB capacity each.

- Only SAS-connected physical disks are allowed. No additional layer of RAID (or any disk subsystem) is supported, whether internal or external.

- Fixed provisioning only for virtual disks; no thin provisioning.

- When creating virtual disks from a clustered storage pool, only simple and mirror storage layouts are supported. Parity layouts are not supported.

- The physical disks used for a clustered pool must be dedicated to that one pool. Boot disks should not be added to a clustered pool.

> **MORE INFO**   For more information about cluster storage pools, visit *http://blogs.msdn* *.com/b/clustering/archive/2012/06/02/10314262.aspx.*

Cluster shared volumes

Cluster shared volumes (CSVs) are a new type of storage used only in failover clusters. CSVs first appeared in Windows Server 2008 R2, so if you earned your last certification before this important feature was introduced, you might have completely missed CSVs. In this case, you need to understand the basics about them before taking the 70-417 exam.

The biggest advantage of CSVs is that they can be shared by multiple cluster nodes at the same time. This is not usually possible with shared storage. Even different volumes created on the same logical unit number (LUN) cannot usually be shared by different cluster nodes at the same time.

CSVs achieve this shared access of volumes by separating the data from different nodes into virtual hard disk (VHD) files. Within each shared volume, multiple VHDs are stored, each used as the storage for a particular role for which high availability has been configured. The CSVs containing these VHDs are then mapped to a common namespace on all nodes in the cluster. On every failover cluster configured with CSVs, the CSVs appear on every node as subfolders in the ClusterStorage folder on the system drive. Example paths are C:\ClusterStorage \Volume1, C:\ClusterStorage\Volume2, and so on.

CSVs are formatted with NTFS, but to distinguish them from typical NTFS volumes, the Windows Server 2012 interface displays them as formatted with CSVFS, or the Cluster Shared Volume File System. An example of a CSV is shown in Figure 10-2.

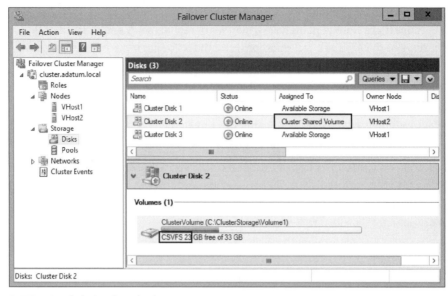

FIGURE 10-2 A cluster shared volume.

To create a CSV in Windows Server 2012, first provision a disk from shared storage, such as from an iSCSI target. Use Server Manager to create a volume from this disk, as shown in Figure 10-3.

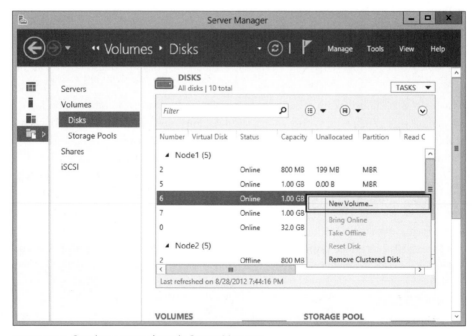

FIGURE 10-3 Creating a new volume in Server Manager.

Assign the new volume to the desired failover cluster, as shown in Figure 10-4. (The name of the cluster appears as a server name.)

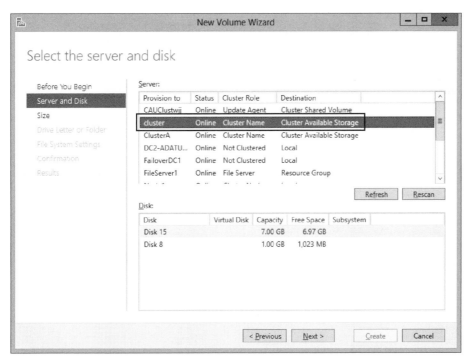

FIGURE 10-4 Assigning a new volume to a cluster.

In Failover Cluster Manager, the new volume will appear as a disk. Right-click the disk and select Add To Cluster Shared Volumes from the shortcut menu, as shown in Figure 10-5.

In Windows Server 2008 R2, CSVs were used as storage for only one type of workload hosted in a failover cluster: a highly available VM. In Windows Server 2012, CSVs are also used as the only storage type for a new role, the Scale-Out File Server, which is described later in this chapter. Another important use for CSVs is with live migration in failover clusters (a feature described later in this chapter). Although CSVs are not required for live migration, they are highly recommended because they optimize the performance of the migration and reduce downtime to almost zero.

FIGURE 10-5 Adding a volume to cluster shared volumes.

How might CSVs appear on the 70-417 exam? If there's a direct question about CSVs, it could come in the form of a requirement that states you want to "minimize administrative overhead" when designing storage for a highly available VM. More likely, you will just see CSV mentioned in the setup to a question that isn't just about CSVs.

> **NOTE** Here is the original problem CSVs were designed to solve: in Windows Server 2008 and earlier versions of Windows Server, only one cluster node could access a LUN at any given time. If any application, service, or VM connected to a LUN failed and needed to be moved to another node in the failover cluster, every other clustered application or VM on that LUN would also need to be failed over to a new node and potentially experience some downtime. To avoid this problem, each clustered role was typically connected to its own unique LUN as a way to isolate failures. This strategy created another problem, however: a large number of LUNs complicated setup and administration.
>
> With CSVs, a single LUN can be accessed by different nodes at a time as long as the different nodes are accessing distinct VHDs on the LUN. You can run these roles on any node in the failover cluster, and when the role fails, it can fail over to any other physical node in the cluster without affecting other roles (services or applications) hosted on the original node. CSVs thus add flexibility and simplify management.

Dynamic quorum

Dynamic quorum configuration is a new feature in Windows Server 2012 in which the number of votes required to reach quorum adjusts automatically to the number of active nodes in the failover cluster. If one or more nodes shut down, the number of votes to reach quorum in Windows Server 2012 changes to reflect the new number of nodes. With dynamic quorum, a failover cluster can remain functional even after half of its nodes fail simultaneously. In addition, with dynamic quorum it's possible for the cluster to remain running with only one node remaining.

The applicability of dynamic quorum to the 70-417 exam is uncertain, mainly because this new feature doesn't require you to remember any configuration settings. However, if you see a question in which nodes in the cluster are running an earlier version of Windows and "you want to have the number of votes automatically adjust based on the number of available nodes at any one time," you know you need to upgrade all nodes to Windows Server 2012. In addition, remember that dynamic quorum works only with the following quorum configurations and not with the Disk Only quorum configuration:

- Node Majority
- Node and Disk Majority
- Node and File Share Majority

EXAM TIP

Remember that the cluster quorum settings determine the number of elements in a failover cluster that must remain online for it to continue running. You access these settings by right-clicking a cluster in the Failover Cluster Manager console tree, selecting More Actions, and then clicking Configure Cluster Quorum Settings.

Node drain

Node drain is a new feature that simplifies the process of shutting down a node for maintenance. In previous versions of Windows, if you wanted to bring a node down for maintenance, you first needed to pause the node and then move all hosted applications and services (now called roles) to other nodes. With node drain, these two steps are combined into one.

To prepare a node to be shut down for maintenance, first navigate to the Nodes container in the Failover Cluster Manager console tree. Then right-click the node you want to shut down in the details pane, point to Pause, and then select Drain Roles, as shown in Figure 10-6.

To achieve this result by using Windows PowerShell, use the Suspend-ClusterNode cmdlet.

FIGURE 10-6 Draining roles from a node.

Cluster-aware updating

Cluster-aware updating (CAU) is a new feature in Windows Server 2012 that addresses the difficulty of performing software updates on failover cluster nodes. This is difficult because updating software usually requires a system restart. To maintain the availability of services hosted on failover clusters in previous versions of Windows, you needed to move all roles off one node, update the software on that node, restart the node, and then repeat the process on every other node, one at a time. Windows Server 2008 R2 failover clusters could include up to 16 nodes, so this process sometimes had to be repeated as many times. In Windows Server 2012, failover clusters can scale up to 64 nodes. At this point, the older, manual method of updating software on failover clusters is no longer practical.

Windows Server 2012 automates the process of updating software. To initiate the process of updating a failover cluster, just right-click the cluster in the list of servers in Server Manager and then select Update Cluster from the shortcut menu, as shown in Figure 10-7.

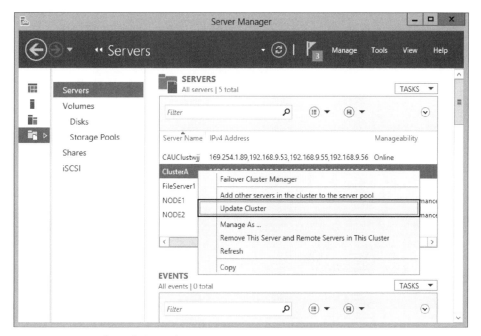

FIGURE 10-7 Manually updating a cluster.

By default, only updates configured through Windows Update are performed. Updates are received as they usually would be, either directly from the Microsoft Update servers or through Windows Software Update Services (WSUS), depending on how Windows Update is configured. Beyond this default functionality, CAU can be extended through third-party plug-ins so other software updates can also be performed.

> **MORE INFO** For more information about how CAU plug-ins work, visit *http://technet .microsoft.com/en-us/library/jj134213*.

The preceding step shows how to manually trigger an update to a cluster. Manually triggering updates might be too straightforward a task to appear on the 70-417 exam. More likely, you could see a question about configuring self-updates. You can access the self-update configuration settings in Failover Cluster Manager by right-clicking the cluster name in the console tree, pointing to More Actions, and then selecting Cluster-Aware Updating, as shown in Figure 10-8.

> **NOTE** Manual updating is called *remote updating mode* when you use this method to update a failover cluster from a remote machine on which the failover cluster management tools have been installed.

FIGURE 10-8 Opening CAU actions.

This step opens the Cluster-Aware Updating dialog box, shown in Figure 10-9.

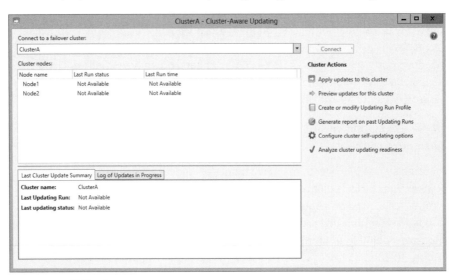

FIGURE 10-9 CAU actions.

To configure self-updating for the cluster, click Configure Self-Updating Options beneath Cluster Actions. This step will open the Configure Self-Updating Options Wizard. You can enable self-updating on the cluster on the second page (Add Clustered Role) of the wizard by selecting the option to add the CAU clustered role with self-updating mode enabled, as shown in Figure 10-10.

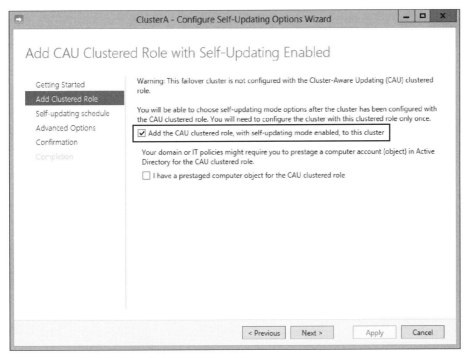

FIGURE 10-10 Enabling self-updating mode for CAU.

> **NOTE** The Cluster-Aware Updating dialog box also enables you to perform the following actions:
>
> - Apply updates to the cluster
> - Preview updates for the cluster
> - Create or modify Updating Run Profile directly (without running a wizard)
> - Generate report on past Updating Runs
> - Analyze cluster updating readiness

The third page (Self-Updating Schedule) of the wizard lets you specify a schedule for updating. The fourth page (Advanced Options) lets you change profile options, as shown in Figure 10-11. These profile options enable you to set time boundaries for the update process and other advanced parameters.

> **MORE INFO** For more information about profile settings for CAU, visit *http://technet .microsoft.com/en-us/library/jj134224.aspx.*

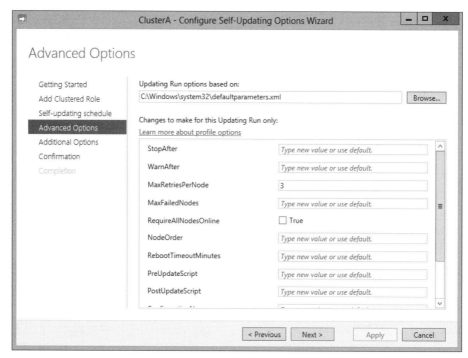

FIGURE 10-11 Configuring advanced options for Cluster-Aware Self-Updating.

> **MORE INFO** For a more detailed description of CAU, visit *http://blogs.technet.com/b* */filecab/archive/2012/05/17/starting-with-cluster-aware-updating-self-updating.aspx.*

EXAM TIP

Even though Network Load Balancing (NLB) hasn't changed significantly since Windows Server 2008 and isn't mentioned in this chapter, be sure to review the feature and its configurable options. For example, remember that in port rules for NLB clusters, the Affinity setting determines how you want multiple connections from the same client handled by the NLB cluster. "Affinity: Single" redirects clients back to the same cluster host. "Affinity: Network" redirects clients from the local subnet to the cluster host. "Affinity: None" doesn't redirect multiple connections from the same client back to the same cluster host.

Objective summary

- In Windows Server 2012, you can create storage pools for failover clusters. Cluster storage pools are compatible only with SAS disks.

- CSVs are a new type of storage used only in some failover clusters. With CSVs, each node on a failover cluster creates its own virtual disk on the volume. The storage is then accessed through paths that are common to every node on the cluster.

- With cluster-aware updating in Windows Server 2012, you can automate the process of updating Windows in a failover cluster.

Objective review

Answer the following questions to test your knowledge of the information in this objective. You can find the answers to these questions and explanations of why each answer choice is correct or incorrect in the "Answers" section at the end of the chapter.

1. You are designing storage for a failover cluster on two servers running Windows Server 2012. You want to provision disks for the cluster that will enable you to create a storage pool for it. Which of the following sets of physical disks could you use to create a storage pool for the failover cluster?

   A. Three individual disks in an iSCSI storage array without any RAID configuration

   B. Four disks in an iSCSI storage array configured as a RAID-5

   C. Three individual disks in a SAS storage array without any RAID configuration

   D. Four disks in a SAS storage array configured as a RAID-5

2. You are an IT administrator for Adatum.com. The Adatum.com network includes 50 servers and 750 clients. Forty of the servers are virtualized. To provide storage for all servers, the Adatum.com network uses an iSCSI-based storage area network (SAN).

   You are designing storage for a new VM hosted in a failover cluster. Your priorities for the storage are simplifying management of SAN storage and minimizing downtime in case of node failure.

   What should you do?

   A. Use Server Manager to create a storage pool.

   B. Keep VM storage on a CSV.

   C. Provision volumes from an external SAS disk array instead of the iSCSI SAN.

   D. Assign a mirrored volume to the cluster.

3. You have configured high availability for a cluster-aware application named ProseWareApp in a two-node failover cluster named Cluster1. The physical nodes in Cluster1 are named Node1 and Node2, and they are both running Hyper-V in Windows Server 2012. Node1 is currently the active node for ProseWareApp.

You want to configure Cluster1 to perform critical Windows Updates with a minimum of administrative effort and a minimum of downtime for ProseWareApp users. What should you do?

A. Drain the roles on Node1 and then start Windows Update on Node1.

B. In Server Manager on Node1, right-click Cluster1 and select Update Cluster.

C. Configure cluster-aware updating to add the CAU clustered role to Cluster1 with self-updating mode enabled.

D. Configure Task Scheduler to run Windows Update daily on Node1 outside business hours.

Objective 10.2: Manage failover clustering roles

This objective covers the configuration of roles in failover clusters. Within this area, there are three new features on which you are likely to be tested: the Scale-Out File Server role, role priority, and VM monitoring.

> **This section covers the following topics:**
> - Create a Scale-Out File Server
> - Assign role priority
> - Configure VM monitoring

Create a Scale-Out File Server

Windows Server 2012 lets you configure two types of file server roles for high availability: a file server for general use (which is the option available in previous versions of Windows Server), and a new Scale-Out File Server For Application Data alternative. Both these options are provided on the File Server Type page of the High Availability Wizard, as shown in Figure 10-12. These clustered file server types are used for different purposes, and they can both be hosted on the same node at the same time.

FIGURE 10-12 Selecting a Scale-Out File Server for the File Server role type.

You will likely see a question or two on the 70-417 exam that tests basic knowledge about Scale-Out File Servers (SoFS). Here's what you need to remember:

- SoFS clusters are not designed for everyday user storage but for applications, such as SQL database applications, that store data on file shares and keep files open for extended periods of time.

- Client requests to connect to an SoFS cluster are distributed among all nodes in the cluster. For this reason, SoFS clusters can handle heavy workloads that increase proportionally to the number of nodes in the cluster.

- SoFS clusters use *only CSVs* for storage.

- SoFS clusters are not compatible with BranchCache, Data Deduplication, DFS Namespace servers, DFS Replication, or File Server Resource Manager.

EXAM TIP

Learn both the benefits and limitations of SoFS well. On the one hand, if a scenario requires a highly available file server for application data in which all added nodes remain online and are able to respond to client requests, an SoFS is a good fit. On the other hand, don't be tricked into selecting SoFS as the file server type for a new clustered file server just because the question states it will host application data. If the file server is also used with incompatible features (such as BranchCache, DFS, or File Server Resource Manager), or if no CSVs are available, you must choose File Server For General Use as the file server type.

MORE INFO   For more information about SoFS, visit *http://technet.microsoft.com/en-us /library/hh831349*.

Assign role startup priority

Unlike previous versions of Windows Server, Windows Server 2012 lets you assign one of four startup priorities to clustered roles: High, Medium, Low, or No Auto Start. Medium is the default priority. In the case of node failure, this priority setting determines the order in which roles are failed over and started on another node. A higher-priority role both fails over and starts before the role of the next-highest priority. If you assign the No Auto Start priority to a role, the role is failed over after the other roles but is not started on the new node. The purpose of startup priority is to ensure that the most critical roles have prioritized access to resources when they fail over to another node.

To change the startup priority of a role, right-click the role in Failover Cluster Manager, point to Change Startup Priority, and select the desired priority, as shown in Figure 10-13.

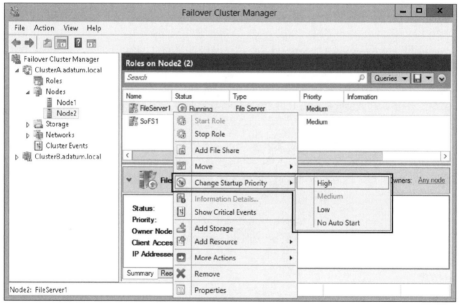

FIGURE 10-13 Setting the startup priority of a role.

Role startup priority is a fairly easy feature to understand and is also likely to appear on the 70-417 exam. Be sure you remember the No Auto Start priority because it's the only priority setting with a meaning that isn't obvious from its name.

EXAM TIP

You need to understand the difference between startup priority settings and preferred owner settings. Startup priority settings determine the order in which roles should be failed over and started after node failure. Preferred owner settings determine *which node*, if available, should handle the client requests for a role both before and after node failure.

Virtual machine application monitoring

Windows Server 2012 introduces the ability for a Hyper-V host to monitor the health of chosen services running on a clustered VM. If the Hyper-V host determines that a monitored service in a guest VM is in a critical state, the host is able to trigger a recovery. The Cluster Service first attempts to recover the VM by restarting it gracefully. Then, if the monitored service is still in a critical state after the VM has restarted, the Cluster Service fails the VM over to another node.

To monitor VM services by using the VM Monitoring feature in Windows Server 2012, the following requirements must be met:

- Both the Hyper-V host and its guest VM must be running Windows Server 2012.
- The guest VM must belong to a domain that trusts the host's domain.
- The Failover Clustering feature must be installed on the Hyper-V host. The guest VM must also be configured as a role in a failover cluster on the Hyper-V host.
- The administrator connecting to the guest through Failover Cluster Manager must be a member of the local administrators group on that guest.
- All firewall rules in the Virtual Machine Monitoring group must be enabled on the guest, as shown in Figure 10-14.

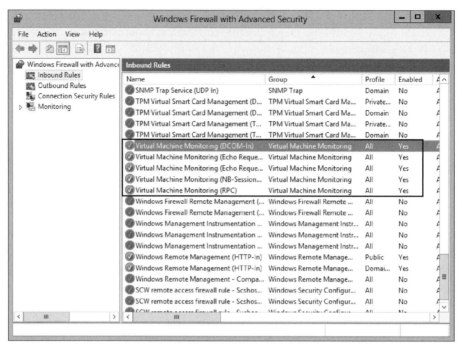

FIGURE 10-14 Enabling firewall rules for VM monitoring.

To configure VM monitoring, right-click the VM in Failover Cluster Manager, point to More Actions, and then select Configure Monitoring, as shown in Figure 10-15.

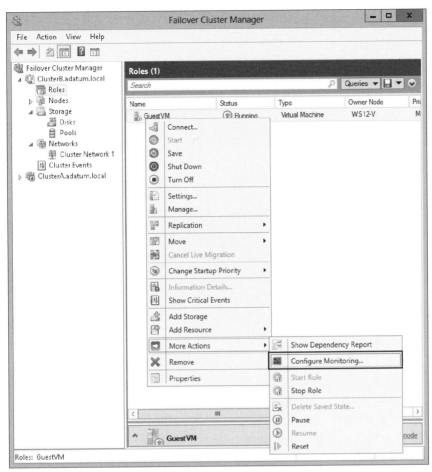

FIGURE 10-15 Configuring monitoring of a VM application.

In the Select Services dialog box that opens, select the services you want to monitor, as shown in Figure 10-16.

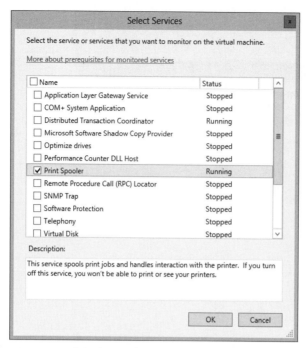

FIGURE 10-16 Selecting services to be monitored in a VM.

By default, the recovery properties for a service are configured so it will automatically attempt to restart the first and second time after it fails. After the third failure, however, the Cluster Service running on the Hyper-V host takes over recovery of the service if you have configured it to do so by selecting the service in the dialog box shown in Figure 10-16.

In some circumstances, you might want to redirect the Cluster Service recovery to a third-party application that allows you more control over the recovery process. In this case, you can disable the default behavior to restart and fail over the VM. To achieve this, first open the resource properties of the guest VM in Failover Cluster Manager, as shown in Figure 10-17.

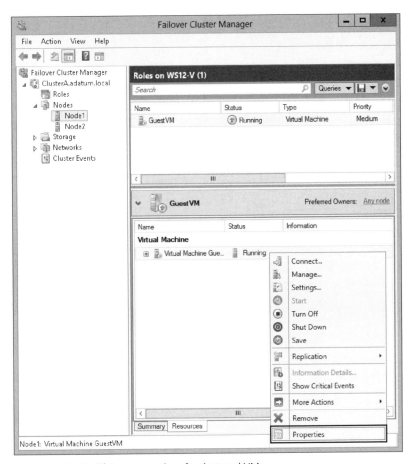

FIGURE 10-17 Modifying properties of a clustered VM.

Then, on the Settings tab of the Properties dialog box shown in Figure 10-18, clear the Enable Automatic Recovery For Application Health Monitoring check box. The Cluster Service will still log an error when a monitored service is in a critical state, but it will no longer attempt to restart or fail over the VM.

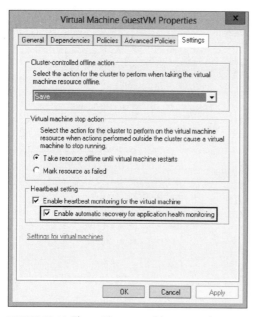

FIGURE 10-18 The setting to enable automatic recovery for a monitored VM application.

Objective summary

- A Scale-Out File Server is a new type of role for which you can configure high availability in a failover cluster. An SoFS can be used to ensure that an application that connects to a file share doesn't generate errors during failover. In addition, an SoFS works on many live nodes at a time, so every node you add enables the cluster to handle more requests. An SoFS is not well suited for use with file storage for users.

- With startup priority, you can determine the order in which roles should be failed over from one node to the next in case of node failure.

- Windows Server 2012 lets you monitor the health of an application running in a guest VM. When a monitored application reaches a critical state, the host computer can trigger the VM to restart. If the application remains in a critical state after the system restart, the host computer will trigger failover to another node.

Objective review

Answer the following questions to test your knowledge of the information in this objective. You can find the answers to these questions and explanations of why each answer choice is correct or incorrect in the "Answers" section at the end of the chapter.

1. You work as a network administrator for Adatum.com. The Adatum.com network includes 25 servers running Windows Server 2012 and 400 clients running Windows 8.

You want to create a failover cluster to support a file share used by a resource-intensive application. Your priorities for the failover cluster are preventing file handling errors in the event of failover and maintaining high performance as the usage of the application grows. Which role and storage type should you configure for the failover cluster? (Choose two. Each answer represents part of the solution.)

A. Configure as the role for the failover cluster a file server for general use.

B. Configure as the role for the failover cluster an SoFS.

C. Store the share on an NTFS volume provisioned from shared storage. Do not add the volume to CSVs.

D. Store the share on a CSV.

2. You work as a network administrator for Fourth Coffee, Inc. The Fourthcoffee.com network spans offices in five cities in North America. All servers in the network are running Windows Server 2012, and all clients are running Windows 8.

   You want to create a failover cluster to support a new file share that will be used by members of the marketing team in all branch offices. Your requirements for the failover cluster and the file share in general are minimizing downtime if a node fails, minimizing storage space needed for the share, reducing or eliminating the possibility of file conflicts, and minimizing the amount of data transferred over wide area network (WAN) links.

   How should you configure the failover cluster and file server? (Choose all that apply.)

   A. Configure as the role for the failover cluster a file server for general use.

   B. Configure as the role for the failover cluster an SoFS.

   C. Enable Data Deduplication on the file share.

   D. Enable BranchCache on the file share.

3. You want to create a two-node failover cluster to provide high availability for a virtual machine. The VM will host an important line-of-business (LOB) application used often throughout the day by members of your organization. You want to configure VM monitoring of the application so that the VM will restart if the application is found to be in a critical state and fail over to the other node if the application still is in a critical state after the system restart.

   Which of the following is NOT a requirement of meeting this goal?

   A. The host Hyper-V server needs to be running Windows Server 2012.

   B. The guest VM needs to be running Windows Server 2012.

   C. The host and the guest need to be members of the same domain.

   D. The guest VM needs to have enabled the firewall rules in the Virtual Machine Monitoring group.

Objective 10.3: Manage virtual machine (VM) movement

Windows Server 2012 both expands and improves on VM migration features that were introduced in Windows Server 2008 R2. The two biggest improvements are the addition of live migration in a nonclustered environment and storage migration.

> **This section covers the following topics:**
> - Configuring and performing live migration in a failover cluster
> - Configuring and performing live migration outside a failover cluster
> - Performing storage migration

Live migration

Live migration is a feature that first appeared in Windows Server 2008 R2. Live migration lets you move a running VM from one Hyper-V host to another without any downtime. Originally, this feature was available only for VMs hosted in failover clusters, but in Windows Server 2012 you can perform live migration of a VM outside a clustered environment. However, the process of performing live migration is different inside and outside clusters, and each of these live migration types has slightly different requirements.

Live migration requires a few configuration steps that you need to understand for the exam. To start configuring this feature, open Hyper-V Settings for each Hyper-V host, as shown in Figure 10-19.

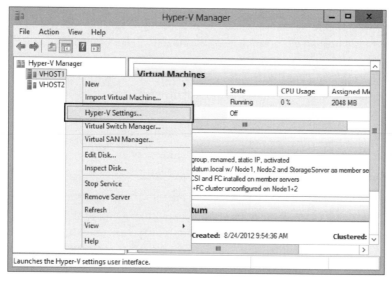

FIGURE 10-19 Configuring Hyper-V settings.

In the Hyper-V Settings dialog box that opens, click Live Migrations on the menu on the left. The associated live migration settings are shown in Figure 10-20.

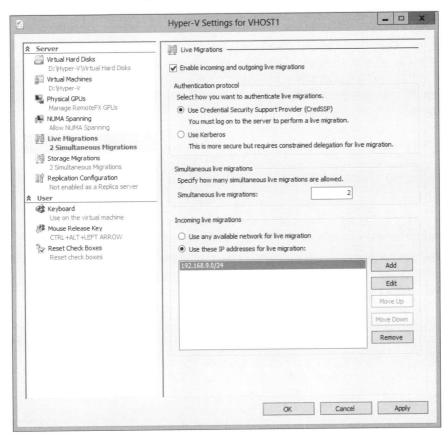

FIGURE 10-20 Live migration settings.

Live migrations are not enabled by default. To enable this feature, perform the following four configuration steps in this dialog box:

1. Select the Enable Incoming And Outgoing Live Migrations check box for both the source and destination hosts.

2. For live migrations outside clustered environments, you need to choose an authentication protocol on both host servers: either Credential Security Support Provider (CredSSP) or Kerberos.

   - **CredSSP** The advantage of this choice is that it requires no configuration. The limitation of choosing CredSSP as the authentication protocol is that you need to be logged on to the source computer when you perform the live migration. You can't perform live migrations through Hyper-V Manager on a remote computer.

- **Kerberos** The advantage of this choice is that you don't need to be logged on to a source computer to perform the live migration. The disadvantage of using Kerberos as the authentication protocol is that it requires configuration. Specifically, in addition to selecting Kerberos in Hyper-V Settings, you need to adjust the properties of the source and destination computer accounts in Active Directory Users and Computers, on the Delegation tab. On each computer account, select the option to trust this computer for delegation, specify the opposite server, and then specify two specified services, CIFS and Microsoft Virtual System Migration Service. The configuration required is shown in Figure 10-21. Note that this configuration step is also known as configuring *constrained delegation*. Expect to see a question about configuring constrained delegation on the 70-417 exam.

3. Set a value for the maximum number of simultaneous live migrations you want to allow on the network. This is a new feature of Windows Server 2012. In Windows Server 2008 R2, you were limited to one live migration at a time. (In the real world, you can estimate 500 Mbps of network bandwidth required per individual live migration. In a Gigabit Ethernet network, you can safely leave the default value of 2.)

4. Add a list of subnets or individual IP addresses from which you want to allow live migrations. Live migration does not provide data encryption of VMs and storage as they are moved across the network, so security is an important consideration. Do not leave the default selection to use any available network for live migration unless you are in a testing environment.

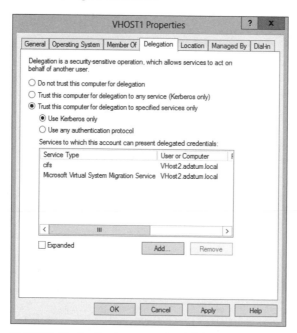

FIGURE 10-21 Configuring constrained delegation.

Live migration in a failover cluster

Although CSVs are not required for VM storage when you perform live migration in a failover cluster, they are highly recommended. If the VM is not already stored in a CSV, you should move it there to prepare for clustered live migration.

MOVING VM STORAGE TO A CSV

To move VM storage to a CSV, right-click the VM in Failover Cluster Manager, point to Move, and then click Virtual Machine Storage, as shown in Figure 10-22.

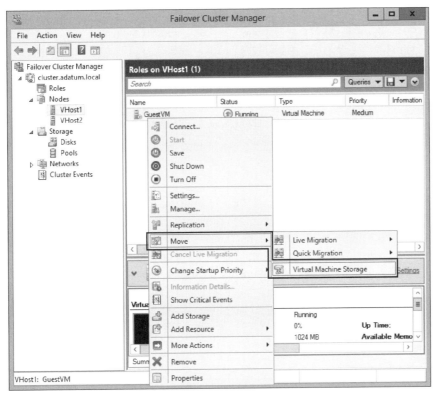

FIGURE 10-22 Moving virtual machine storage.

Then, in the Move Virtual Machine Storage dialog box that opens, shown in Figure 10-23, select the VM in the top pane and drag it to a CSV folder in the bottom-left pane. Click Start to begin the copy operation.

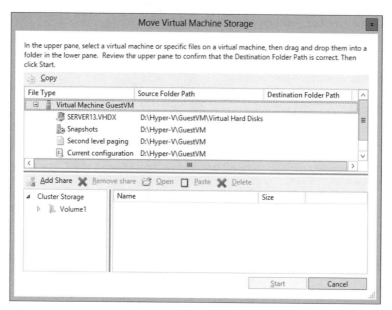

FIGURE 10-23 Moving VM storage to a CSV.

PERFORMING LIVE MIGRATION

After the transfer is complete, you can perform a live migration as long as the Hyper-V environments, including the names of virtual switches, are the same on the source and destination nodes. To perform the live migration, in Failover Cluster Manager, right-click the clustered VM, point to Move, then point to Live Migration, and then click Select Node from the shortcut menu, as shown in Figure 10-24.

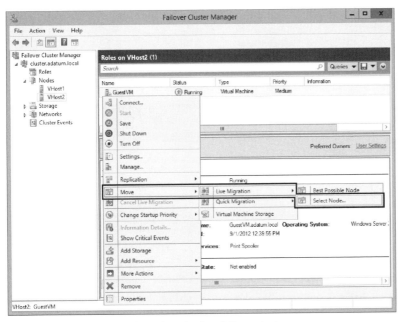

FIGURE 10-24 Performing a live migration in a failover cluster.

In the Move Virtual Machine Dialog box that opens, shown in Figure 10-25, select the destination node in the failover cluster to which you want to transfer the running VM and then click OK to start the process.

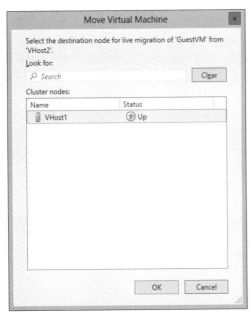

FIGURE 10-25 Selecting a destination node for live migration.

You can keep track of the migration status in Failover Cluster Manager, as shown in Figure 10-26.

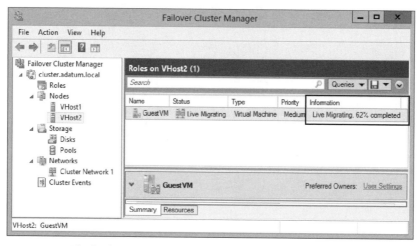

FIGURE 10-26 Viewing live migration status.

During and after migration, the VM continues to operate without interruption.

> **NOTE** First introduced in Windows Server 2008, Quick Migration is still an option when you choose to move a clustered VM from one node to another in Windows Server 2012. Quick Migration saves the VM state and resumes the machine on the destination node. The advantages of Quick Migration are that it is a faster process from start to finish for the VM you are migrating and requires less network bandwidth. The disadvantage of Quick Migration is that the VM is briefly brought offline during the migration process. If minimizing downtime is not a priority and you want to transfer a VM as quickly as possible, then Quick Migration is the best option.

Live migration outside a clustered environment

Nonclustered live migration is a new feature in Windows Server 2012 in which you can move a running VM from one Hyper-V host to another, with no downtime, outside a clustered environment. The feature requires that the source and destination Hyper-V hosts belong to domains that trust each other. However, it doesn't require SAN storage or a clustered environment. It's also worth noting that a disadvantage of nonclustered live migration, compared to clustered live migration, is that the process takes much longer because all files are copied from the source to the destination host. (An exception to this is if the VM and its storage are kept on a file share and do not need to be copied from one host to the other during the migration process.)

Once you have configured live migration settings in Hyper-V Manager on the source and destination computers, you can perform the live migration. It's a simple procedure. In Hyper-V Manager, right-click the running VM you want to live migrate and then select Move from the shortcut menu, as shown in Figure 10-27.

FIGURE 10-27 Initiating a live migration outside a clustered environment.

In the wizard that opens, select the Move The Virtual Machine option, as shown in Figure 10-28.

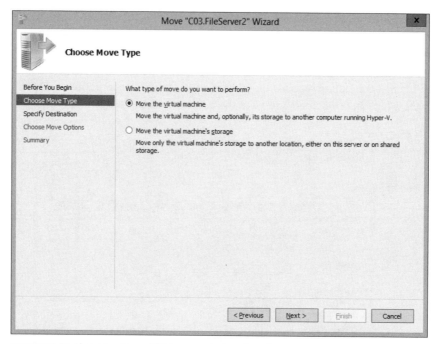

FIGURE 10-28 Live migrating a VM in a nonclustered environment.

Then, specify the destination server, as shown in Figure 10-29.

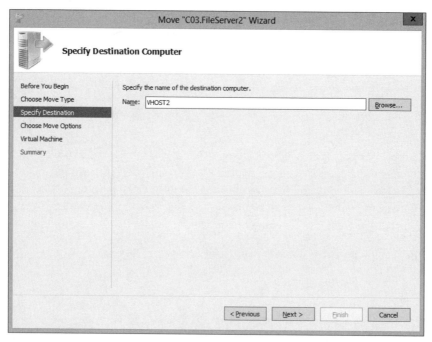

FIGURE 10-29 Choosing a destination host for live migration in a nonclustered environment.

You have three options for how to move the VM's items when you perform the live migration, as shown in Figure 10-30. First, you can move all the VM's files and storage to a single folder on the destination computer. Second, you can move different items to different folders in a particular way that you specify. Third, you can migrate just the VM while leaving the storage in place. Note that this option requires the VM storage to reside on shared storage such as an iSCSI target, a fact that could easily serve as the basis for an incorrect answer choice on a test question.

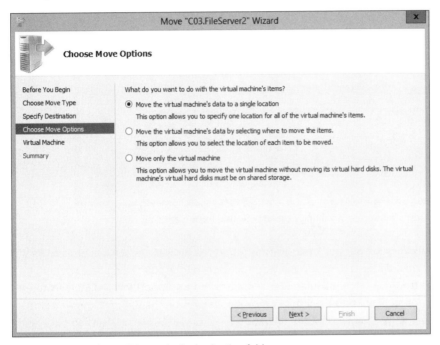

FIGURE 10-30 Moving a VM to a single destination folder.

Processor compatibility

One potential problem that can arise when you perform a live or quick migration is that the processor on the destination Hyper-V host supports different features than the processor on the source host. In this case, you might receive the error message shown in Figure 10-31, and the migration fails. (A failed migration does not negatively affect the running VM. The result of the failure is just that the VM is left running on the source computer.)

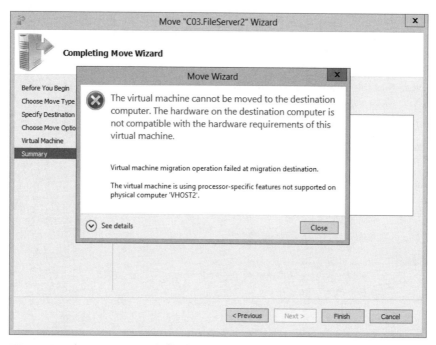

FIGURE 10-31 An error message indicating processor feature incompatibility.

Neither live migration nor quick migration is supported between hosts with processors from different manufacturers. However, if the processors on the source and destination computers are from the same manufacturer and are found to support incompatible features, you have the option of limiting the virtual processor features on the VM to maximize compatibility and improve the chances that the migration will succeed. (Again, this setting does not provide compatibility between different processor manufacturers.)

To enable processor compatibility, expand the Processor settings in the VM's settings dialog box and select the Compatibility node, as shown in Figure 10-32. Then, select the Migrate To A Physical Computer With A Different Processor Version check box. Alternatively, you can run the following command at a Windows PowerShell prompt:

```
Set-VMProcessor VMname -CompatibilityForMigrationEnabled $true
```

It's worth noting that this setting is very easy to construct a test question around. If you see a question about live migration in which you receive an error message indicating trouble related to processor-specific features, you now know how to handle it: just enable the processor compatibility setting.

FIGURE 10-32 Enabling processor compatibility for migration.

EXAM TIP

Look for trick questions about VM migration in which the fact that the source and destination hosts have different processor manufacturers is buried somewhere in the middle of a table or list. When the processor manufacturers are different, your best option for migration is to manually export it from the source machine and import it on the destination machine. You can't use live migration or quick migration.

Virtual switch name matching

Another common problem that can occur when you attempt to perform a live migration is that the destination Hyper-V environment doesn't provide virtual switches with names identical to those in the Hyper-V environment on the source computer. This problem is detected as you complete the Move Wizard. For each snapshot of the source VM that defines a virtual switch without an exact equivalent on the destination Hyper-V host, you are given an opportunity to choose another virtual switch on the destination that the VM should use in place of the original. This step is shown in Figure 10-33.

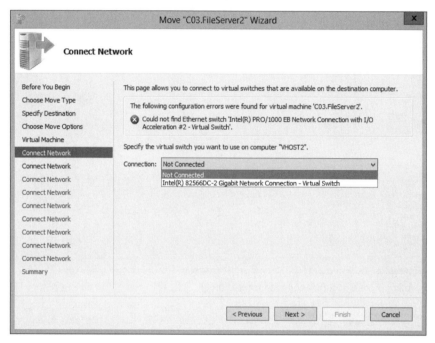

FIGURE 10-33 Matching a virtual switch on a destination host for live migration.

After you make the required substitutions, the wizard begins the live migration when you click Finish on the final page, as shown in Figure 10-34.

> **MORE INFO**   For more information about live migration in Windows Server 2012, visit
> *http://technet.microsoft.com/en-us/library/jj134199.aspx.*

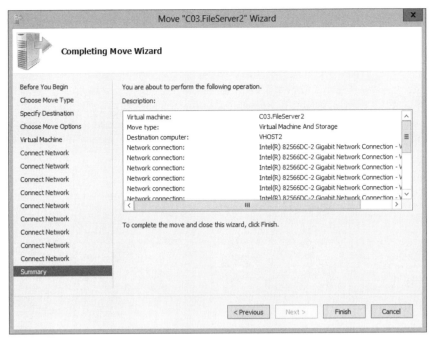

FIGURE 10-34 A live migration in progress in a nonclustered environment.

Storage migration

Another useful new feature in Windows Server 2012 is the live migration of VM storage. With this option, you can move the data associated with a VM from one volume to another while the VM remains running. This option is useful if storage space is scarce on one volume or storage array and is more plentiful on another storage source. An important advantage of storage-only live migration to remember for the exam is that unlike live migration, it can be performed in a workgroup environment because the source and destination servers are the same.

To perform storage migration, use the Move option to open the Move Wizard, as you would to begin the process of live migrating the VM. Then, on the Choose Move Type page of the wizard, select Move The Virtual Machine's Storage, as shown in Figure 10-35.

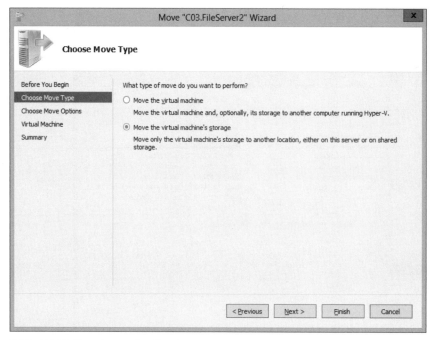

FIGURE 10-35 Choosing a migration type.

You have three options for how to migrate the storage of the VM, as shown in Figure 10-36. The first option is to move all storage to a single folder on the destination volume.

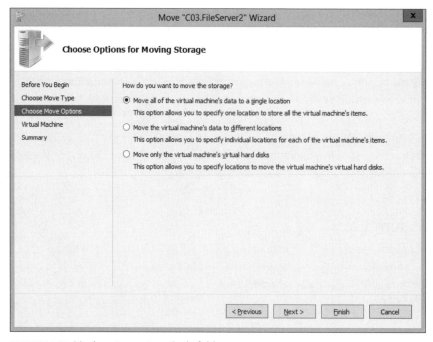

FIGURE 10-36 Moving storage to a single folder.

The second option allows you to select which particular storage items you want to migrate, such as snapshot data or the smart paging folder, as shown in Figure 10-37. The third option allows you to specify particular VHDs to migrate only.

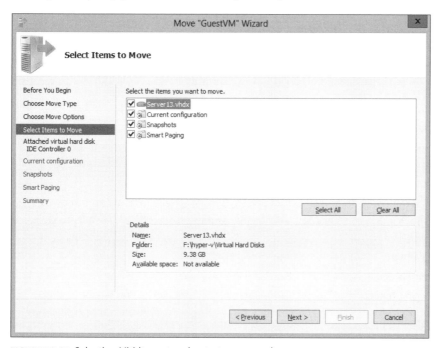

FIGURE 10-37 Selecting VM items to migrate to a new volume.

For the exam, what's most important to remember about storage migration is that this feature provides an option that is often the best way to solve a problem. If space runs out for a running VM, it's not necessarily a good idea to migrate that VM to another server. No other server might be available, for example, and you might want to spare your organization the unnecessary expense of buying a new one. In this case, it's often more prudent to just attach a new disk array to the server and move the VM storage to this newly available space.

> **MORE INFO**   For a good review of Live Migration and Storage Migration, see the TechEd Australia session on the topic at http://channel9.msdn.com/Events/TechEd/Australia/2012 /VIR314.

Objective summary

- Live migration is a feature in which a running VM is transferred from one host computer to another without any downtime. In Windows Server 2012, live migration can be performed inside or outside a failover cluster, but live migration within a failover cluster is much faster.

- When configuring servers for live migration outside a failover cluster, you must choose an authentication protocol either CredSSP or Kerberos. CredSSP needs no configuration, but it requires you to trigger the live migration while logged on to the source host. Kerberos allows you to trigger the live migration from a remote host, but it requires you to configure constrained delegation for the source and destination hosts.

- Windows Server 2012 introduces storage migration for VMs. By using storage migration, you can move all the storage associated with a running VM from one disk to another without any downtime.

Objective review

Answer the following questions to test your knowledge of the information in this objective. You can find the answers to these questions and explanations of why each answer choice is correct or incorrect in the "Answers" section at the end of the chapter.

1. You are a network administrator for Contoso.com. You have recently upgraded all your servers to Windows Server 2012. Your manager has indicated that he wants to start testing the live migration feature in a nonclustered environment so you can eventually take advantage of this functionality in production.

   You create a small test network consisting of two Hyper-V servers running Windows Server 2012 named Host1 and Host2. The hardware and software settings on these two physical servers exactly match those of two physical servers in your production network. Host1 is currently hosting a guest VM named VM1.

   You enable live migration on both servers and configure CredSSP as the authentication protocol. You then log on locally to Host1 and initiate a live migration of VM1 from Host1 to Host2. You receive an error message indicating that the VM is using processor-specific features not supported on the destination physical computer.

   You want to successfully perform a live migration in your test network so you will know what is required to successfully use this feature in production. What should you do?

   A. Configure constrained delegation for Host1 and Host2.

   B. Disable VM monitoring on VM1.

   C. Configure Kerberos as the authentication protocol on Host1 and Host2.

   D. On Host1, run the following command:

   ```
   Set-VMProcessor VM1 -CompatibilityForMigrationEnabled $true
   ```

2. You are a network administrator for Adatum.com. You have recently upgraded all your servers to Windows Server 2012. Your manager has indicated that she wants to start testing the live migration feature so you can eventually take advantage of this functionality in production.

   You create a small test network consisting of two Hyper-V servers running Windows Server 2012 named VHost1 and VHost2. The hardware and software settings on these two physical servers exactly match those of two physical servers in your production network. VHost2 is currently hosting a guest VM named VM2.

You enable live migration on both servers and configure Kerberos as the authentication protocol. You then log on locally to Host1 and initiate a live migration of VM1 from VHost2 to VHost1. The live migration fails, and you receive an error indicating "No credentials are available in the security package."

You want to successfully perform a live migration in your test network so you will know what is required to successfully use this feature in production. You also want to initiate live migrations when you are not logged on to the source host server. What should you do next?

A. Configure constrained delegation for VHost1 and VHost2.

B. Disable VM monitoring on VM2.

C. Configure CredSSP as the authentication protocol on VHost1 and VHost2

D. On VHost1, run the following command:

```
Set-VMProcessor VM2 -CompatibilityForMigrationEnabled $true
```

3. You are a network administrator for Proseware.com. One of your servers is named HV1 and is running Windows Server 2012 with the Hyper-V role. HV1 is hosting 10 virtual machines on locally attached storage. It is not a member of any domain.

The available storage used by the 10 guest VMs on HV1 is nearly depleted. At the current rate of growth, the physical disks now attached to HV1 will run out of space in three months.

You want to provide more space to your guest VMs. How can you solve the storage problem with minimal financial expense and minimal impact on users?

A. Perform a quick migration of the VMs on HV1 to a new server with more space.

B. Perform a live migration of the VMs on HV1 to a new server with more space.

C. Perform a storage migration of the VMs on HV1 to a new storage array with ample storage space.

D. Attach a new storage array with ample storage space to HV1 and expand the VHD files used by the guest VMs.

Thought experiment

You are a network administrator for Proseware.com, a software company with offices in several cities. You are designing high availability for certain applications and services at the Philadelphia branch office. You have the following goals:

- You want to ensure that two domain controllers from the Proseware.com domain remain online with high availability in the Philadelphia branch office, even if one server experiences a catastrophic failure or is brought down for maintenance. (The domain controllers will not host any operations master roles.)

- You want to ensure that a heavily used LOB application can withstand the failure of one server without experiencing any downtime or file handling errors, even during failover. The LOB application is not cluster-aware. It also frequently reads and writes data stored on a network share.

With these details in mind, answer the following questions:

1. How many physical servers will you need to support your requirements at a minimum?

2. How can you best provide high availability for file sharing?

3. How can you best provide high availability for the LOB application?

4. Which of your goals require Windows Server 2012 as opposed to an earlier version of Windows Server?

Answers

This section contains the answers to the Objective Reviews and the Thought Experiment.

Objective 10.1: Review

1. **Correct Answer:** C

   A. **Incorrect:** A cluster storage pool can only be created from SAS disks.

   B. **Incorrect:** A cluster storage pool can only be created from SAS disks. In addition, a cluster storage pool is incompatible with external RAIDs.

   C. **Correct**: To create a cluster storage pool, you need three independent SAS disks that are not configured with any RAID or governed by any disk subsystem.

   D. **Incorrect**: You cannot create a cluster storage pool from disks that are configured as part of a RAID or governed by any disk subsystem.

2. **Correct Answer:** B

   A. **Incorrect:** Creating a storage pool might simplify management of SAN storage, but it won't minimize downtime in case of node failure. In addition, the SAN storage cannot be configured as a storage pool for the cluster because it is iSCSI-based. Only SAS storage can be used for a cluster storage pool.

   B. **Correct:** Keeping VM storage on a CSV will optimize live migration of the VM in case of node failure and minimize downtime. CSVs will also simplify management of SAN storage by allowing multiple failover cluster nodes to share LUNs.

   C. **Incorrect:** Provisioning volumes from a SAS array will enable you to create a storage pool for the cluster, which might simplify management of storage. However, using a SAS array will not minimize downtime in case of node failure.

   D. **Incorrect:** Assigning a mirrored volume to the cluster might prevent node failure if one disk fails, but it will not minimize downtime if a node fails. In addition, it will not simplify management of SAN storage.

3. **Correct Answer:** C

   A. **Incorrect:** This solution performs updates only once on Node1 only, not the entire cluster.

   B. **Incorrect:** This solution only updates the cluster once. It doesn't minimize administrative effort because you would need to do it repeatedly.

   C. **Correct**: This solution configures Cluster1 to perform Windows Updates automatically and regularly on both nodes in the cluster.

   D. **Incorrect**: This solution performs updates only on Node1, not the entire cluster.

Objective 10.2: Review

1. **Correct Answers:** B, D

   A. **Incorrect:** A traditional file server for general use is best suited for users, not resource-intensive applications. In addition, a traditional file server would not easily allow you to handle an increased load as the usage of the file share increased.

   B. **Correct:** A Scale-Out File Server allows an application to maintain file handles even during failover, which minimizes application errors. In addition, an SoFS allows you to keep all nodes active and to add nodes as needed to handle an increased load.

   C. **Incorrect**: A Scale-Out File Server requires CSV storage. Choosing this storage type would not allow you to meet your requirements of reducing errors and maintaining high performance.

   D. **Correct**: A Scale-Out File Server requires CSV storage.

2. **Correct Answers:** A, C, D

   A. **Correct:** A File Server for general use is the more suitable role to provide high availability for a file share that users (as opposed to applications) will use for file storage. In addition, only the File Server role is compatible with Data Deduplication and BranchCache.

   B. **Incorrect:** An SoFS is not compatible with Data Deduplication or BranchCache, two features that will help you meet your requirements for the share.

   C. **Correct:** Data Deduplication will help minimize storage space requirements.

   D. **Correct:** BranchCache will minimize the amount of data transferred over WAN links and prevent file conflicts.

3. **Correct Answer:** C

   A. **Incorrect:** VM monitoring requires Windows Server 2012 to be running on the host Hyper-V server and failover cluster node.

   B. **Incorrect:** VM monitoring requires Windows Server 2012 to be running on the clustered VM.

   C. **Correct:** The host and guest do not need to be members of the same domain. However, the two domains need to trust each other.

   D. **Incorrect:** The firewall rules in the Virtual Machine Monitoring group need to be enabled on the clustered VM.

Objective 10.3: Review

1. **Correct Answer:** D

   A. **Incorrect:** Constrained delegation is required for Kerberos authentication. You have configured CredSSP as the authentication protocol. In addition, you have received an error related to processor compatibility, not authentication.

   B. **Incorrect:** VM monitoring isn't incompatible with live migration, so it wouldn't generate an error like this.

   C. **Incorrect:** There is no reason to change the authentication protocol to Kerberos under these circumstances. CredSSP allows you to initiate a live migration when you are logged on locally to the source host.

   D. **Correct:** If you enable processor compatibility on the VM, the virtual processor will use only the features of the processor that are available on all versions of a virtualization-capable processor by the same processor manufacturer. You would see this error if each host server used a different processor from the same manufacturer.

2. **Correct Answer:** A

   A. **Correct:** When you choose Kerberos as the authentication protocol, you need to configure constrained delegation on the computer accounts for the source and destination computers.

   B. **Incorrect:** VM monitoring is not incompatible with live migration and would not generate an error like this.

   C. **Incorrect:** CredSSP as an authentication protocol would not enable you to initiate live migrations when you are not logged on to the source host server.

   D. **Incorrect:** The error received is not related to processor compatibility, so this step would not fix the problem.

3. **Correct Answer:** C

   A. **Incorrect:** A quick migration is possible only in a failover cluster environment. In addition, purchasing a new server with ample new storage is unnecessarily costly compared to purchasing only new storage.

   B. **Incorrect:** You cannot perform a live migration from a computer outside a domain environment. In addition, purchasing a new server with ample new storage is unnecessarily costly compared to purchasing only new storage.

   C. **Correct:** This option avoids the unnecessary expense of purchasing a new server and lets you transfer storage to the new storage array live, without taking your VMs offline.

   D. **Incorrect:** This option will not solve your problem. If you purchase a new disk array, you need to find a way to move the VMs onto the new storage. You will be able to expand the size of the VHD files only to the point at which they will use up the space on the old disks.

Thought experiment

1. Three. You need to have two highly available domain controllers even after one server is brought down. You can provide high availability for all workloads on those three servers.

2. Use an SoFS with CSVs so the LOB application can remain connected to files even during failover.

3. You should host the LOB application in a highly available VM because the application isn't cluster-aware.

4. A virtualized domain controller is not recommended in older versions of Windows Server. In addition, an SoFS is available only in Windows Server 2012.

CHAPTER 11

File and storage solutions

The File and Storage Solutions domain includes just one objective, but it's a big one: Implement Dynamic Access Control.

Access permissions for files have traditionally been controlled by a combination of share permissions and NTFS permissions. Dynamic Access Control (DAC) is a set of features new to Windows Server 2012 that adds to these two access controls an optional third security gate for file access. DAC controls access in a way that is dependent not on group memberships or file locations, but instead on object attributes cited in access rules. The advantage of DAC is that it can provide highly customized and simplified management of file security, especially in a large organization.

Objectives in this chapter:

- Objective 11.1: Implement Dynamic Access Control

Objective 11.1: Implement Dynamic Access Control

DAC relies on file classifications, user and device attributes called claims, and rules and policies built from these elements. DAC can be very complex. The good news is that on the 70-417 exam, you will likely need to understand only the fundamentals about this feature. The bad news is that these concepts are new, so even learning the fundamentals well enough for the exam requires some effort.

> **This section covers the following topics:**
> - Configuring claims-based authentication
> - Configuring file classification
> - Configuring access policies

Introduction to DAC

DAC is a new way to control access to files. It doesn't replace NTFS and share permissions but is sometimes combined with them. When DAC permissions are combined with the NTFS and share permissions, the most restrictive permissions always apply to the account requesting access.

You can think of DAC as being based on *access rules*. These rules are if–then statements built on the attributes of files, users, and devices. An expression to serve as the basis for an access rule could be "If a user is a member of the finance department with an office on Floor 10 and is connecting from a device that is located in the company HQ, then that user can access finance department files and folders designated as having a high business impact." Before you can create such an access rule, you need to create and assign the needed attributes to all the objects mentioned in that rule. The user and device attributes are called *claims*. The file attributes are called *classifications* (or *resource properties*).

The way these three attribute types relate to an access rule is illustrated in Figure 11-1.

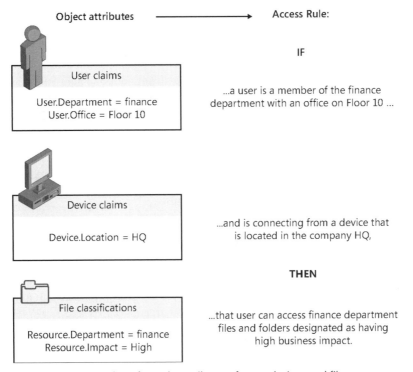

FIGURE 11-1 Access rules refer to the attributes of users, devices, and files.

DAC has a number of advantages. First, it allows administrators to manage file access centrally, in a way that impacts all file servers in the organization. (It should be noted, however, that you cannot enforce access rules centrally through DAC; you can only make access rules available for enforcement.) Second, it enables you to dramatically reduce the number of user groups you would otherwise need to create and manage to implement a particular access policy. Third, it enables you to construct access rules in a way that is both more flexible and more likely to correspond to the needs of your organization. Instead of access control lists (ACLs) based only on user and group accounts, you can create rules based on location, office, country, telephone number, or any other parameter that is most useful to you.

To implement DAC, you need at least one Windows Server 2012 file server, at least one Windows Server 2012 domain controller (one at each site is recommended), and Windows 7 clients or higher. In addition, specific features such as access-denied assistance require Windows 8. The domain functional level must also be set to Windows Server 2012.

Even more than most new features on which you will be tested for the 70-417 exam, DAC is best understood by working with it hands-on. This isn't the easiest new Windows Server 2012 feature to master, but without implementing it on a test network, it can seem more complicated than it really is. To prepare for the exam, then, use the following sections as a general walk-through for hands-on configuration, if at all possible. Plan to walk through these steps at least twice, and it will all begin to make sense.

EXAM TIP

Expect to see questions on the 70-417 exam for which you need to remember the exact order of steps necessary to configure DAC. Use this chapter to help understand the concepts in DAC and to learn the main steps as they are presented in each section.

Configuring claims-based authentication

DAC relies on an expanded Kerberos token. This Kerberos token includes more than the usual data, which is (as you remember) the user's ID and group memberships. Besides this information, the expanded Kerberos token used in DAC includes certain attribute values, called claims, about the user, additional claims about the device to which the user is signed on, and that device's own group memberships. The expanded Kerberos token used in DAC is illustrated in Figure 11-2.

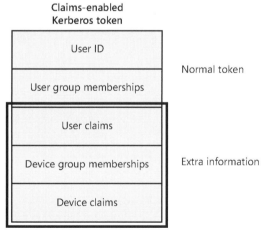

FIGURE 11-2 The Kerberos token used in DAC.

To configure a DAC policy, you need to perform the following steps:

1. Define the types of claims about users and devices you want to include in Kerberos tokens.

2. Configure Active Directory Domain Services to use the expanded Kerberos tokens that include these claims.

Step 1: Define user and device claims types

In this step, you choose the specific user and device properties that will be presented as claims in the Kerberos token whenever access permissions are evaluated. User and device claim types correspond to names of Active Directory attributes (such as "Department" or "City") for user and computer account objects. The actual claim values included in a token are copied from the corresponding Active Directory attribute values. Because access rules refer to these claim types in their specifications about who is allowed or denied access to a given resource, you want to define claims types you will need later when you create access control rules.

You can use Active Directory Administrative Center to configure the user and device claim types. In the console tree, select tree view, and then navigate to Dynamic Access Control\Claim Types. Right-click Claim Types, click New, and then select Claim Type, as shown in Figure 11-3.

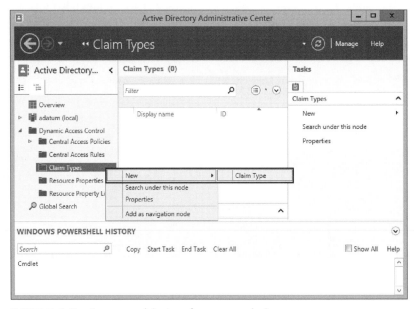

FIGURE 11-3 Creating a new claim type for a user or device.

The Create Claim Type page that opens is shown in Figure 11-4.

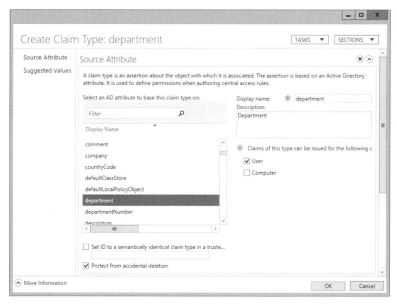

FIGURE 11-4 Creating a claim type for a user object.

In the Source Attribute section, click the Active Directory object attribute name you want to use as the basis of the claim type. You can also specify whether you want this claim type to be issued for users, computers (devices), or both. For example, if you plan to define rules that include references to the department of either the user or the device to which a user is signed on, you should select both User and Computer when you create the Department claim type.

In the Suggested Values section, you can provide a list of suggested matching values that you will later be able to supply in access rules. For example, if you plan to create access rules that specify user or device Department values such as "Finance," "Engineering," "Operations," "Marketing," and "Sales," you can precreate these strings as suggested values when you are creating the claim type. Note that if you define any suggested values, those values will be the only ones available to select when you create rules that refer to the claim type.

Step 2: Enable Kerberos support for claims-based access control

In this step, you use Group Policy to enable Kerberos support for claims on domain controllers. This step ensures that Kerberos tokens include claims information that can be evaluated by domain controllers for access authorization.

In the Group Policy Management Console, create or edit a group policy object (GPO) linked to the Domain Controllers organizational unit (OU) and then enable the following setting: Computer Configuration/Policies/Administrative Templates/System/KDC/KDC Support For Claims, Compound Authentication, And Kerberos Armoring. (Within the Policy Setting dialog box, leave selected the default option of Supported.)

The requirement that you set this policy for claims-based authorization, and that you should do so at the Domain Controllers OU level, is one of the most likely aspects about DAC on which you will be tested during the 70-417 exam. Learn to recognize not only the full name of this policy but also the possible ways its name might be shortened. (For example, an answer choice might just say "Use Group Policy to enable Kerberos armoring on the Domain Controllers OU.") The location of this policy setting within a GPO is shown in Figure 11-5.

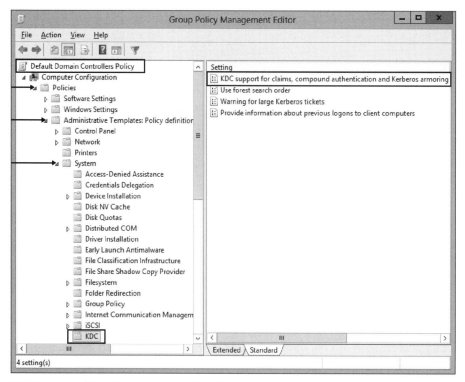

FIGURE 11-5 Enabling Kerberos support for claims.

Configuring file classification

File classification refers to the process of adding attributes to the properties of files and folders. These attributes enable you to construct access rules that apply to these resources. Configuring file classification can be broken down into the following four steps:

1. Enable or create selected resource properties.
2. Add resource properties to a resource property list.
3. Update Active Directory file and folder objects.
4. Classify files and folders.

Step 1: Enable or create selected resource properties

You perform this step on a domain controller running Windows Server 2012 in Active Directory Administrative Center. In the console tree, select tree view (the right tab in the navigation pane) and then the Resource Properties container, as shown in Figure 11-6.

Resource properties correspond to attribute categories, such as Department, that you can make appear on the Classification tab of the Properties dialog box of files and folders. You make a resource property appear on this Classification tab by first enabling the property and then performing steps 2 and 3 described later in this section. Generally, you should enable only the resource properties you plan to use later in access rules. For example, if your eventual goal is to create and apply the access rule shown in Figure 11-1, you should enable the Department and Impact resource properties.

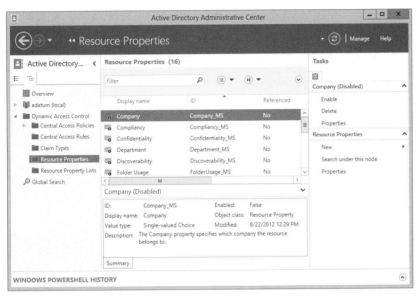

FIGURE 11-6 Resource properties.

Windows Server 2012 includes 16 predefined resource properties, including Department, Impact, Compliancy, Intellectual Property, and Confidentiality. These resource properties include predefined suggested values you can eventually assign to objects, such as the specific names of departments; High, Medium, or Low; and Yes or No. However, if a resource property you need isn't predefined (such as City or Country), you can create it and define suggested values you need, such as London, New York, UK, US, and so on. Any new resource properties you create are enabled automatically.

Step 2: Add resource properties to a resource property list

After you enable your desired resource properties, you have to add them to a resource property list before they can be applied to objects. Begin by selecting the Resource Property Lists container in Active Directory Administrative Center. One predefined list is available: Global

Resource Property List. If you want the same classifications to be available for all objects, use this list. To add the resource properties you have enabled, right-click the list and select Add Resource Properties, as shown in Figure 11-7. In the Select Resource Properties dialog box that opens, add the desired resource properties that you have enabled and then click OK.

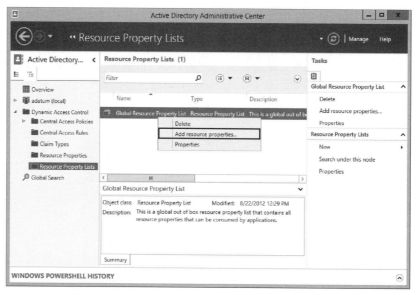

FIGURE 11-7 Adding resource properties to a resource property list.

EXAM TIP

Beware of answer choices that suggest you need to *create* a resource property list when you configure file classification. You don't need to create a resource property list. You just need to add the resource properties to a list (usually the built-in Global Resource Property List).

Step 3: Update Active Directory file and folder objects

To update Active Directory Domain Services with the new classifiable properties, you need to run the following cmdlet on a file server on which the File Server Resource Manager (FSRM) component of the File Server role has been installed:

```
Update-FSRMClassificationPropertyDefinition
```

After you perform this step, the resource properties you chose in step 1 appear on the Classification tab of every file and folder on that file server. The Classification tab is shown in Figure 11-8.

Note that this cmdlet is one of the most likely items related to DAC to appear on the 70-417 exam. Make sure you understand its function.

FIGURE 11-8 Resource properties on the Classification tab.

Step 4: Classify files and folders

Objects in the file structure can be classified manually or automatically. The following sections provide instructions on how to classify files by using these strategies.

MANUAL CLASSIFICATION

To classify file objects manually, you can select and apply a resource property value on the Classification tab directly on selected files or on their parent folder. For example, for the folder shown in Figure 11-9, the Finance and High values have been selected for the Department and Impact properties, respectively. When you click Apply, these classifications will automatically be applied to all child objects within the folder.

Note that child objects keep these classification settings until they are reapplied. Files do not automatically inherit the values of other parent folders if they are moved into those other folders. The classifications remain applied to those objects even when you copy them from computer to computer. However, you can only see and read the classifications that have been applied to objects after you install FSRM and run the Update-FSRMClassificationPropertyDefinition cmdlet.

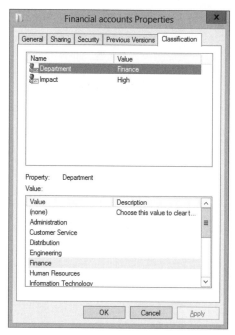

FIGURE 11-9 Classification values set on a parent folder.

AUTOMATIC CLASSIFICATION

Windows Server 2012 includes a built-in file classifier that can be configured to automatically classify files within targeted folders. You can classify all files within targeted folders automatically or restrict this function to a subset of the files, limiting classification to Microsoft documents with contents that include a match of a specified expression. You can also restrict classification to the files selected by a custom Windows PowerShell script. Besides this built-in functionality, automatic classification (and DAC in general) can be extended greatly through third-party applications.

To start configuring automatic file classification, you first need to install the FSRM component of the File Server role. Then, in the File Server Resource Manager console tree, navigate to Classification Management\Classification Rules. In the Actions pane, click Create Classification Rule, as shown in Figure 11-10.

This step opens the Create Classification Rule dialog box. On the General tab, enter a name and description for the new rule. The General tab also includes an Enabled check box, which is selected by default.

On the Scope tab, shown in Figure 11-11, click Add to select the folders where this rule will apply. The classification rule applies to all folders and their subfolders in the list. Alternatively, you can target *all* folders that store *any* of the following selected classifications of data: Application Files, Backup And Archival Files, Group Files, and User Files.

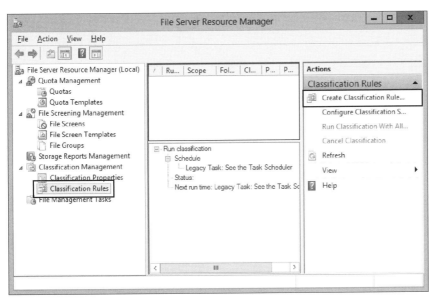

FIGURE 11-10 Creating a classification rule.

FIGURE 11-11 Setting the scope for a classification rule.

On the Classification tab, shown in Figure 11-12, choose a classification method along with the classification value for one selected property the rule will assign.

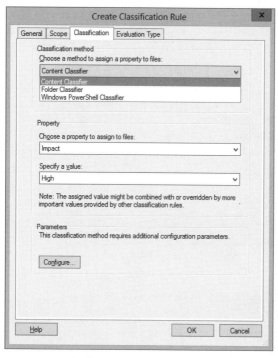

FIGURE 11-12 Configuring a classification method and property value.

For a classification method, there are three options:

- The Folder Classifier option assigns the property value to all files that fall within the scope of the rule.

- The Windows PowerShell Classifier prompts you to specify a script to determine the target files within the scope of the rule.

- The Content Classifier option searches Microsoft documents for a text or regular expression string. Click Configure to further configure this option with the Classification Parameters dialog box, shown in Figure 11-13.

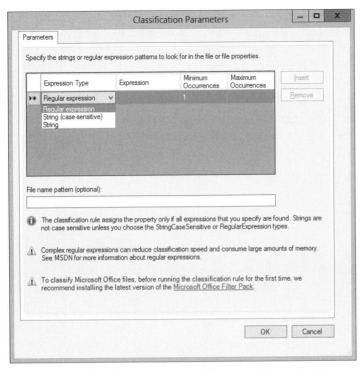

FIGURE 11-13 Configuring a content search for automatic classification.

This dialog box lets you specify an expression that will be searched for in the content of Microsoft documents that fall within the scope of the rule. If the content search results in a match for the specified expression, the file is tagged with the property value specified on the Classification tab of the Create Classification Rule dialog box.

You can choose one of three expression types to search for: string, case-sensitive string, or *regular expression*. A regular expression, sometimes called a regex, is used in programming to match *patterns* of text strings rather than exact sequences of specific numbers or letters. A regular expression is often a useful matching mechanism for classifying files that include sensitive numbers, such as credit card numbers.

The following is an example of a regular expression. It matches credit card numbers from most vendors:

```
^((4\d{3})|(5[1-5]\d{2})|(6011)|(34\d{1})|(37\d{1}))-?\d{4}-?\d{4}-?\d{4}|3[4,7]
[\d\s-]{15}$
```

The Evaluation Type tab is the final tab of the Create Classification Rule dialog box. On this tab, you choose how to handle files that already exist within the scope of the rule. By default, the classification rule does not apply to preexisting files. You can choose, however, to run the rule against existing files. If matches are found, you can either overwrite any existing classification that conflicts with the new value or attempt to aggregate them.

After you create the desired classification rule, click Configure Classification Schedule in File Server Resource Manager to determine how often you want the rule to run. This step opens the File Server Resource Manager Options dialog box. On the Automatic Classification tab, shown in Figure 11-14, select the Enable Fixed Schedule check box. You must then specify days and times at which you want the rule to run. In addition, you can select the Allow Continuous Classification For New Files check box to run the rule on newly created or edited files that fall within the scope of the rule and on existing files that are moved to a new location that falls within the scope of the rule. (Be sure to remember the option for continuous classification for the exam.)

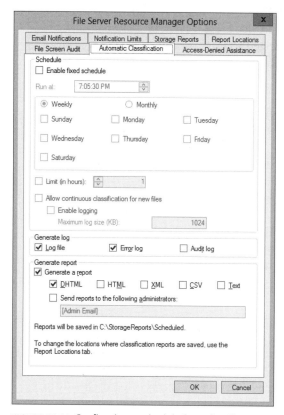

FIGURE 11-14 Configuring a schedule for a classification rule.

After configuring the schedule, you can click Run Classification With All Rules Now in the Actions pane of File Server Resource Manager. This step will run all rules immediately and classify the targeted files.

ACCESS-DENIED ASSISTANCE

The File Server Resource Manager Options dialog box shown in Figure 11-14 also includes an Access-Denied Assistance tab. You can use this tab to enable the local file server to provide helpful information to a user whose access to a file or folder has been denied.

To enable this functionality, on the Access-Denied Assistance tab, select the Enable Access-Denied Assistance check box. In the Display The Following Message text box, you can type a custom message that users will see when they are denied access to a file or folder. You can also add certain variables in brackets that will insert customized text, such as the following:

- **[Original File Path]**   The original file path that was accessed by the user
- **[Original File Path Folder]**   The parent folder of the original file path that was accessed by the user
- **[Admin Email]**   The administrator email recipient list
- **[Data Owner Email]**   The data owner email recipient list

You can also configure the file server to provide a Request Assistance button in access-denied messages, which enables the user denied access to send an email to a predefined user. To configure this option, click Configure Email Requests, select the Enable Users To Request Assistance check box, and then click OK.

> **MORE INFO**   If your network environment includes an Active Directory Rights Management Service server, you can use FSRM to automatically apply RMS encryption to files in designated folders. This feature is configured through the File Management Tasks node. For more information, visit *http://technet.microsoft.com/en-us/library/hh831572.aspx*.

Configuring access policies

You are ready to create access policies after you have assigned attributes to users, devices, and files. To configure access policies, you need to perform the following steps:

1. Create a claims-based central access policy.
2. Use Group Policy to deploy this central access policy to your file servers.

Step 1: Create a central access policy that includes claims

This step consists of two parts, both of which you can perform in Active Directory Administrative Center. First, you create one or more central access rules that include claims. Then, you add those rules to a central access policy.

> **EXAM TIP**
> Normally you would want to create access rules and then create the central access policy to which to add them.

CREATE A NEW CENTRAL ACCESS RULE

A central access rule is similar to an ACL in that it describes which conditions must be met for access to be granted to a resource.

To create a new central access rule, in Active Directory Administrative Center, select tree view in the navigation pane and then select Central Access Rules. In the Tasks pane, click New and then click Central Access Rule. This step opens the Create Central Access Rule page, shown in Figure 11-15.

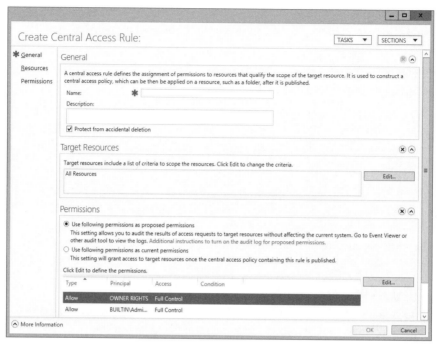

FIGURE 11-15 Creating a new central access rule.

Use the following instructions to complete the page:

1. In the Name text box, type the name you want to give the rule.

2. In the Target Resources section, click Edit, and in the Central Access Rule dialog box, add the conditions that match the target resources for which you want to define access. For example, if your goal is to define access permissions to resources that have been configured with both a Department classification property of Finance and an Impact classification property of High, then you want to add the two conditions configured as shown in Figure 11-16.

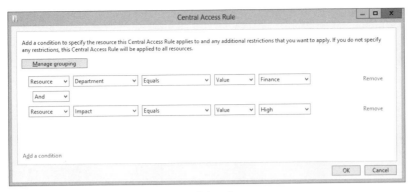

FIGURE 11-16 Configuring matching conditions for target resources.

3. In the Permissions section of the Create Central Access Rule page, select Use Following Permissions As Current Permissions and then click Edit. In the Advanced Security Settings For Permissions dialog box, click Add to open the Permission Entry For Permissions dialog box, shown in Figure 11-17. In this dialog box, do the following:

A. Near the top of the dialog box, click Select A Principal. A principal is another name for a user or group account. To configure DAC, you usually want to select Authenticated Users as the principal. (Remember this point for both the real world and the exam.)

B. In the middle of the dialog box, beneath Basic Permissions, select the permissions you want to assign to users who match the conditions in your rule.

C. Near the bottom of the dialog box, add conditions that match the users for whom you want to define access. For example, if you want to provide access only to users whose accounts in Active Directory have defined a Department value of Finance and an Office value of Floor 10 and who are signed on to computers with accounts in Active Directory that have defined a Location value of HQ, then you want to add the three conditions configured as shown in Figure 11-17. Remember that if Authenticated Users attempt to access the target resource and do *not* match these conditions, the users will be denied access completely (with the exception of the file owner).

EXAM TIP

As an alternative to step 3, you can leave selected the Use Following Permissions As Proposed Permissions option, which you can see in Figure 11-15. This option is used to stage a policy rule. Staging policies can be used to monitor the effects of a new policy entry before you enable it. You can use this option with the Group Policy setting named Audit Central Access Policy Staging. For more information, see the procedure described at *http://technet.microsoft.com/en-us/library/hh846167.aspx#BKMK_1_2.*

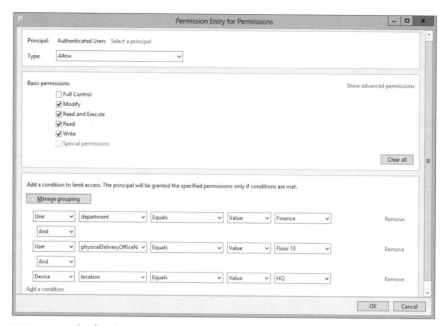

FIGURE 11-17 Configuring permissions and matching conditions for users and devices.

4. Click OK three times to finish and return to Active Directory Administrative Center.

ADD CENTRAL ACCESS RULE(S) TO A CENTRAL ACCESS POLICY

In the navigation pane of Active Directory Administrative Center, select tree view and then click Central Access Policies. In the Tasks pane, click New and then click Central Access Policy.

On the Create Central Access Policy page that opens, do the following:

1. In the Name text box, type the name you want to assign to the policy.
2. In Member Central Access Rules, click Add and then add the desired central access rules you have created. Click OK twice to return to Active Directory Administrative Center.

> **NOTE** When you include multiple access rules in a policy, all the rules will be applied with that policy when the policy is applied. The most restrictive access permissions always take effect when two rules provide different levels of access to the same user.

Step 2: Deploy central access policy to file servers

In this step, you configure a policy setting at the domain level that will deliver chosen central access policies to your file servers. Note that you can't actually *enforce a central access policy* by using Group Policy. You use Group Policy only to make desired central access policies available for selection in the Advanced Security Settings dialog box of all objects within the folder structure on file servers. The policy must then be applied manually to the object (usually a folder).

To make your central access policies available to objects on file servers, in a GPO linked to the domain, navigate to Computer Configuration\Policies\Windows Settings\Security Settings\File System and then click Central Access Policy. On the Action menu, select Manage Central Access Policies. In the Central Access Policies Configuration dialog box, add the central access policies you want to make available to file servers and then click OK.

When this Group Policy policy setting is enforced, the central access policies appear on a new Central Policy tab of this dialog box, shown in Figure 11-18. A particular central access policy applies to a folder or file object only when an administrator selects and applies it manually in these advanced security settings.

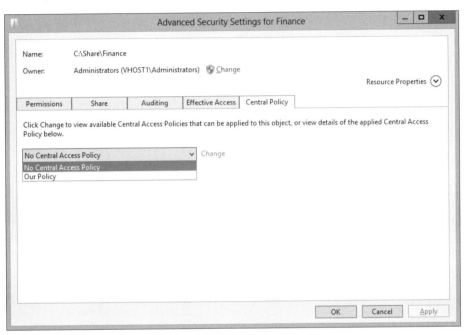

FIGURE 11-18 The Central Policy tab of the Advanced Security Settings dialog box.

MORE INFO For more practice implementing DAC, you can complete the Windows Server 2012 virtual lab "Using Dynamic Access Control to Automatically and Centrally Secure Data" at *http://go.microsoft.com/?linkid=9806471*, or perform the DAC walkthrough named "Deploy a Central Access Policy (Demonstration Steps)" at *http://technet.microsoft.com/en-us/library/hh846167.aspx*.

EXAM TIP

The Configure and Optimize Storage objective is one of the original objectives in the File and Storage Solutions domain on the 70-412 exam. The Configure and Optimize Storage objective mostly covers iSCSI support in Windows Server 2012, and although this objective hasn't been identified as a topic on the 70-417 exam, it's recommended that you learn the basics about configuring iSCSI in Windows Server 2012. For example, be sure you know the steps required to configure the iSCSI Target and iSCSI Initiator as a way to provide and provision storage in Windows Server 2012. You should also understand the function of iSNS, a DNS-like feature used for locating iSCSI resources. To practice implementing iSCSI on Windows Server 2012, complete the virtual labs at *http://go.microsoft.com/?linkid =9806468* and *http://go.microsoft.com/?linkid=9813223*.

Objective summary

- Dynamic Access Control is a new option for setting access permissions to file and folder objects in Windows Server 2012. DAC works by assigning file classifications to target resources, configuring user and device claims, and then creating rules that describe conditions for access.

- DAC relies on a modified form of Kerberos in which user tokens are expanded to include information called claims about the user and the device from which the user is connecting. To support this functionality, you need to enable Key Distribution Center support for claims-based authentication in Group Policy at the Domain Controllers OU level. You also need to define the claims types you will include in the Kerberos token for each user.

- To assign file classifications, first enable chosen resource properties in Active Directory and add the properties to a property list. Next, run the Update-FSRMClassificationPropertyDefinition cmdlet. Then, configure classification values of desired file or folder objects on the Classification tab of the Properties dialog box. You can also use File Server Resource Manager to configure file classification rules that classify files automatically, for example, on the basis of an expression found in the contents of the file.

- A central access rule includes one or more conditional expressions that match target resources and one or more conditional expressions that match users or devices and defines permissions to the target resources. One or more central access rules must be added to a central access policy before it can be deployed to file servers.

- You use Group Policy to make central access policies available to file and folder objects. A central policy must be selected and enforced manually on a file or folder.

Objective review

Answer the following questions to test your knowledge of the information in this objective. You can find the answers to these questions and explanations of why each answer choice is correct or incorrect in the "Answers" section at the end of the chapter.

1. You are a network administrator for Adatum.com. The Adatum.com network consists of a single domain that spans branch offices in New York and London. Within the Adatum.com domain, the users and computers within the New York office are contained in an OU named US, and the users and computers within the London office are contained in an OU named UK.

    You want to be able to classify data as originating from either the New York or London office. You create a resource property named Country and configure the suggested values "US" and "UK." You want administrators in both the New York and London offices to see the Country resource property appear on the Classification tab of files and folder properties.

    What should you do next?

    A. Run the Update-FSRMClassificationPropertyDefinition cmdlet.

    B. Enable the Country resource property.

    C. Create a classification rule.

    D. Add the Country property to a resource property list.

2. Your organization's network consists of a single Active Directory domain. All servers are running Windows Server 2012, and all clients are running Windows 8.

    You want to enable claims-based access authorization for users in your domain. Which of the following steps should you take to take to achieve this goal?

    A. Enable the policy setting KDC Support For Claims, Compound Authentication, And Kerberos Armoring in a GPO at the Domain Controllers OU level.

    B. Enable the policy setting KDC Support For Claims, Compound Authentication, And Kerberos Armoring in a GPO at the domain level.

    C. Enable the policy setting Kerberos Support For Claims, Compound Authentication, And Kerberos Armoring in a GPO at the Domain Controllers OU level.

    D. Enable the policy setting Kerberos Support For Claims, Compound Authentication, And Kerberos Armoring in a GPO at the domain level.

3. You are a network administrator for Proseware.com. The Proseware.com network consists of a single Active Directory domain. All servers in the network are running Windows Server 2012, and all clients are running Windows 8.

    On a file server named FileSrv1, your manager has created five new file shares named Finance, Marketing, Sales, Operations, and Legal. On each share, your manager has assigned Full Control to Authenticated Users for both the NTFS and share permissions.

Your manager now asks you to configure permissions to the contents of each departmental file share so that Full Control access is restricted to members of the corresponding department, and no other users are allowed any access. Your manager also wants you to ensure that files within each departmental share can be traced to their origin even when they are moved from their original share location.

Which of the following steps will enable you to meet these goals? (Choose two. Each answer represents part of the solution.)

A. On each new shared folder, remove all currently configured NTFS permissions and then grant Full Control NTFS permissions to a security group that includes all the members of only the corresponding department.

B. On each new shared folder, remove all currently configured share permissions and then grant Full Control share permissions to a security group that includes all the members of only the corresponding department.

C. On each department's shared folder, configure a Department classification property value that corresponds to the name of the department.

D. On each department's shared folder, apply a central access policy that assigns to members of the appropriate department Full Control permissions on files assigned with a matching Department value classification.

 Thought experiment

You are a network administrator for Adventure Works, Inc., a rapidly growing company based in Seattle that has just opened its first branch office in Denver. The network consists of a single Active Directory domain, Adventureworks.com. All servers are running either Windows Server 2008 R2 or Windows Server 2012, and all clients are running either Windows 7 or Windows 8. The two sites are linked by a site-to-site VPN.

The Seattle and Denver offices each include a main file server, named FSSeattle1 and FSDenver1, respectively, that is shared by all users in the local office location. DFS has been configured so that the same five shares are available to authorized users in both offices. Each share is used by one of the company-wide departments: Finance, Sales and Marketing, Operations, Human Resources, and Research and Development.

Both office locations include employees from each of the five departments.

A goal for the IT department is to address security concerns about confidential information while making all other information available to members of each department.

With the preceding information in mind, answer the following questions. You can find the answers to these questions in the "Answers" section at the end of the chapter.

1. If you wanted to limit access to some files within each department share to members of each office site, how can you best achieve this goal by using NTFS file permissions?

2. Given the information provided about the network, what changes might you need to make to ensure that DAC can be implemented on the network?

3. You want to make sure that when employees at one office designate a file in their department share as highly confidential the file can be viewed only from computers with account properties in Active Directory that indicate the same physical delivery office name as the user. How might you achieve this goal by using DAC permissions only? (Describe or list resource properties, claims types, and the central access rules you would need to create. You can assume that all informational fields are filled out in the properties of both user and computer accounts at both locations.)

4. What changes must you make to the network before you can configure detailed assistance to all users who are denied access to a resource?

Answers

This section contains the answers to the Objective Review and the Thought Experiment.

Objective 11.1: Review

1. **Correct Answer:** D

   A. **Incorrect:** You should run this cmdlet after you add the new resource property to a resource property list.

   B. **Incorrect:** You don't need to enable new resource properties that you create. They are already enabled when you create them.

   C. **Incorrect**: Creating a classification rule to automatically classify files and folders is an option. However, you can take this step only after you have updated file and folder objects.

   D. **Correct**: After you create or enable a resource property, you need to add it to a resource property list. Only then can you update file and folder objects so they include this resource property on the Classification tab.

2. **Correct Answer:** A

   A. **Correct:** To enable claims-based authorization in your domain, you should enable this policy setting at the domain controller level.

   B. **Incorrect:** You should enable this policy setting at the domain controller level, not at the domain level.

   C. **Incorrect:** This policy setting enables computers to request claims. It is used for policy auditing, not for enabling claims-based authorization.

   D. **Incorrect:** This policy setting enables computers to request claims. It is used for policy auditing, not for enabling claims-based authorization.

3. **Correct Answers:** C, D

   A. **Incorrect:** Changing the NTFS permissions will restrict access to members of the appropriate department, but it will not provide any information about files that will enable them to be traced when they are moved outside the shared folder.

   B. **Incorrect:** Changing the share permissions will restrict access to members of the appropriate department when they connect over the network, but it will not provide any information about files that will enable them to be traced when they are moved outside the shared folder.

   C. **Correct**: Configuring a Department property value will enable you to classify the files in each departmental shared folder as belonging to that department, even when they leave that folder.

   D. **Correct**: Applying this type of central access policy to each shared folder will configure the files within these folders with appropriate access permissions.

Thought experiment

1. You should create a security group for members of each site-specific department, such as Seattle-Finance and Denver-Finance. Then you could create a folder in each department share to which only members of each site-specific department had access.

2. You might need to install a Windows Server 2012 domain controller at each site.

3. You can configure the following:

   - Resource property: Confidentiality

   - Claims types: Office name (Physical-Delivery-Office-Name) for both users and computers

   - Access rule, target resource conditional expression: Resource.Confidentiality Equals High

   - Access rule, permissions: Authenticated users = Full Control Conditional expression: Device.physicalDeliveryOfficeName Equals User.physicalDeliveryOfficeName.

4. You must first upgrade all clients to Windows 8.

CHAPTER 12

Implement business continuity and disaster recovery

This domain includes two objectives that, on the 70-417 upgrade exam, will each empha-size one feature new to Windows Server 2012. For the Configure and manage backups objective, the new feature is Windows Azure Online Backup. (This feature is actually an optional add-on to Windows Server Backup in Windows Server 2012.) For the Configure site-level fault tolerance objective, the new feature is one of the most interesting Windows features ever: Hyper-V Replica.

Objectives in this chapter:

- Objective 12.1: Configure and manage backups
- Objective 12.2: Configure site-level fault tolerance

Objective 12.1: Configure and manage backups

Windows Azure Online Backup (also called Microsoft Online Backup or Windows Online Backup) is an optional cloud backup feature new to Windows Server 2012. Windows Azure Online Backup enables you to schedule selected volume, folder, and file backups from your local server over the Internet to cloud storage on Microsoft premises.

As with all new features, Windows Azure Online Backup is a topic that's likely to appear in an exam question. Fortunately, it's an easy topic to learn and understand.

> **This section covers the following topic:**
> - Configuring online backups

Configure online backups

You can begin configuring online backups from the Windows Server Backup console, but you must visit the Windows Azure Online Backup website to configure an account. The entire procedure is described in the following sections.

Create a Windows Azure Online Backup account

The first step in configuring online backups in Windows Server 2012 is to create a user ID on the Windows Azure Online Backup website. You can access the site by opening the Windows Server Backup console and clicking Continue in the Online Backup section of the details pane, as shown in Figure 12-1.

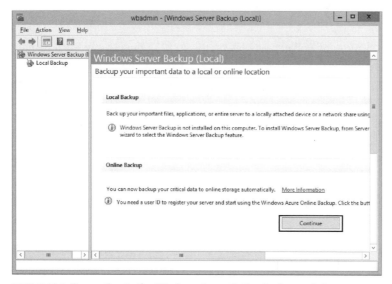

FIGURE 12-1 Connecting to the Windows Azure Online Backup website.

Download and install the Windows Azure Online Backup Agent

After you create an account on the Windows Azure Online Backup website, you can download the Windows Azure Online Backup Agent and install it locally. An Online Backup node appears in the navigation pane of the Windows Server Backup console, as shown in Figure 12-2.

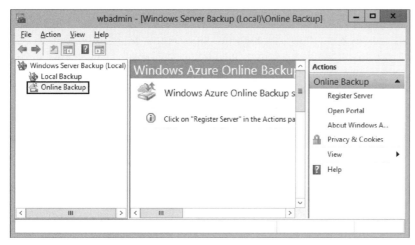

FIGURE 12-2 The Online Backup node in the Windows Server Backup console.

If you prefer, you can configure online backups from the Windows Azure Online Backup console, which becomes available after you install the agent. The Windows Azure Online Backup console provides the same set of options as the Online Backup node in the Windows Server Backup console.

Register server

The next step is to register your server. Registering a server enables you to perform backups from that server only. (Remember this point for the exam.) To register the server, from the Actions menu, select Register Server.

The Register Server Wizard includes two configuration steps. First, you are given an opportunity to specify a proxy server if desired. Second, you are asked to provide a passphrase that will be used to encrypt your backup data and a location to save this passphrase in a file. You need to provide this passphrase when you perform a restore operation, so it's essential that you don't lose it. (Microsoft doesn't maintain a copy of your passphrase.) A Generate Passphrase option automatically creates the passphrase for you.

After you register a server, new options for Online Backup appear in the Actions pane, including Schedule Backup, Recover Data, Change Properties, and Unregister Server.

EXAM TIP

Remember this sequence of steps: create an account, download and install the agent, and *then register the server.*

Create schedule

Here's an unexpected detail about online backups that could appear on the 70-417 exam: you are required to create a schedule for your online backup. Unlike with local backups in the Windows Server Backup utility, you can't perform a one-time online backup until you have created an automated backup schedule for the items.

To start the Schedule Backup Wizard, click Schedule Backup in the Actions pane, as shown in Figure 12-3.

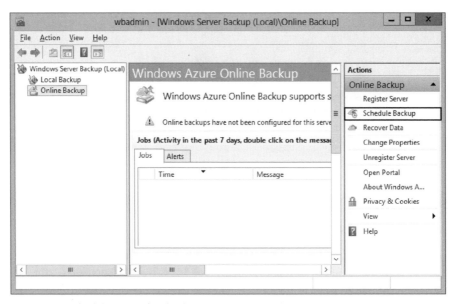

FIGURE 12-3 Scheduling an online backup.

SELECTING ITEMS FOR BACKUP

The items you can select to back up in the Schedule Backup Wizard are shown in Figure 12-4. Remember that in Windows Server 2008, you could back up only entire volumes, not folders or files. Beginning in Windows Server 2008 R2 and continuing in Windows Server 2012, you can back up selected individual volumes, folders, or files. This improved granularity of backup sets might be difficult for the exam writers to work into a test question, but you should be aware of it for both the exam and your job.

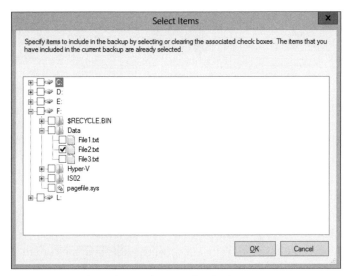

FIGURE 12-4 Backup selection for an online backup.

There is a limitation related to selecting items in online backup sets compared to local backup sets. The Select Items dialog box for local backups is shown in Figure 12-5. Compare this to Figure 12-4. Notice that the local backup lets you select three sets unavailable for online backups: Bare Metal Recovery, System State, and Hyper-V data (individual virtual machines or the host component).

Local backup only. (Not available for online backup.)

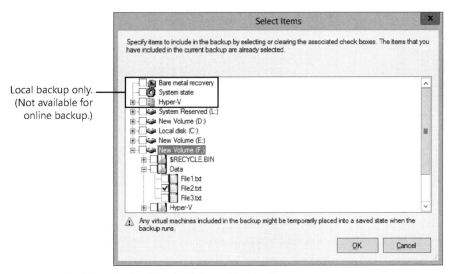

FIGURE 12-5 Backup selection for a local (not online) backup.

EXAM TIP

Remember that you can't use Windows Azure Online Backup for Bare Metal Recovery, System State, or Hyper-V data. There is no restriction on individual folders or files.

EXCLUDING ITEMS FROM BACKUP

Beginning in Windows Server 2008 R2 and continuing in Windows Server 2012, you can exclude files or subfolders from a volume or folder you have selected for backup. A good example of a folder you might want to exclude from a backup set is a temp folder. When you choose to exclude a folder from your backup set, you are also given an opportunity to exclude its subfolders, as shown in Figure 12-6.

It's possible that you will see a question on the 70-417 exam that requires some understanding of backup exclusions. Such a question might set up a scenario in which you need to perform a backup more quickly, with less space, or with less network traffic than the current backup set. The correct answer might be to exclude a folder with temporary data from the current backup set.

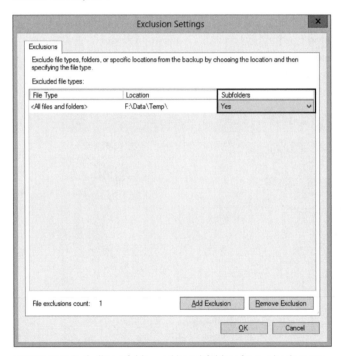

FIGURE 12-6 Excluding a folder and its subfolders from a backup set.

SPECIFYING RETENTION SETTINGS

Another feature relevant for the exam can be found on the Specify Retention Setting page of the Schedule Backup Wizard, shown in Figure 12-7. The retention setting, also called the retention range, is the number of days the backup cannot be overwritten or deleted to make space for another backup. You can set the retention range for a backup at 7 days (the default), 15 days, or 30 days.

If your Windows Azure Online Backup account runs out of free space and your retention settings prevent a new backup from overwriting any of the existing backups, the new backup will fail. For example, imagine that the storage quota for your account is 300 GB and you have scheduled a weekly backup job of 200 GB. If you set the retention range of the backup job for 15 days, the backup will fail in the second week. At the default retention setting of 7 days, however, the backup will succeed every week.

FIGURE 12-7 Backup retention settings.

Back Up Now

The Back Up Now option appears in the Actions pane for online backups, as shown in Figure 12-8, but only after you first complete the Schedule Backup Wizard. As stated earlier, Back Up Now for online backups enables you to perform additional online backups only of online backup sets that have been previously defined and scheduled. You *cannot* use this option to select a new set of volumes, folders, or files and then perform an online backup of that new set.

Aside from this critical difference, the Back Up Now option for online backups resembles the Back Up Once option for local backups.

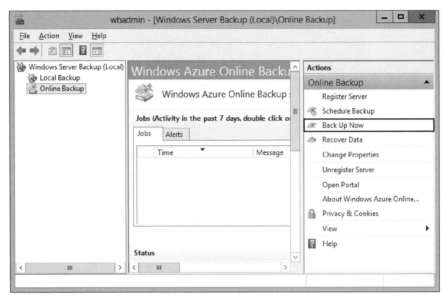

FIGURE 12-8 Performing an additional backup of a scheduled backup.

Recover Data

To restore data that has been backed up, choose the Recover Data option in the Actions pane. Nothing about this option is likely to confuse you, either in the real world or in the exam world. However, it's worth remembering that you can restore online backups to an alternate location such as another volume, a file share, or another server.

Bandwidth throttling

You can restrict the amount of bandwidth used during your online backup operations in a way that depends on when the backup occurs. To enable bandwidth throttling, click Change Properties in the Actions pane, click the Throttling tab, and then select the Enable Internet Bandwidth Usage Throttling For Backup Operations check box, as shown in Figure 12-9.

Bandwidth throttling works by letting you set different bandwidth speeds for work and nonwork hours. First, you define the hours that should be considered work hours and the days of the week to which these hours apply. You can then specify how much Internet bandwidth you want to use for online backup operations during these work hours and during the remaining nonwork hours.

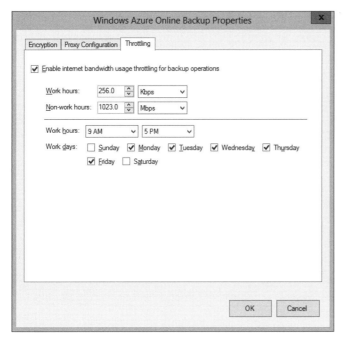

FIGURE 12-9 Configuring bandwidth throttling for online backups.

Bandwidth throttling might be the most likely feature about online backups to appear on the exam. For example, you could see a question that displays the Throttling tab and an accompanying scenario in which you need to adjust the settings to reduce the impact of online backups on your users. In such a case, you might need to redefine the work hours (perhaps by lengthening the work day). Alternatively, you might need to decrease the bandwidth currently assigned to work hours if you want to prevent work day disruption, or increase the bandwidth currently assigned to nonwork hours if you want the online backups to be performed as quickly as possible.

EXAM TIP

Be sure to review topics related to backing up and restoring that have remained the same since Windows Server 2008. For example, remember that when you enable and configure Shadow Copies settings on a file server, users can use the Previous Versions tab to restore older versions of files, and you can use the VSSAdmin tool to manage this feature. Also remember the function of the Backup Operators group: it grants users not only the right to perform backups but also the right to restore and shut down the system.

Objective summary

- Windows Server 2012 provides an option that enables you to back up selected volumes, folders, and files of the local server over the Internet to cloud storage on Microsoft-owned premises. This functionality is provided by an optional add-on service called Windows Azure Online Backup, also called Microsoft Online Backup or Windows Online Backup.

- To use Windows Azure Online Backup, you need to create an account on the Windows Azure Online Backup website and then download and install the Windows Azure Online Backup Agent.

- After you install the Windows Azure Online Backup Agent, you can administer online backups in either the Windows Server Backup console or the Windows Azure Online Backup console. The first step to configuring online backups for a particular server is to register that server online.

- With online backups, you need to create a backup schedule for any backup sets you define. When you run the Schedule Backup Wizard, you select the volumes, folders, and files in the backup, specify any exclusions, set retention settings, and determine the times during the week you want the backup to run.

- Bandwidth throttling is a feature that enables you to limit the amount of Internet bandwidth consumed during your online backups. To use bandwidth throttling, you define the hours in the week to be considered work hours and then specify the bandwidth in Kbps or Mbps you want online backups to use during these work hours and during the remaining nonwork hours.

Objective review

Answer the following questions to test your knowledge of the information in this objective. You can find the answers to these questions and explanations of why each answer choice is correct or incorrect in the "Answers" section at the end of the chapter.

1. You configure a Hyper-V host running Windows Server 2012 named VHost01 to perform a Windows Azure Online Backup at 11:00 P.M. every Wednesday. The organization's Internet connection is capable of download speeds of 5 MB per second and isn't used for any other operations until 8:00 A.M. the following day. After running the online backup for the first time, you discover that the backup operation completes at 10:00 A.M. Thursday, after the start of the work day. You open the bandwidth throttling settings for the server and see the configuration shown in Figure 12-10.

   You want the online backup of VHost01 to complete before 8:00 A.M. on Thursday. Which of the following solutions is most likely to help you accomplish your goal with the minimum disruption for workers?

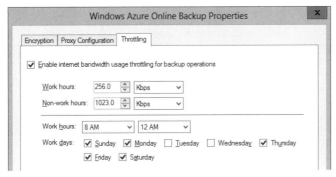

FIGURE 12-10 Bandwidth throttling settings on VHost01.

A. Change the bandwidth setting assigned to work hours.

B. Change the bandwidth setting assigned to nonwork hours.

C. Change the hours defined as work hours.

D. Change the days defined as work days.

2. You have a Windows Azure Online Backup account with a storage quota of 300 GB. You use this account to configure a single weekly backup of a file server running Windows Server 2012 named FileSrv01. The total amount of data on FileSrv01 does not change significantly from week to week. No other backups are configured with your account.

The online backup of FileSrv01 completes successfully the first week, but the second week, the backup fails. You receive an error indicating that the usage associated with your Windows Azure Online Backup account has exceeded its quota.

The Windows Azure Online Backup console displays the information shown in Figure 12-11 about the backup.

FIGURE 12-11 Backup settings and destination usage.

You want to be able to perform the weekly backup of FileSrv01 without failure. Which of the following actions is most likely to allow you to accomplish your goal?

A. Configure an exclusion for C:\Windows\Temp, and choose to exclude its subfolders.

B. Configure an exclusion for C:\Windows\Temp, and choose not to exclude its subfolders.

C. Change the retention range to 7 days.

D. Change the retention range to 30 days.

3. You want to configure a file server running Windows Server 2012 named FS02 to perform a daily Windows Azure Online Backup at 3:00 A.M. You also want to ensure that if the online backup operation extends into the beginning of the next work day at 9:00 A.M. it will have a minimal impact on network performance for users. The work week in your organization runs from Monday through Friday.

You enable Internet bandwidth usage throttling for backup operations and find the default settings shown in Figure 12-12. What should you do next?

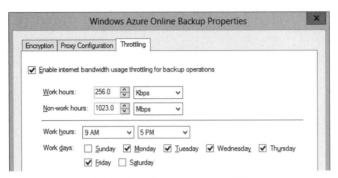

FIGURE 12-12 Bandwidth throttling settings on FS02.

A. Leave the default settings.

B. Increase the bandwidth setting assigned to work hours.

C. Increase the bandwidth setting assigned to nonwork hours.

D. Change the selected work days.

Objective 12.2: Configure site-level fault tolerance

Hyper-V Replica is a new feature in Windows Server 2012 that gives a virtual machine (VM) a warm standby copy (or *replica virtual machine*) that can exist anywhere in the world. If the primary VM fails, you can manually fail over to the replica VM. Hyper-V Replica can thus provide fault tolerance for a VM even if an entire host site goes offline.

Unlike a failover cluster, Hyper-V Replica doesn't rely on shared storage between the VMs. Instead, the replica VM begins with its own copy of the primary VM's virtual hard disk. The primary VM then sends updates of its changes (called *replication data*) every 5 to 15 minutes, and this data is saved repeatedly by the replica VM. The replica thus remains up to date.

Hyper-V Replica is one of the most important features of Windows Server 2012, and it will certainly appear on the 70-417 exam. In fact, you will probably see more than one question about it. Fortunately, it's a relatively easy feature to understand and implement, so your study efforts in this area will likely reap large dividends on the test.

Configuring Hyper-V physical host servers

It's important to understand the sequence of steps in configuring Hyper-V Replica. The first step is to configure the server-level replication settings for *both* physical Hyper-V hosts, called the primary server and replica server. You can access these settings in Hyper-V Manager by right-clicking a host server in the navigation pane, selecting Hyper-V Settings, and then selecting Replication Configuration in the left column of the Hyper-V Settings dialog box, as shown in Figure 12-13. By default, replication is not enabled, and no options are selected or configured.

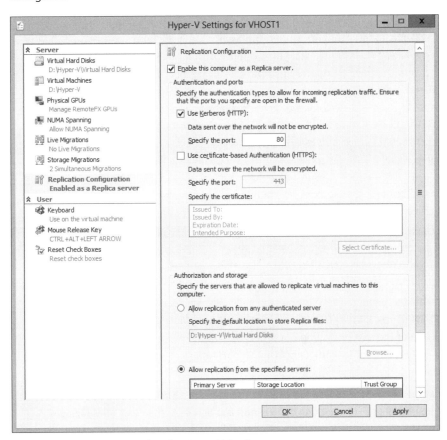

FIGURE 12-13 Host server settings for Hyper-V Replica.

To enable a physical host for Hyper-V Replica, first select the Enable This Computer As A Replica Server check box. Then, configure settings in the Authentication And Ports area and the Authorization And Storage area shown in Figure 12-13. You need to take these configuration steps on both primary and replica servers before configuring a VM for replication.

- **Authentication And Ports** In this area you choose which authentication methods you want to be available later when you configure a locally hosted VM for replication. You can enable Kerberos (HTTP), Certificate-Based Authentication (HTTPS), or both.

  - You can enable Kerberos (HTTP) only if the local server is domain-joined. The advantage of choosing Kerberos is that it requires no further configuration. The two disadvantages are that it doesn't encrypt data sent over the network and that it can be used for authentication only when the remote host server is located in a trusted domain. Note also that when you choose this authentication protocol, you need to enable the firewall rule named Hyper-V Replica HTTP Listener (TCP-In).

  - You can enable Certificate-Based Authentication (HTTPS) regardless of whether the local server is domain-joined. When the local server is a standalone server, this is the only authentication protocol option. The two advantages of enabling Certificate-Based Authentication (HTTPS) are that it encrypts replication data and that it allows you to replicate with a remote host when there is no trust relationship with that host through Active Directory. The disadvantage of this authentication method is that it is more difficult to configure. It requires you to provide an X.509v3 certificate for which Enhanced Key Usage (EKU) must support both Client Authentication and Server Authentication (through the Computer certificate template, for example) and that typically specifies the fully qualified domain name (FQDN) of the local server in the Subject Name field. The certificate can be self-signed or issued through a public key infrastructure (PKI). When you choose this authentication protocol, you need to enable the firewall rule named Hyper-V Replica HTTPS Listener (TCP-In).

  Remember that Windows Server 2012 doesn't automatically enable the firewall rules you need for the authentication protocols you choose. Depending on which protocol(s) you have enabled, you also need to enable the firewall rule Hyper-V Replica HTTP Listener (TCP-In), Hyper-V Replica HTTPS Listener (TCP-In), or both. You can enable a rule either in Windows Firewall with Advanced Security or by using the Enable-NetFirewallRule -DisplayName command in Windows PowerShell followed by the name of the rule (including quotation marks).

EXAM TIP

Remember that encrypted replication of a VM requires the host servers to have installed a certificate including both Client Authentication and Server Authentication extensions for EKU.

MORE INFO   For more information about configuring certificate-based authentication with Hyper-V Replica, search for Hyper-V Replica - Prerequisites for certificate-based deployments, or visit *http://blogs.technet.com/b/virtualization/archive/2012/03/13 /hyper-v-replica-certificate-requirements.aspx.*

- **Authorization And Storage**   This area allows you to configure security settings on the local server that are used when the local server acts as a replica server. Your choice here determines the remote primary servers from which the local server will accept replication data. Even if you are configuring your local server as the primary server, the settings here are required so that if you ever need to fail over to a remote replica you can later fail back to the local server.

  You need to choose one of two security options, both of which also provide a default path you can modify to store replication data:

  - **Allow Replication From Any Authenticated Server**   This option is the less secure of the two. When you choose this option, the local server can receive replication data from any authenticated server.

  - **Allow Replication From The Specified Servers**   This option requires you to specify the primary server(s) authorized for the local replica server. You can add multiple entries to authorize different primary servers by DNS name. To add an entry authorizing a primary server address, click Add, as shown in Figure 12-14. This step opens the Add Authorization Entry dialog box shown in Figure 12-15.

  For each entry, a default storage path (the middle field) is already provided, but the other two fields must be filled in manually. In the Specify The Primary Server field, you enter an FQDN that can include a wildcard character (for example, "*.adatum.com"). You also have to provide a tag called a trust group. If you want to allow replication traffic from a set of primary servers, you should assign those primary servers the same trust group name.

FIGURE 12-14 Authorizing primary servers for the local replica server.

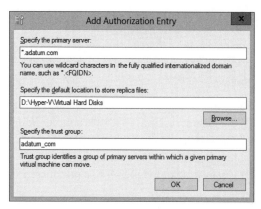

FIGURE 12-15 Adding an authorized primary server address.

How might the settings in the Authorization And Storage area appear on the 70-417 exam? A question could be based on an unsuccessful failover. In such a question, authorization settings might not be configured on the replica server. Or the FQDN provided in the Specify The Primary Server field (shown in Figure 12-15) might be configured incorrectly, and the correct answer fixes that problem. Another possible question could involve a new organizational requirement that security be tightened on a replica server. Incorrect answer choices might refer to IPsec or other security-tightening methods, but the correct answer will refer to adding an authorization entry on the replica server.

Configuring VMs

After you configure both physical host servers, the next step in configuring Hyper-V Replica is to configure the chosen VM for replication on the primary server. Begin by right-clicking the VM and selecting Enable Replication, as shown in Figure 12-16.

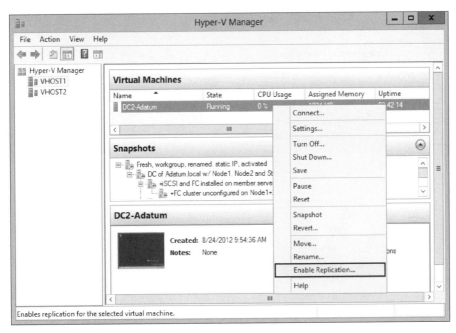

FIGURE 12-16 Creating a replica of a VM.

This step opens the Enable Replication wizard. The wizard includes the following five configuration pages:

1. **Specify Replica Server page**   Use this page to specify the remote replica server by name.

2. **Specify Connection Parameters page**   This page, shown in Figure 12-17, asks you to specify which of the authentication types enabled at the server level in Hyper-V Settings you want to use to support this replicated VM. If you have enabled only one of the two authentication methods at the server level, that method is the only option given. The replica server must support the same authentication method.

   This page also provides an option that could be part of an exam question: the Compress The Data That Is Transmitted Over The Network check box. This compression option reduces bandwidth requirements for replication at the expense of increased processor usage. If this option appears on the exam, this trade-off is likely to be the key to the correct answer.

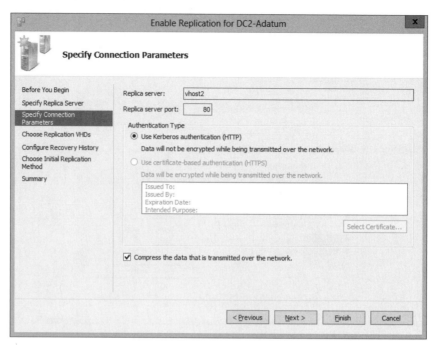

FIGURE 12-17 Selecting authentication and compression settings for a replicated VM.

EXAM TIP

If both authentication types are available for the VM and you later want to switch to certificate-based authentication (HTTPS), you have to remove replication and complete the Enable Replication Wizard again. Before you do, make sure that certificate-based authentication is also enabled in the Hyper-V Settings on the remote host server.

---

3. **Choose Replication VHDs page** By default, all virtual hard disks (VHDs) attached to the VM are enabled for replication. You can use this page to deselect any VMs that you don't want to be replicated.

4. **Configure Recovery History page** This page, shown in Figure 12-18, includes the settings to configure recovery points. These are among the most likely Hyper-V Replica settings to appear on the 70-417 exam. By default, the Only The Latest Recovery Point option is selected, and no other options are enabled or configured.

    Recovery points are VM snapshots saved on a replica server. Replication traffic sends a new snapshot from the primary to the replica server every 5 to 15 minutes, but only the latest is saved on the replica by default. Selecting the Additional Recovery Points option configures the replica server to keep one extra snapshot per hour. If you later perform a failover operation at the replica server, you then have the option of recovering either the most recent version of the VM, which is always available, or one of these earlier, hourly snapshots.

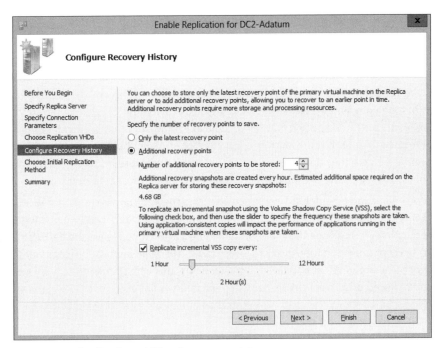

FIGURE 12-18 Configuring additional recovery points.

A menu of available recovery points on a replica server is shown in Figure 12-19. If the Configure Recovery History page was left at the default setting (Only The Latest Recovery Point), only the first option, named Latest Recovery Point, would appear in this menu.

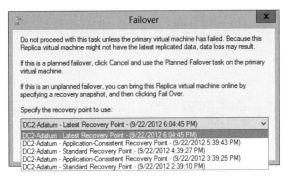

FIGURE 12-19 The latest recovery point and previous hourly snapshots of a VM that can be restored in a failover on the replica server.

When you enable the Additional Recovery Points option on the Configure Recovery History page, the replica server by default will keep an hourly snapshot for each of the past four hours in addition to the latest recovery point. However, you can change this setting if you want to store more (or fewer) of these recovery points on the replica server. The main drawback to keeping many recovery points is the storage resources required to do so.

The last configuration settings on the Configure Recovery History page relate to *incremental Volume Shadow Copy Service (VSS) copies*, also known as *application-consistent recovery points*. These are high-quality snapshots taken during moments in which the VM momentarily "quiesces" (gracefully pauses) activity in VSS-aware applications such as Microsoft Exchange and SQL Server. The advantage of these snapshot types is that they help ensure that the failover will be free of errors in these applications. The disadvantage is that they are more processor-intensive and cause important applications to pause briefly. (However, the pause is usually too brief for users to detect.)

You enable incremental VSS copies by selecting the Replicate Incremental VSS Copy Every check box, and then selecting the frequency of the application-consistent recovery point. (You can see these options in Figure 12-18.) If you leave the default frequency of one hour, then every recovery point will be an application-consistent recovery point. If you select a frequency of two hours, then the standard recovery point will be replaced by an application-consistent recovery point every two hours, and so on. Figure 12-20 shows the snapshots stored on a replica server for which incremental VSS copies are scheduled every two hours.

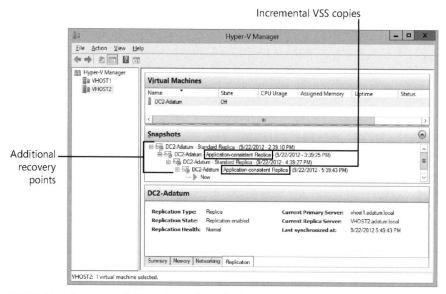

FIGURE 12-20 Incremental VSS copies and standard recovery points.

EXAM TIP

Expect to see a question about application-consistent snapshots on the 70-417 exam.

5. **Choose Initial Replication Method page** This page, shown in Figure 12-21, enables you to specify how the initial copy of the VHDs attached to the primary VM will be sent to the replica server. By default, the VHDs are sent over the network. Sending very large files over a network such as the Internet isn't always a realistic option, however. As an alternative, you can choose the second option: to export the VHDs to external media (and then physically transport them to the replica server). The final option is to use an existing VM on the replica server as the initial copy. You can choose this option if you have restored an exact copy of the VM and its VHDs on the replica server.

This page also enables you to configure the initial network transfer to take place at a specified future time. You can use this option to minimize user disruption.

NOTE Typically, the initial transfer of the VHD is far more bandwidth-intensive than the updates sent through replication. After the initial copies of the VHDs are sent, only the changes (deltas) to these VHDs are sent during replication, which occurs every 5 to 15 minutes.

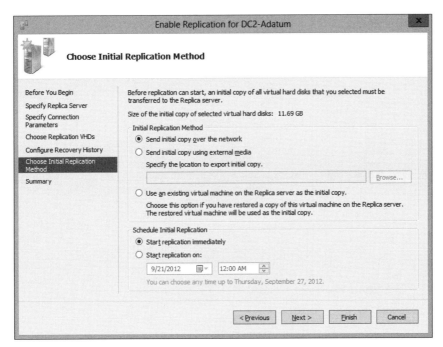

FIGURE 12-21 Determining how to send the base copy of the VHDs attached to a primary VM.

Failover TCP/IP settings

After you enable replication on a VM, you might need to specify the TCP/IP settings that will apply to the replica VM after failover. By default, the replica VM will inherit the same IPv4 and IPv6 configuration as the primary VM. In many cases, however, the replica VM will need a different IP configuration to communicate in its environment.

To assign a different IP configuration to the replica VM, in Hyper-V Manager on the replica server, right-click the replica VM and select Settings from the shortcut menu. In the Settings dialog box, expand Network Adapter in the left column and then select Failover TCP/IP, as shown in Figure 12-22. In the right pane, assign the new IP configuration as appropriate.

Then, on the primary server, assign the original IP configuration in the same settings area. If you don't take this step, the replica settings will persist if you fail back to the original location. (Remember this point for the exam.)

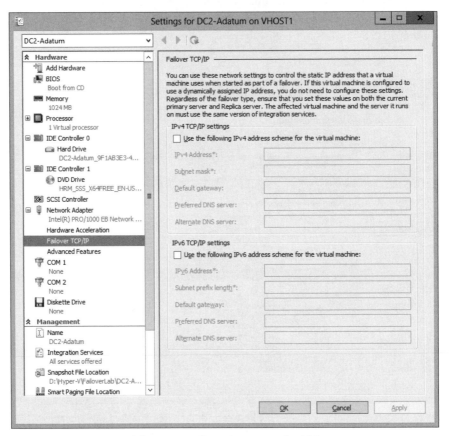

FIGURE 12-22 Assigning a different IP configuration to a replica VM.

Resynchronizing the primary and replica VMs

After you complete the Enable Replication wizard, you can modify the replication settings for a VM in the Settings dialog box for that VM. Replication settings appear in the Management category in the menu on the left, as shown in Figure 12-23.

One configuration setting appears here that does not appear in the Enable Replication wizard: Resynchronization. Resynchronization is a resource-intensive operation that is performed occasionally between a primary and replica VM. By default, resynchronization can occur at any time. You have the option, however, to restrict resynchronization to selected off-peak hours. Alternatively, you can opt to perform resynchronization manually.

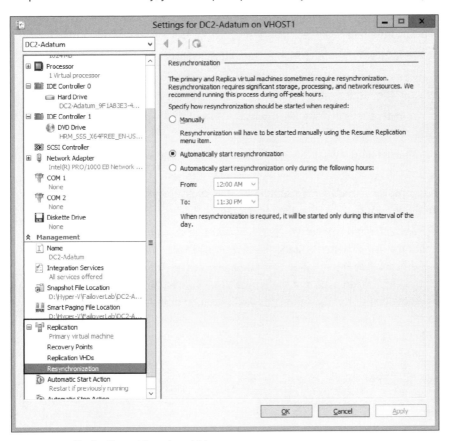

FIGURE 12-23 Replication settings for a VM.

Performing Hyper-V Replica failover

You can perform three types of failovers with Hyper-V Replica after it is configured: planned failovers, unplanned failovers, and test failovers. It's likely you will see an exam question in which you need to understand the differences among them and when they are used.

- **Planned failover** A planned failover is the only failover you initiate from the primary server. You use this method whenever you can manually shut down the primary VM, and the primary and replica servers can still communicate.

    A planned failover is the preferred failover type because no data is lost. In fact, you cannot use this option to fail over to the latest, or any earlier, recovery point. With a planned failover, only an exact copy of the current primary VM and its VHDs can be failed over to the replica server.

    A planned failover is a good option in the following situations:

    - You want to perform host maintenance on the primary server and want to temporarily run the VM from the replica.

    - Your primary site is anticipating a possible power outage and you want to move the VM to the replica site.

    - You are expecting a weather emergency such as a flood and you want to ensure business continuity.

    - Your compliance requirements mandate that you regularly run your workloads for certain periods of time from the replica site.

    To perform a planned failover, you begin by *shutting down the primary VM*. You then right-click the VM in Hyper-V Manager, click Replication, and then click Planned Failover, as shown in Figure 12-24. The latest updates are then sent to the replica server, the VM is failed over, and the replica VM is started automatically on the remote server. At the end of this operation, the replication relationship is reversed, so what was the replica server becomes the primary server, and vice versa.

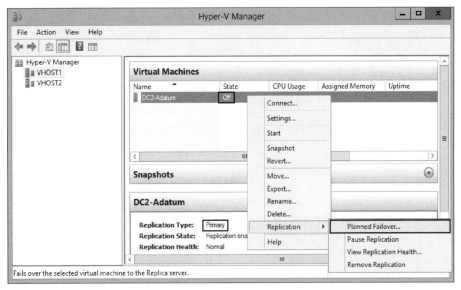

FIGURE 12-24 Performing a planned failover from the primary server.

- **(Unplanned) failover**   This type of failover is called an unplanned failover in the Windows Server 2012 documentation, but in the interface, it's called just "failover." On the 70-417 exam, you might see it referred to either way.

An unplanned failover is performed at the replica server. You perform this failover type when the primary VM fails suddenly and cannot be brought back online.

An unplanned failover is a good option in the following situations:

- Your primary site experiences an unexpected power outage or a natural disaster.

- Your primary site or VM has had a virus attack, and you want to restore your business quickly with minimal data loss by restoring your replica VM to the most recent recovery point before the attack.

To perform an unplanned failover, in Hyper-V Manager on the replica server, right-click the replica VM, click Replication, and then click Failover, as shown in Figure 12-25.

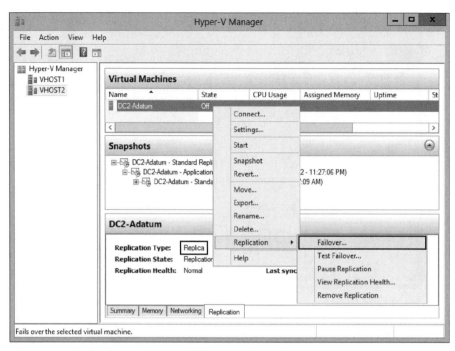

FIGURE 12-25 Performing an unplanned failover on the replica server.

When you perform an unplanned failover, you have to choose a recovery point, as shown earlier in Figure 12-19. The VM is then started on the replica server.

After the replica VM is started, the replica relationship with the primary VM is broken, and replication stops. If at some later point you can bring the original primary VM online, you can resume replication by reversing the replication relationship. After you perform this operation, the local replica server becomes the new primary, and the remote primary becomes the new replica. To reverse replication, right-click the VM on the replica server, click Replication, and then click Reverse Replication, as shown in Figure 12-26. This step starts the Reverse Replication Wizard, which enables you to reenter the settings for the replica.

Another option you can see on the Replication submenu in Figure 12-26 is Cancel Failover. You can safely choose this option after you perform an unplanned failover as long as no changes have been made to the replica. After you cancel a failover, you have to manually resume replication on the primary VM by right-clicking it and selecting Resume Replication. Cancelling a failover is a good idea if you discover soon after performing an unplanned failover that the primary VM can be brought online.

EXAM TIP

Remember the Reverse Replication and Cancel Replication options for the exam.

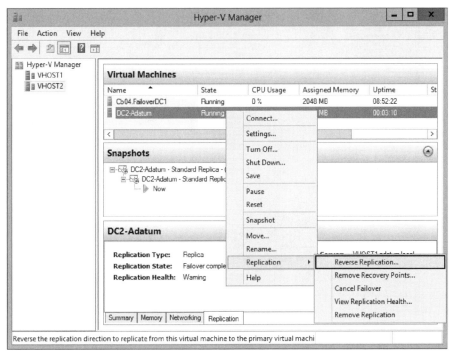

FIGURE 12-26 Reversing replication.

- **Test failover** A test failover is the only failover operation you can perform while the primary VM is running. The purpose of this failover type is to simulate an unplanned failover to ensure that it will function as planned in case of an emergency.

  To perform a test failover, in Hyper-V Manager on the replica server, right-click the replica VM, click Replication, and then click Test Failover. You then have to select a recovery point, just as you do with an unplanned failover. Next, a local, disposable copy of the replica VM is created on the replica server. The new copy of the VM appears in Hyper-V Manager in a stopped state with the tag "- Test." For example, a test failover of a VM named "MyVM1" would result in a new VM called "MyVM1 - Test." You can then start the new VM manually to see if it works as expected.

  By default, the virtual network adapters of the test VM are disconnected from all virtual switches. If desired, you can preattach the adapter(s) of the test VM to a virtual switch of your choice. To do so, open the settings of the base replica VM, expand Network Adapter, and then click Test Failover, as shown in Figure 12-27. Make sure you choose a virtual switch that will not create any conflicts in a production network.

  After you examine the functioning of the test VM, you can safely delete it in Hyper-V Manager.

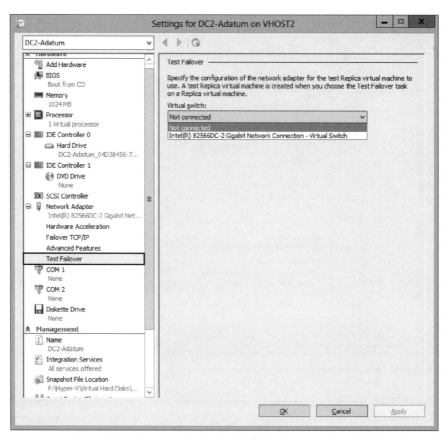

FIGURE 12-27 Preattaching the network adapter of a failover test VM to a virtual switch.

Using Hyper-V Replica in a failover cluster

The configuration steps previously described apply to VMs that are not hosted in a failover cluster. However, you might want to provide an offsite replica VM for a clustered VM. In this scenario, you would provide two levels of fault tolerance. The failover cluster is used to provide local fault tolerance; for example, if a physical node fails within a functioning data center. The offsite replica VM could be used to recover only from site-level failures; for example, in case of a power outage, weather emergency, or natural disaster.

The steps to configure a replica VM for a clustered VM differ slightly from the normal configuration, but they aren't complicated. The first difference is that you begin by opening Failover Cluster Manager, not Hyper-V Manager. In Failover Cluster Manager, you then have to add a failover cluster role named *Hyper-V Replica Broker* to the cluster. (Remember, in this context the word "role" describes a hosted service in a failover cluster.)

To add the Hyper-V Replica Broker role, right-click the Roles node in Failover Cluster Manager and select Configure Role. This step opens the High Availability Wizard. In the High Availability Wizard, select Hyper-V Replica Broker, as shown in Figure 12-28.

FIGURE 12-28 Adding the Hyper-V Replica Broker role to a failover cluster.

When you choose this role, the High Availability Wizard asks you to provide a NetBIOS name and IP address to be used as the connection point to the cluster (called a client access point, or CAP). This step is shown in Figure 12-29.

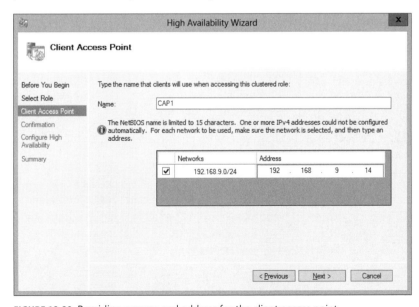

FIGURE 12-29 Providing a name and address for the client access point.

Next, you configure the equivalent of the server replication settings shown earlier in Figure 12-13. To do so, right-click the Hyper-V Replica Broker node in Failover Cluster Manager and select Replication Settings from the shortcut menu, as shown in Figure 12-30. The difference between the settings here and the settings in Figure 12-13 is that in this case the settings apply to the cluster as a whole.

FIGURE 12-30 Configuring replication settings for the cluster.

On the remote Replica server, you configure replication as you usually would: by configuring Hyper-V Settings in Hyper-V Manager as described in the earlier section named "Configuring Hyper-V physical host servers." However, if you want the remote Replica to also be a multinode failover cluster, then you would need to configure that remote failover cluster through Failover Cluster Manager (by adding and configuring the Hyper-V Replica Broker role).

After you configure the host server settings, you can configure replication on the VM in Failover Cluster Manager just as you would in Hyper-V Manager. Right-click the clustered VM, click Replication, and then click Enable Replication, as shown in Figure 12-31.

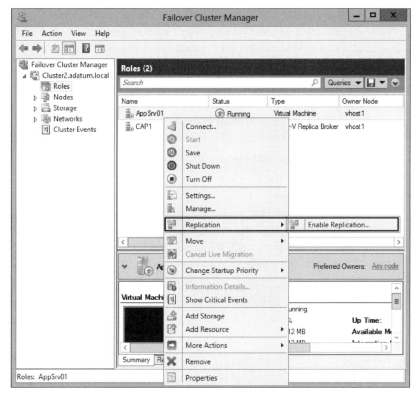

FIGURE 12-31 Enabling replication on a clustered VM.

This step opens the same Enable Replication wizard you see when you configure replication on a nonclustered VM. The remaining configuration steps are therefore identical.

For the 70-417 exam, there's a good chance you will be asked about basic concepts related to configuring replication on clustered VMs. First, remember that you use Failover Cluster Manager to configure replication for a clustered VM at the primary site but use Hyper-V Manager at the replica site. Second, remember that in Failover Cluster Manager at the primary site, you need to add the Hyper-V Replica Broker role to the failover cluster, and that this role is used to configure Hyper-V Replica "server" settings for the cluster. Finally, remember that when you configure Hyper-V Replica in a failover cluster, the CAP name and address are used as the server name and address.

Objective summary

- Hyper-V Replica is a new feature in Windows Server 2012 that creates an offline copy (replica) of a running VM and its storage. This replica can exist anywhere in the world. The online original (called the primary VM) sends the replica updates of any changes every 5 to 15 minutes. In case the primary VM fails, you can fail over to the replica and bring it online.

- To configure Hyper-V Replica, you first configure authentication and authorization settings for both physical host servers, called the primary server and replica server. Then, in Hyper-V Manager on the primary server, you run the Enable Replication wizard for the desired VM.

- By default, you can fail over only to the most recent recovery point, which is usually no more than 5 to 15 minutes old. However, you can choose to store additional, older recovery points that enable you to return to point-in-time snapshots of the primary VM.

- A planned failover is performed on the primary server after you shut down the primary VM. A planned failover brings the replica VM online with no loss of data. You can perform an unplanned failover on the replica server if the primary server fails without warning. With an unplanned failover, the replica VM recovers a copy of the primary VM that is usually no more than 5 to 15 minutes old. You can also perform a test failover while the primary VM is running. A test failover brings a copy of the replica VM online in a state that is disconnected from the network.

- If you want to configure Hyper-V Replica for a VM that is hosted in a failover cluster, you need to add the Hyper-V Replica Broker role to the cluster. You also need to provide a CAP name and address for the cluster that will act as the server name.

Objective review

Answer the following questions to test your knowledge of the information in this objective. You can find the answers to these questions and explanations of why each answer choice is correct or incorrect in the "Answers" section at the end of the chapter.

1. You are configuring Hyper-V Replica on a VM that is hosting Microsoft Exchange. You want to help ensure that if you fail over to the replica VM, the application data will remain in a consistent state.

   What should you do? (Choose all that apply.)

   A. Configure the replica server to save additional recovery points.

   B. Configure the primary server to replicate incremental VSS copies.

   C. Configure a resynchronization schedule for the primary and replica VMs.

   D. Configure Hyper-V Replica Broker.

2. You have configured Hyper-V Replica for a VM named AppSrv1, which is hosted on a primary server named VMhost1 located in Cleveland. The replica server is named RepHost1 and is located in Denver.

An unexpected power outage suddenly brings the entire Cleveland site offline. You perform a failover at the Denver site and start the replica VM on RepHost1. The Cleveland site regains power after several hours, but only after changes have been made to AppSrv1.

You are able to bring VMhost1 back online and now want to return AppSrv1 to its original host. Which step should you take next?

- **A.** Perform an unplanned failover.
- **B.** Choose the option to cancel the failover.
- **C.** Perform a planned failover.
- **D.** Choose the option to reverse replication.

3. Within your organization, a clustered VM named SQL1 is hosting SQL Server. The failover cluster hosting SQL1 is named Cluster1 and includes three nodes, named Node1, Node2, and Node3. Node1 is the preferred owner of the SQL1 VM. All three nodes are located in the same data center.

You want to configure an offsite replica of SQL1 to protect the VM in case the entire failover cluster is brought down because of a power outage or other emergency.

You deploy a physical server named RepSrv2 at a remote site. You want to configure RepSrv2 as the replica server. You install Windows Server 2012 and then install the Hyper-V role on RepSrv2. You then connect the server to the Internet and establish a VPN connection between the two sites.

Which of the following steps should you take? (Choose two.)

- **A.** At the primary site, configure Hyper-V Replica Broker and provide a CAP name.
- **B.** At the replica site, configure Hyper-V Replica Broker and provide a CAP name.
- **C.** In the replication settings on Cluster1, restrict authorization to the CAP.
- **D.** In the replication settings on RepSrv2, restrict authorization to the CAP.

Thought experiment

You are a network administrator for Adatum.com, an organization with headquarters in San Francisco and a branch office in Montreal. You are designing fault
tolerance and business continuity for a new application server and VM that will be
named AppVM1. AppVM1 will be hosted in the San Francisco office.

You have the following goals:

- You want to prevent any disruption of service and data loss in case an individual server fails unexpectedly.

- You want to be able to resume service with minimal data loss in case a catastrophe such as an earthquake brings the main office offline for an extended
  period.

- You always want to retain daily backups from the previous two weeks.

With these goals in mind, answer the following questions:

1. Which feature(s) in Windows Server 2012 enable you to meet the first goal?

2. How might you design fault tolerance so you can meet the first goal even after a
   catastrophe brings the main office offline for an extended period?

3. Describe two ways you might design fault tolerance for AppVM1 so you can continue to meet the third goal even if a catastrophe brings the main office offline
   for an extended period.

Answers

This section contains the answers to the Objective Reviews and the Thought Experiment.

Objective 12.1: Review

1. **Correct Answer:** B

    A. **Incorrect:** Changing the bandwidth assigned to the work hours will not help you achieve your goal of having the backup operation complete before the work day begins at 8:00 A.M.

    B. **Correct:** The bandwidth setting assigned to nonwork hours is restricted to 1023.0 Kbps, which is much lower than the connection's stated capability of 5 MB per second. This low setting could be unnecessarily limiting the bandwidth allowed at night. If you raise this value, the backup operation could proceed much more quickly.

    C. **Incorrect:** Adjusting the work hours could potentially cause disruption for workers, and it will not help you meet your goal of completing the backup operation before 9:00 A.M.

    D. **Incorrect:** The work days are not currently affecting the backup because the backup is being performed outside work hours. If you include Wednesday as a work day, you would actually apply bandwidth throttling to the first hour of the backup operation and slow the procedure down for that hour.

2. **Correct Answer:** C

    A. **Incorrect:** This step would exclude the C:\Windows\Temp folder and its subfolders from the backup set, but it would not meet your goal of allowing the backup to be performed weekly. This folder is too small to significantly reduce the size of the backup.

    B. **Incorrect:** This step would exclude the C:\Windows\Temp folder but not its subfolders from the backup set, but it would not meet your goal of allowing the backup to be performed weekly. Too little data is stored in this folder to significantly reduce the size of the backup.

    C. **Correct:** This setting would allow the previous week's backup to be deleted to make space for the current week's backup. The size of the backup from the previous week is approximately 220 GB, and your storage quota is 300 GB. Consequently, you need to be able to remove the previous week's backup to make room for the current week's backup.

    D. **Incorrect:** This setting would not fix your problem. It would require all backups to be kept at least 30 days on Microsoft servers. If there is insufficient space to allow a new backup, as is the case in this scenario, the new backup will fail.

3. **Correct Answer:** A

   A. **Correct:** You don't need to modify the default settings. The bandwidth of the backup operation will be throttled to 256 Kbps beginning at 9:00 A.M. every weekday.

   B. **Incorrect:** You don't want to increase the bandwidth settings assigned to work hours because this would increase the impact on network performance for users during work hours.

   C. **Incorrect:** Increasing the bandwidth setting assigned to nonwork hours would not help you achieve your goal of minimizing impact on users if the backup operation continues into the work day.

   D. **Incorrect:** You don't need to adjust work days because the current selection reflects the Monday through Friday schedule of the organization.

Objective 12.2: Review

1. **Correct Answers:** A, B

   A. **Correct:** You need to enable the option to save additional recovery points. This step enables you to configure some of these additional recovery points as incremental VSS copies, which are application-consistent.

   B. **Correct:** Incremental VSS copies are snapshots that are application-consistent for VSS-aware applications like Microsoft Exchange.

   C. **Incorrect:** Resynchronization does not affect the consistency of applications within recovery point snapshots.

   D. **Incorrect:** Hyper-V Replica Broker is used for failover clustering, not for application consistency.

2. **Correct Answer:** D

   A. **Incorrect:** You have already performed an unplanned failover. You cannot perform a failover to the other site until replication is reestablished between the two servers.

   B. **Incorrect:** It's too late to cancel the failover because changes have already been made to AppSrv1.

   C. **Incorrect:** You cannot perform a planned or unplanned failover to the other site until replication is reestablished between the two servers.

   D. **Correct:** Choosing the option to reverse replication starts the Reverse Replication Wizard. This wizard enables you to reestablish replication between the two servers, with the local server in Denver acting as the new primary. After you complete this wizard, you can perform a planned failover to return the VM to the site in Cleveland.

3. **Correct Answers:** A, D

   A. **Correct:** You need to configure the Hyper-V Replica Broker role for the failover cluster if you want to add an offsite replica to a clustered VM.

   B. **Incorrect:** To configure the Hyper-V Replica Broker at the replica site, you would need to create a failover cluster at the replica site. This step is unnecessary because you want to configure RepSrv2 as the replica server. Your goal is not to create a replica cluster.

   C. **Incorrect:** In the replication settings for Cluster1, you want to restrict authorization to RepSrv2. However, this step would be required only if the VM were failed over to the replica site, and you later wanted to fail back to the original site.

   D. **Correct:** The server-level replication settings enable you to limit which remote servers can act as a primary server to the local replica server. In this case, you need to configure the CAP as the name of the primary server.

Thought experiment

1. Only failover clustering can prevent any disruption of service and data loss in case of an individual server failure.

2. You can configure Hyper-V Replica on failover clusters in both the San Francisco and Montreal offices. The failover cluster in the San Francisco office can act as the primary server, and the failover cluster in the Montreal office can act as the replica server.

3. One option is to use a cloud backup service such as Windows Azure Online Backup to back up AppVM1 daily and specify a retention range of 15 days. Another option is to perform daily backups of AppVM1 to local file storage on a file server that is itself a VM. You can then configure this file server as a primary VM with a replica VM in the replica site (Montreal). In case of site-level failure at the primary site, the replica VMs of AppVM1 and the file server at the replica site will continue to operate as before with no loss of backup data.

CHAPTER 13

Configure network services

The Configure Network Services domain includes a single objective: Deploy and manage IP Address Management (IPAM). IPAM is a new feature used for managing your organization's entire IP address space, public and private.

For the 70-417 exam, IPAM is a bit of a wildcard. It's a large topic, but because it is a new feature, the questions you will see will most likely be fair and not require unusually deep knowledge. That said, be sure to supplement the information in this chapter with some hands-on practice to develop a feel for how IPAM works.

Objectives in this chapter:

- Objective 13.1: Deploy and manage IPAM

Objective 13.1: Deploy and manage IPAM

On the surface, IPAM seems easy. Here's how it works: you have an IPAM server that automatically collects information from your infrastructure servers about the IP address ranges used on your network. You then use the IPAM interface as a reference about these same address ranges. It doesn't sound complicated at all.

Unfortunately, IPAM is not as easy to master as it might first appear. The difficulty is not conceptual; rather, it is a result of the large number of component features and functionalities that IPAM includes. The first official Microsoft white paper about IPAM is almost 100 pages long, which gives you some idea of the feature's depth. There's a lot there—too much to be covered in one objective.

The best way to handle the large subject of IPAM is to focus on three basic topics: What can you use the feature to accomplish? How do you configure it? And finally, how do you use it?

> **This section covers the following topics:**
> - Configure IPAM
> - Create and manage IP blocks and ranges
> - Delegate IPAM administration

What is IPAM?

IPAM is a useful new feature in Windows Server 2012 that lets you centrally view, manage, and configure the IP address space in your organization. By using IPAM, you can look at all your address blocks and ranges, find free IP addresses, manage DHCP scopes across multiple servers, create DHCP reservations and DNS host records, and even search for address assignments by device name, location, or other descriptive tag.

IPAM works by first discovering your infrastructure servers and importing from them all available IP address data. You then manually add whatever data you need to complete the picture of your organization's IP address assignments. Once you have this information in place, you can track updates to your IP address space.

Problems solved by IPAM

IPAM has many component features that help you manage IP addressing. To better understand the purpose and functionality of IPAM and these many aspects, it's helpful to view IPAM as a means to solve the following kinds of administrative questions:

- How can I track my organization's address space and know the addresses that are either in use or available across different locations?
- How can I find a free static IP address for a new device and register it in DNS?
- How can I find out which DHCP scopes in my organization are full or close to full?
- How can I efficiently change a DHCP option across dozens of scopes residing on multiple servers?
- How can I find an unused address range within my organization's address space to dedicate to a new subnet?
- How can I determine which public and private address ranges are used by my organization?
- How can I determine which portion of the address space used by my organization is dynamically assigned and which portion is statically assigned?
- How can I search for and locate an IP address or set of addresses by name, device, location, or another descriptive tag?

Limitations of IPAM

IPAM is a new feature, so it's important to recognize some of the limitations in this first release:

1. IPAM can import data only from Windows servers running Windows Server 2008 and later that are members of the same Active Directory forest.
2. IPAM does not support management and configuration of non-Microsoft network elements.
3. IPAM does not check for IP address consistency with routers and switches.

4. A single IPAM server can support up to 150 DHCP servers for a total of 6,000 scopes, and 500 DNS servers for a total of 150 zones.

5. Address utilization trends and reclaiming support are provided only for IPv4.

6. IPAM does not support auditing of IPv6 stateless address autoconfiguration on an unmanaged machine to track the user.

Installing and configuring IPAM

To install the IPAM feature in Windows Server 2012, you can use the Add Roles and Features Wizard or the following Windows PowerShell command:

```
Install-WindowsFeature IPAM -IncludeManagementTools
```

Once IPAM is installed, you configure and manage the feature through the IPAM client in Server Manager, as shown in Figure 13-1, or by using Windows PowerShell cmdlets from the IpamServer module. (There is no other graphical IPAM console.)

EXAM TIP

You can install the IPAM client tool without installing the server component. To accomplish this by using the Add Roles and Features Wizard, select IPAM in the wizard, choose to install the prerequisite features of IPAM, clear the selection of IPAM you have just selected, and then complete the wizard. The IPAM client doesn't appear by default in Server Manager, however. To make the IPAM client appear, you need to add the remote IPAM server to Server Manager by using the Add Other Servers To Manage option (visible in Figure 13-1).

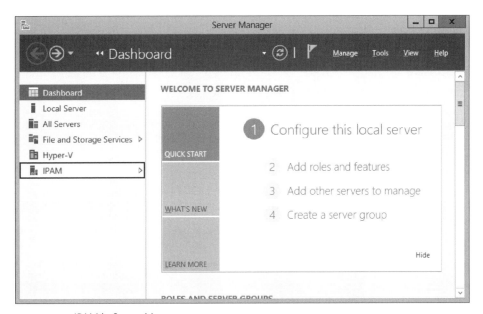

FIGURE 13-1 IPAM in Server Manager.

When you click IPAM in the navigation pane of Server Manager, the navigation pane narrows and the details pane reveals the IPAM Overview page, shown in Figure 13-2.

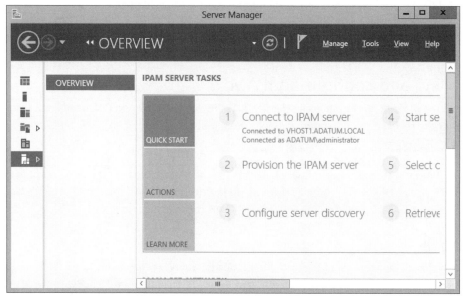

FIGURE 13-2 The IPAM Overview page preconfiguration.

The Overview page presents the following six links that help guide you through configuration:

1. Connect To IPAM Server
2. Provision The IPAM Server
3. Configure Server Discovery
4. Start Server Discovery
5. Select Or Add Servers To Manage And Verify IPAM Access
6. Retrieve Data From Managed Servers

We'll use these same steps to cover the configuration process in the next sections.

1. Connect To IPAM Server

You use this link only if you need to connect to a remote IPAM server. By default, Server Manager is connected to the local IPAM server.

2. Provision The IPAM Server

Clicking this link on the Overview page starts the Provision IPAM Wizard. Provisioning the IPAM server is a term that describes preparing the IPAM server by performing steps such as automatically creating the IPAM database, creating IPAM security groups, and configuring access to IPAM tasks and folders.

You also use this wizard to determine how you want to configure the infrastructure servers that IPAM will manage. You can either configure the infrastructure servers manually or by using Group Policy, as shown in Figure 13-3. If you choose to use Group Policy, you specify a prefix for the three group policy objects (GPOs) that will later be created automatically when you use the Invoke-IpamGpoProvisioning cmdlet.

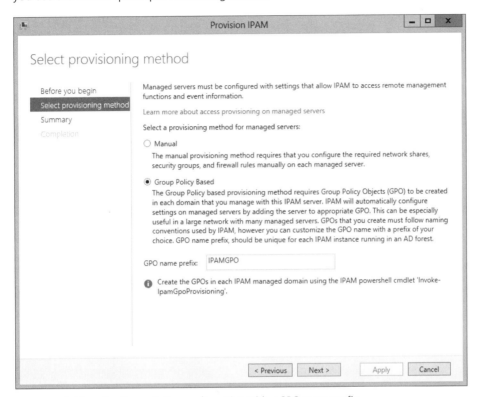

FIGURE 13-3 Choosing Group Policy configuration with a GPO name prefix.

You wouldn't select Manual here unless an unusual factor made the Group Policy Based option impossible or ineffective. Despite the limited real-world applicability of the Manual option, configuring IPAM manually is one of the tasks officially mentioned in the Deploy and manage IPAM objective. (The process of manual configuration is discussed in section 5, "Select Or Add Servers To Manage," later in this chapter.)

EXAM TIP

You can't change the provisioning method after you complete the Provision IPAM Wizard. To change from manual provisioning to Group Policy–based provisioning, or from Group Policy–based to Manual, you have to uninstall and reinstall IPAM.

3. Configure Server Discovery

Clicking this link on the Overview page opens the Configure Discovery Settings dialog box, shown in Figure 13-4. You use this step to specify which types of infrastructure servers you want to discover. By default, all three possible infrastructure types are selected: Domain Controller, DHCP Server, and DNS Server.

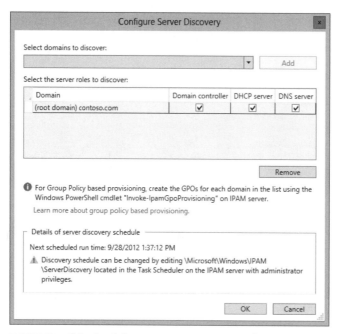

FIGURE 13-4 Selecting infrastructure server types to discover.

4. Start Server Discovery

This link begins the process of discovering infrastructure servers in your environment. To determine when the process is complete, you can click the notification flag in Server Manager and then click Task Details. The process is complete when the IPAM ServerDiscovery task displays a status of Complete, as shown in Figure 13-5.

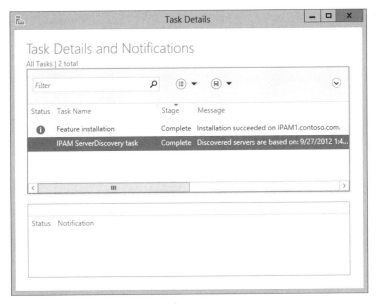

FIGURE 13-5 Server discovery complete.

5. Select Or Add Servers To Manage

Clicking this link on the Overview page displays the SERVER INVENTORY page in the IPAM client of Server Manager. This page shows the servers that have been discovered by the server discovery task in the previous step. Initially, the discovered servers display a Manageability Status of Unspecified and an IPAM Access Status of Blocked, as shown in Figure 13-6. This status means you still need to configure the servers for IPAM management. To perform this step, you need to run a Windows PowerShell command and then designate the desired servers as managed. (You need to perform this step if you have chosen the Group Policy Based option on the Select Provisioning Method page shown in Figure 13-3. If you have chosen the Manual option, the entire IPAM configuration process is different. For instructions on manual configuration, see the sidebar "Manual configuration of managed servers" later in this chapter.)

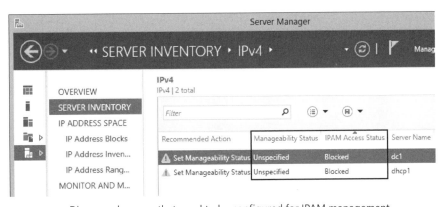

FIGURE 13-6 Discovered servers that need to be configured for IPAM management.

To configure the servers by using the Group Policy Based provisioning method, you need to create IPAM GPOs. You can do this by running the following Windows PowerShell command:

```
Invoke-IpamGpoProvisioning [-Domain] <String> [-GpoPrefixName] <String> [-IpamServerFqdn <String> ]
```

The GPO prefix name should be the same one you specified in the Provision IPAM Wizard. For example, if you specified a prefix of IPAMGPO in the Provision IPAM Wizard, you could enter the following command at an elevated Windows PowerShell prompt:

```
Invoke-IpamGpoProvisioning –Domain contoso.com –GpoPrefixName IPAMGPO –IpamServerFqdn ipam1.contoso.com
```

This command creates the three GPOs shown in Figure 13-7.

FIGURE 13-7 GPOs created for IPAM.

These three new GPOs apply only to servers that you designate as managed, but no servers are designated as managed by default. (Remember this last point for the exam because it could easily serve as the basis for a test question.) To change the manageability status of servers, right-click each server you want to manage on the SERVER INVENTORY page and then click Edit Server. In the Add Or Edit Server dialog box that opens, in the Manageability Status drop-down list, select Managed (as shown in Figure 13-8) and then click OK.

> **NOTE** The IPAM provisioning process creates a domain security group named IPAMUG. This group is used to grant permissions on managed servers.

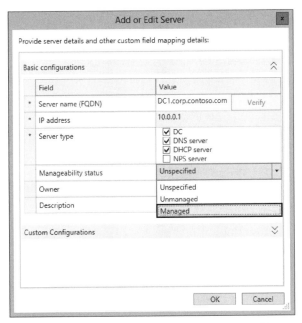

FIGURE 13-8 Setting a server's manageability status to Managed.

You then need to force an update of Group Policy on all the servers you have designated as managed. You can do this by running Gpupdate /force on each of these servers, by restarting them, or by invoking Gpupdate centrally in the methods described in Chapter 9, "Configure and manage Group Policy."

Next, click the refresh icon in Server Manager in the menu bar next to the notification flag. (Alternatively, you can right-click your servers on the SERVER INVENTORY page and select the Refresh Server Access Status option. You can see this option on the shortcut menu in Figure 13-10.) After you refresh the server status, the Manageability Status of the servers will appear as Managed, and the IPAM Access Status will appear as Unblocked on the SERVER INVENTORY page, as shown in Figure 13-9. If the status is not immediately updated, wait several minutes and refresh the server status again.

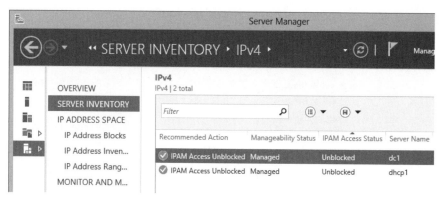

FIGURE 13-9 Servers that are configured to be managed by IPAM.

MANUAL CONFIGURATION OF MANAGED SERVERS

Configuring IPAM manually from start to finish without using Group Policy is a far more elaborate and cumbersome process than you are usually required to learn for Microsoft certification exams.

However, there are aspects of manual configuration that are easily summarized and could plausibly appear on the exam, shown in Table 13-1. The most likely elements to appear in an exam question are the firewall ports created on each server and the security groups the IPAM server needs to join.

If you want to learn the full step-by-step procedure for configuring IPAM manually, consult the document entitled "Understand and Troubleshoot IP Address Management (IPAM) in Windows Server '8' Beta," available at *http://www.microsoft.com/en-us/download/details.aspx?id=29012*. (The steps for manual configuration appear in the first appendix.)

TABLE 13-1 Manual configuration steps for managed infrastructure servers in IPAM

On this Managed Server...	Perform this configuration step	Enable these Firewall Rules	Associated IPAM functionality
DHCP	Add the IPAM server to the local DHCP Users security group.	DHCP Server (RPC-In) DHCP Server (RPCSS-In)	DHCP address space, settings, and utilization data collection
	Assign to the IPAM server Read access in the DHCP Server service access control list (ACL).	Remote Service Management (RPC) Remote Service Management (RPC-EPMAP)	DHCP Service monitoring
	Add the IPAM server to the local Event Log Readers security group.	Remote Event Log Management (RPC) Remote Event Log Management (RPC-EPMAP)	DHCP configuration event monitoring
	Create a network share named DHCPAudit for %windir%\system32\dhcp and assign Read access to the IPAM server on this share.	File and Printer Sharing (NB-Session-In) File and Printer Sharing (SMB-In)	DHCP lease event collection for IP address tracking
DNS	For DNS servers that are also domain controllers, assign to the IPAM server Read access in the domain-wide DNS ACL* OR For DNS servers that are not domain controllers, add the IPAM server to the local Administrators group.	DNS Service RPC DNS Service RPC Endpoint Mapper	DNS zone configuration collection
	Add the IPAM server to the local Event Log Readers security group. Assign to the IPAM server Read access in the ACL stored in the DNS CustomSD registry key.	Remote Event Log Management (RPC) Remote Event Log Management (RPC-EPMAP)	DNS zone event collection for DNS zone monitoring
	Assign to the IPAM server Read access in the DNS Server service ACL.	Remote Service Management (RPC) Remote Service Management (RPC-EPMAP)	DNS service monitoring
DC/NPS	Add the IPAM server to the local Event Log Readers security group.	Remote Event Log Management (RPC) Remote Event Log Management (RPC-EPMAP)	Logon event collection for IP address tracking
IPAM (local server)	Add the local Network Service to the local Event Log Readers security group.	N/A	IPAM configuration event monitoring

6. Retrieve Data From Managed Servers

The final step in configuring IPAM is to load data from your managed servers into the IPAM database. To do so, on the Overview page, click Retrieve Data From Managed Servers. Then, click the notification flag and wait for all tasks to complete.

Alternatively, you can select and right-click the Managed servers on the SERVER INVENTORY page and then select Retrieve All Server Data from the shortcut menu, as shown in Figure 13-10.

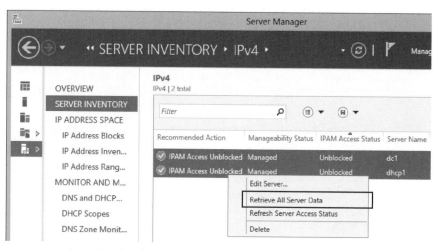

FIGURE 13-10 Retrieving data from managed servers.

Managing address space

The most basic function of IPAM is to let you view, monitor, and manage the IP address space in your organization. By using IPAM, you can search and sort IP blocks, ranges, and individual addresses based on built-in fields or user-defined custom fields. You can also track IP address utilization within scopes or display utilization trends.

Adding your IP address space to the IPAM database

You can browse and search your organization's address space in the IPAM client in Server Manager, but only after you add this data to the IPAM database. In IPAM, the IP address space is broken down into blocks, ranges, and addresses. Blocks represent the largest sections of IP address space used by a company, such as 10.0.0.0/8. Ranges are portions of blocks that typically correspond to DHCP scopes. IP addresses exist within ranges.

How are these elements added to IPAM? IPAM discovers DHCP scopes automatically, and it automatically imports the corresponding address ranges into the IPAM database. However, IPAM doesn't automatically import blocks or addresses into its database; you have to add them manually or import them from a comma-delimited file. (You can also export addresses to a file in comma-delimited format.) In addition, you might want to create additional ranges that have not been discovered by IPAM. These address ranges might correspond to space reserved for statically assigned addresses, or they might be used by DHCP servers that are not members of the local Active Directory forest.

To add an IP address block, range, or address to the IPAM database, click IP Address Blocks in the IPAM navigation menu and then, from the Tasks menu, select Add IP Address Block, Add IP Address Range, or Add IP Address, as shown in Figure 13-11.

NOTE Although IPAM doesn't automatically import addresses associated with DHCP leases into the IPAM database, you can use the EVENT CATALOG page and the IP Address Tracking tool to directly search the DHCP server log for DHCP leases by client name or address.

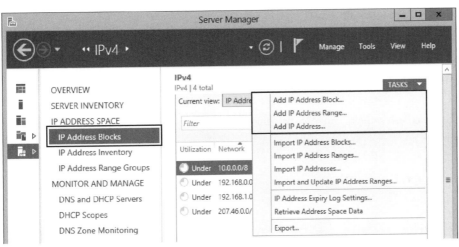

FIGURE 13-11 Adding a block, range, or address to the IPAM database.

After this step, you can view the elements you have added by selecting the appropriate category (IP addresses, address blocks, or address ranges) in the Current View drop-down list, as shown in Figure 13-12.

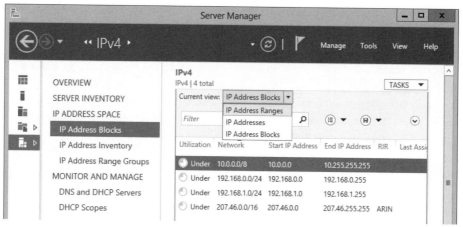

FIGURE 13-12 Viewing added blocks, addresses, or ranges.

EXAM TIP

Remember that only address ranges that correspond to DHCP scopes on managed DHCP servers are automatically imported into the IPAM database.

Creating custom fields

You can create custom data fields that you can later apply to your blocks, ranges, and individual addresses. You can then use these fields to sort or locate IP address information in a way that is useful to you, such as by office location, building, floor, or department.

To create a custom field for IPAM, first select IPAM Settings from the Manage menu in Server Manager, as shown in Figure 13-13.

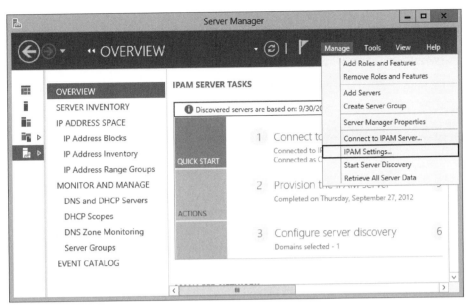

FIGURE 13-13 Opening IPAM settings.

The IPAM Settings dialog box is shown in Figure 13-14. In this dialog box, select Configure Custom Fields.

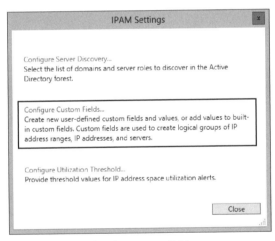

FIGURE 13-14 Configuring custom fields.

This step opens the Configure Custom Fields dialog box, shown in Figure 13-15. Use this dialog box to create a custom field name, such as Building, and then possible values for that field, such as Headquarters, Sales, Operations, and Data Center.

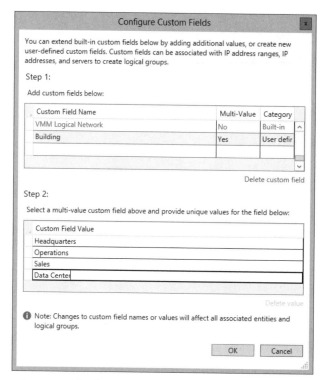

FIGURE 13-15 Configuring custom fields.

EXAM TIP

Remember that you can use custom fields to categorize the IP addresses and ranges in your IPAM database.

Applying a custom field to addresses and ranges

To add a custom field to an IP address range or IP address, right-click the element and select the option to edit it. (You can edit multiple ranges or addresses simultaneously.) Then, click Custom Configuration in the associated dialog box and provide the desired field and value.

Creating IP address range groups

An IP address range group is a view of IP addresses or ranges sorted by stacked categories, as shown in Figure 13-16. In this figure, an IP address range group named Building/Floor has been created. When you select this IP address range group, you can view or search ranges and address by building name and then by floor name.

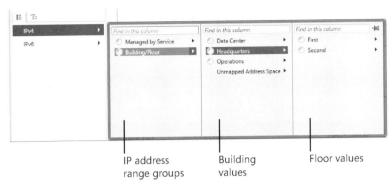

FIGURE 13-16 An IP address range group.

To create an IP address range group, select the IP Address Range Groups page in the IPAM navigation pane in the IPAM client in Server Manager. Then, from the Tasks menu, select Add IP Address Range Group, as shown in Figure 13-17. A dialog box will then open that allows you to specify parent and child values for your new address range group.

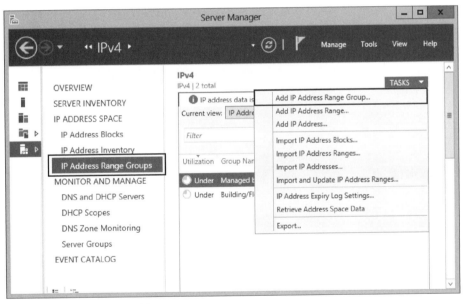

FIGURE 13-17 Adding an IP address range group.

Finding and allocating an address from a range

Finding an unused address to allocate to a device is a common task for a network administrator. IPAM enables you to perform this task within a chosen IP address range and verifies that the IP address is unused.

To perform this function, select the IP Address Blocks page in the IPAM client in Server Manager and verify that IP Address Ranges is selected in Current View. Then, right-click the desired IP Address range and select Find And Allocate Available IP Addresses, as shown in Figure 13-18.

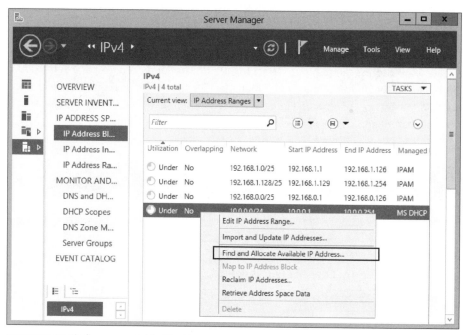

FIGURE 13-18 Finding an available IP address.

Viewing and configuring IP utilization thresholds

When you select the IP Address Blocks page, the first column in the list of blocks or ranges displayed is Utilization, as shown in Figure 13-19. This value indicates the percentage of a displayed address block or range that is already assigned to devices. By default, if fewer than 20 percent of the addresses defined in the range are in use, the status reads Under. If over 80 percent of the addresses are in use, the status reads Over. Optimal utilization is shown when the IP address usage is between 20 percent and 80 percent.

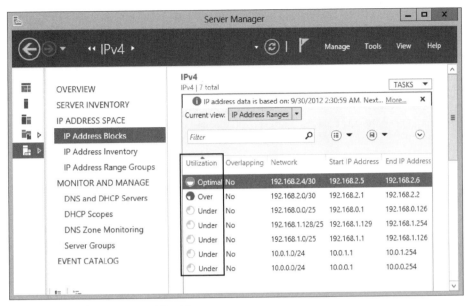

FIGURE 13-19 Utilization rates of IP address ranges.

You can alter the 20 percent and 80 percent parameters that define Under, Optimal, and Over status. To do so, in Server Manager, select IP Settings from the Manage menu, and then select the Configure Utilization Threshold option in the IPAM Settings dialog box. (You can see these options in Figures 13-13 and 13-14 earlier in this chapter.) In the Configure IP Address Utilization Threshold dialog box that opens, shown in Figure 13-20, adjust the percentage for Under Utilized or Over Utilized, as desired.

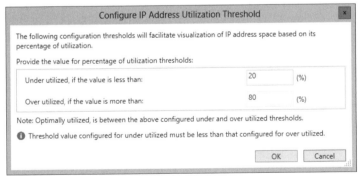

FIGURE 13-20 Changing the overutilization and underutilization thresholds.

Delegating IPAM administration

IPAM setup creates on the IPAM server the five local security groups shown in Table 13-2. You can use these groups to delegate aspects of IPAM administration to different users.

Make sure you learn these five groups for the 70-417 exam. You could see a question in which each answer choice corresponds to an IPAM security group.

TABLE 13-2 Local security groups created on the IPAM server

Group Name	Description
IPAM Users	Members of this group can view all information in server inventory, IP address space, and server management consoles of IPAM. They can view IPAM and DHCP server operational events but cannot view IP address tracking information.
IPAM MSM Administrators	Members of this group have all the privileges of the IPAM Users group and can manage DHCP and DNS server instance-specific information. Such users are Multi Server Management (MSM) Administrators.
IPAM ASM Administrators	Members of this group have all the privileges of the IPAM Users group and can perform add and modify address space management operations. Such users are Address Space Management (ASM) Administrators.
IPAM IP Audit Administrators	Members of this group have all the privileges of the IPAM Users group and can view IP address tracking information.
IPAM Administrators	Members of this group have privileges to view all IPAM information and perform all IPAM tasks.

MORE INFO For more in-depth information about IPAM, refer to the IPAM Step-by-Step Guide at *http://technet.microsoft.com/en-us/library/hh831622.aspx*, the IPAM Test Lab Guide at *http://www.microsoft.com/en-us/download/details.aspx?id=29020*, and the IPAM virtual lab at *http://channel9.msdn.com/Events/TechEd/Europe/2012/WSV14-HOL*.

EXAM TIP

The original Configure Network Services domain on the 70-412 exam includes additional objectives about DHCP and DNS. Don't be surprised if you see a question or two about these topics, even though they are not officially listed for the 70-417 exam. For DNS, review the basics about primary and secondary zones, DNS on DCs, zone properties, and basic DNS files such as the zone file and Netlogon.dns. For DHCP, be sure to study a new feature in Windows Server 2012 called DHCP failover. By using DHCP failover, you can configure a second DHCP server in hot standby mode (taking over from the DHCP server in case the main DHCP fails) or load sharing mode (sharing the DHCP requests). For more information about DHCP failover, visit *http://technet.microsoft.com/en-us/library /hh831385.aspx*.

Objective summary

- IPAM is a new feature that enables you to centrally manage the IP addressing information in your organization. IPAM works only with Microsoft servers in a domain environment.

- To configure IPAM, you run the Provision IPAM Wizard, start a process to automatically discover your infrastructure servers, mark chosen servers as Managed, and then run a special cmdlet (Invoke-IpamGpoProvisioning) to create GPOs that automatically configure required settings on those servers.

- DHCP scopes discovered on the network are automatically imported into the IPAM database as IP address ranges. You can add larger IP address blocks and individual IP addresses to these IP address ranges.

- IPAM includes many features for IP address management. These features enable you to describe data in a way that helps you sort and find information about your address space. They also help you keep track of the addresses used in available ranges and update DHCP and DNS servers directly.

- You can delegate aspects of IPAM administration to different users by assigning these users to any of five IPAM security groups.

Objective review

Answer the following questions to test your knowledge of the information in this objective. You can find the answers to these questions and explanations of why each answer choice is correct or incorrect in the "Answers" section at the end of the chapter.

1. You have installed the IPAM feature on a server named IPAM1 that is a member of the Contoso.com domain. You want to configure the IPAM server to retrieve data from all DHCP servers, DNS servers, and domain controllers in the domain.

   You choose the option to use the Group Policy–based provisioning method to discover the servers, and you select all three server roles to discover. You start server discovery, and all the DHCP servers, DNS servers, and domain controllers in the domain are discovered. However, they appear in the Server Manager with an IPAM Access Status of Blocked.

   You want the IPAM Access Status of the discovered infrastructure servers to appear as Unblocked. What should you do? (Choose all that apply.)

   A. Run the Invoke-IpamGpoProvisioning cmdlet.

   B. Mark the servers as Managed.

   C. Add the IPAM server to the local Event Log Readers security group.

   D. Refresh Group Policy on the discovered servers.

2. You work as a network administrator for Fabrikam.com, a company with 2,500 employees and offices in New York, London, Paris, and Munich. Each office site includes its own Active Directory Domain Services domain within the Fabrikam.com forest.

As an administrator, you occasionally need to know the IP address ranges used in various parts of your organization. You want to be able to browse the IP address ranges assigned to each city.

You install IPAM on a server running Windows Server 2012 named IPAM2 in your local office. You then configure IPAM; perform server discovery of the DHCP servers, DNS servers, and domain controllers in your organization; and finally retrieve addressing data from these servers.

Your goal is to use Server Manager to browse the IP address ranges assigned to each city. Which of the following steps do you need to take? (Choose all that apply.)

   A. Configure a custom field.

   B. Create an IP address range group.

   C. Assign custom values to IP address ranges.

   D. Edit the Description field in IP address ranges.

3. You have installed the IPAM feature on a server named IPAM3 that is a member of the Litwareinc.com domain. You want to allow a certain user named Pam to view the IPAM database, server inventory, DHCP events, and IP address tracking.

You don't want to assign any additional rights to Pam. To which security group on IPAM3 should you add her?

   A. IPAM Users

   B. IPAM MSM Administrators

   C. IPAM ASM Administrators

   D. IPAM IP Audit Administrators

Thought experiment

You are a network administrator for Adatum.com. The Adatum.com network is spread over four buildings on a single campus near Sydney, Australia. The network consists of 1,000 clients and 60 servers, including the following infrastructure servers:

- 12 DHCP servers, including the following:
  - 8 running Windows Server 2012 (four scopes)
  - 2 running Windows Server 2008 R2 (one scope)
  - 1 running Windows Server 2003 R2 (one scope)
  - 1 running CentOS distribution of Linux (one scope)
- 4 domain controllers that are also DNS servers, including the following:
  - 2 running Windows Server 2012
  - 2 running Windows Server 2008 R2
- 2 DNS servers running Debian Linux

All clients and servers on the network that are running Windows are also members of the Adatum.com domain.

As a network administrator, you want to use the IPAM feature in Windows Server 2012 to manage the company's address space. The 12 DHCP servers are used to support seven /24 IPv4 networks within the 10.0.0.0/16 address block. The first 10 addresses in each scope are configured as exclusions and are reserved for static IP assignments. Twelve public servers are hosted on a /28 IPv4 network obtained from the APNIC regional registry. All 12 of these public addresses are statically assigned.

With this information in mind, answer the following questions:

1. How many of the infrastructure servers are not compatible with IPAM?
2. Assuming you want to add all the organization's public and private addresses to the IPAM database, how many IP address blocks should you add? How many IP address ranges must be added manually?
3. Server Manager displays the public IP address range utilization as Over. Your organization isn't intending to assign any more public IP addresses to servers. What step can you take to allow your IP ranges to use 90 percent of the available addresses before displaying the Over status?
4. You want to assign a static IP address to a new device in the logical subnet that contains the DHCP server running Windows Server 2012. What is the most efficient way to discover an unused address in this range?

Answers

This section contains the answers to the Objective Review and the Thought Experiment.

Objective 13.1: Review

1. **Correct Answers:** A, B, D

   A. **Correct:** You use this cmdlet to create the GPOs needed to configure discovered servers for IPAM management.

   B. **Correct:** The GPOs created by running the Invoke-IpamGpoProvisioning cmdlet apply only to servers you mark as Managed in IPAM.

   C. **Incorrect**: This setting needs to be configured on the domain controller you want to manage in IPAM, but it is automatically configured by the GPO created by the Invoke-IpamGpoProvisioning cmdlet. You therefore don't need to take this step.

   D. **Correct**: After running the Invoke-IpamGpoProvisioning cmdlet, you need to refresh Group Policy on the discovered infrastructure servers so the settings in the newly created GPOs are applied to these servers.

2. **Correct Answers:** A, B, C

   A. **Correct:** You need to configure a custom field that includes the values New York, London, Paris, and Munich. You can create a new custom field for these values and name it City, or you can use an existing custom field such as Location and add the four cities as new custom values.

   B. **Correct:** An IP address range group enables you to sort and browse your IP address ranges by any field you choose.

   C. **Correct:** You need to tag each IP address range with the City (or Location) value of New York, London, Paris, or Munich.

   D. **Incorrect:** You cannot browse IP addresses based on the values included in the Description tag. To accomplish that, you need an IP address range group.

3. **Correct Answer:** D

   A. **Incorrect:** The IPAM Users group will assign all the rights Pam needs except the ability to use IP address tracking.

   B. **Incorrect:** The IPAM MSM Administrators group doesn't provide the ability to use IP address tracking. It also provides unnecessary rights for managing DHCP and DNS servers.

   C. **Incorrect**: The IPAM ASM Administrators group doesn't provide the ability to use IP address tracking. It also provides the unnecessary right to perform add and modify address space management operations

   D. **Correct**: The IPAM IP Audit Administrators group provides exactly the user rights (and no others) that are required by the scenario.

Thought experiment

1. Four: one running Windows Server 2003 R2 and three running Linux.

2. You should add two IP address blocks: one for the 10.0.0.0/16 private address block and one for the public /28 address block. You need to add three IP address ranges manually: one for the public address range, one for the scope hosted on the Windows Server 2003 R2 server, and one for the scope hosted on the CentOS Linux server. (The others are imported automatically.)

3. Change the Over Utilized utilization threshold in IPAM Settings to 90 percent.

4. Use the Find And Allocate Available IP Addresses function in IPAM.

CHAPTER 14

Configure identity and access solutions

In its original form on the 70-412 exam, the Configure Identity and Access Solutions domain covers three general topics: Active Directory Federation Services (AD FS) 2.1, Active Directory Certificate Services (AD CS), and Active Directory Rights Management Services (AD RMS). However, of these three, just AD FS 2.1 has been tagged as a 70-417 exam topic.

AD FS 2.1 is essentially AD FS 2.0 built into Windows Server 2012. AD FS 2.0 first appeared as a downloadable update to Windows Server 2008 and Windows Server 2008 R2. In those operating systems, the built-in version of AD FS was 1.1.

The purpose of AD FS is to use claims (described in Chapter 11, "File and storage solutions") to securely extend the reach of Active Directory authentication across multiple networks and platforms. Compared to AD FS 1.1, the biggest change in AD FS 2.0 and AD FS 2.1 (known collectively as AD FS 2.x) is how they work behind the scenes. AD FS 2.x can issue security tokens by using various industry-standard protocols, including WS-Trust, WS-Federation, and Security Assertion Markup Language (SAML) 2.0. AD FS 2.x can thus create and issue tokens containing claims information for almost any application that requests them, and as a result, the server role can be used in a greater range of contexts than ever before.

However, this leap in functionality isn't easily captured in exam questions. From the perspective of exam preparation, the biggest change to AD FS is a *revamped AD FS console*. In this chapter, we will briefly examine this new console and indicate any topics within this domain that you're likely to encounter on the exam.

Objectives in this chapter:

- Objective 14.1: Implement Active Directory Federation Services 2.1

Objective 14.1: Implement Active Directory Federation Services 2.1

AD FS helps authenticate your Active Directory users outside the corporate network in a way that protects your organization's internal security infrastructure.

The main functionality of AD FS 1.0 and 1.1 was to support Active Directory users in your network who needed to access an application in a partner network (or vice versa). Because AD FS 2.x is built on interoperability with standards-based tokens and claims, it can support new scenarios. For example, AD FS 2.x supports *enterprise applications that are hosted in the cloud.* AD FS 2.x also uses industry standards to offer improved support for web single sign-on (SSO) to applications across different organizations and platforms, including non-Microsoft environments.

For the 70-417 exam, this is probably more than you need to know about AD FS tokens and compatibility with industry standards. Instead, you just need to concentrate on some basic new features in AD FS 2.1 configuration, which represent the focus of this chapter.

This section covers the following topics:

- Initial configuration of AD FS
- New features of the AD FS console
- Installing certificates for AD FS

The new AD FS console in AD FS 2.1

The AD FS console installs automatically when you install the AD FS server role in Windows Server 2012, but the console tree remains unpopulated until you run the AD FS Federation Server Configuration Wizard. You can access this wizard by clicking the notification flag in Server Manager. To complete the wizard successfully, a Secure Sockets Layer (SSL) certificate must be installed on the Default Web Site of the local instance of Internet Information Services (IIS).

Figure 14-1 shows the new AD FS console in Windows Server 2012 after you run the AD FS Federation Server Configuration Wizard. You can use the AD FS console to configure services and policies related to the deployment of a federation server.

NOTE The central pane in Figure 14-1 indicates that you need to add a trusted relying party. This message appears on a freshly configured installation of AD FS in Windows Server 2012, and its associated link corresponds to the first action listed in the Actions pane, Add Relying Party Trust. (The Add Relying Party Trust action corresponds to a wizard of the same name.)

A relying party (RP) is a new concept in AD FS 2.x that refers to an application or other agent that "consumes" (requests and uses) claims in security tokens issued by the local Federation Service. When you run the Add Relying Party Trust Wizard, you configure AD FS to provide claims for a specific application in the form of industry-standard tokens.

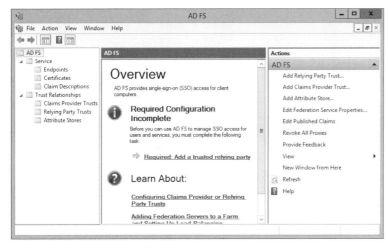

FIGURE 14-1 The AD FS console in AD FS 2.1.

The AD FS 2.1 console tree includes two main nodes: the Service node and the Trust Relationships node.

Service node

You use the Service node in the AD FS console for the following general purposes:

- Managing the services provided through endpoints
- Configuring the certificates used for issuing and receiving tokens and publishing metadata
- Configuring claims types

ENDPOINTS NODE

In AD FS, endpoints are URLs that provide access to various services, such as issuing tokens and publishing federation metadata. You use the Endpoints node to enable or disable various endpoints and to control whether the endpoint is published to federation server proxies. (The AD FS Proxy is a service that brokers a connection between external users and your internal AD FS server.)

As shown in Figure 14-2, when the Endpoints node is selected, the details pane reveals a Token Issuance section and a Metadata section. The Metadata section includes the path to the local federation server's metadata XML file. This metadata file defines the data format for communicating configuration information between a claims provider (such as Active Directory Domain Services) and an RP. You might need to provide this address or XML file to a resource partner when you are establishing a federated trust.

EXAM TIP

You need to know that the Endpoint node contains a path to the federation metadata of your organization. You provide this data to a partner organization to configure a federated trust.

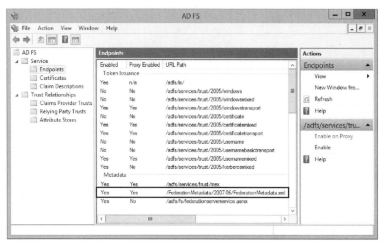

FIGURE 14-2 The Endpoints node and Federation Metadata file.

CERTIFICATES NODE

The Certificates node in the AD FS console shows the three certificates you need to run AD FS. All three of these certificates are based on the Web Server template.

- **Service communications** This certificate is used for Windows Communication Foundation (WCF) message security. Before you can configure AD FS, this certificate must be installed as an SSL certificate on the Default Web Site of the local instance of IIS. To prepare for this step, from the local computer's Personal certificate store, request a new certificate based on the Web Server template.

- **Token-decrypting** This certificate is used to decrypt tokens the Federation Service receives. It is created by default as a self-signed certificate, but you can replace it with a certificate issued by an enterprise certificate authority (CA).

- **Token-signing** This certificate is used to sign tokens the Federation Service issues. As with the Token-decrypting certificate, this certificate is created by default as a self-signed certificate, but you can replace it with a certificate issued by an enterprise CA.

The Certificates node and the three AD FS certificates are shown in Figure 14-3.

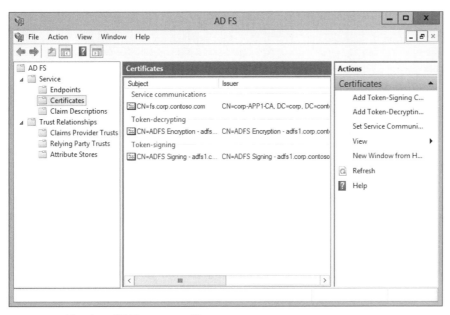

FIGURE 14-3 The three AD FS server certificates.

EXAM TIP

For the 70-417 exam, you need to know that all three AD FS certificates are based on the Web Server template and that you should import these certificates into the Personal certificate store for the local computer (not the current user).

CLAIM DESCRIPTIONS

Through this node you can find information about the claims the local server is currently able to assert about identities. The description of each claim is found at a specified URL. More claims can be added by clicking Add Claim Description in the Actions pane.

> **NOTE** AD FS 2.1 is the only version of AD FS that can be integrated with Windows Server 2012 Dynamic Access Control. This integration enables AD FS to consume Active Directory Domain Services claims that are included in Kerberos tickets as a result of domain authentication.

Trust Relationships node

The Trust Relationships node in the AD FS console enables you to manage the trust relationships of the Federation Service. The three child nodes enable you to add and configure policies for claims providers, relying parties, and attribute stores.

Windows PowerShell cmdlets for AD FS 2.1

Windows Server 2012 includes an AD FS module for Windows PowerShell that includes approximately 50 cmdlets. These cmdlets were not available out of the box in Windows Server 2008 or Windows Server 2008 R2. You could see a question about AD FS that includes one or more of these Windows PowerShell cmdlets, so it's worth browsing the list of available AD FS cmdlets by using the following command:

```
Get-Command -Module ADFS
```

Although encountering Windows PowerShell in an AD FS question on the 70-417 exam is possible, it is not probable. AD FS is an advanced topic, and any question that would add the complication of Windows PowerShell would likely miss the target level of difficulty appropriate for this exam.

However, one new Windows PowerShell cmdlet relevant to AD FS that is not too challenging is Install-WindowsFeature. To install AD FS at the Windows PowerShell prompt, use the following command:

```
Install-WindowsFeature AD-Federation-Services
```

EXAM TIP

Although Certificate Services is not included in the objectives of this domain for the 70-417 exam, you will likely see at least one question on the exam related to this topic. If your knowledge of Certificate Services is rusty, be sure to review features such as enrollment, autoenrollment, user and computer templates, and public key infrastructure (PKI) components.

Objective summary

- Active Directory Federation Services (AD FS) is a claims-based identity access solution that enables you to securely authenticate your Active Directory users outside the company network. AD FS 2.x introduces the ability to create and issue industry-standard tokens containing claims, which makes AD FS interoperable with other systems.

- AD FS 2.x allows your Active Directory users to use their native credentials to sign in to a cloud-hosted application. This is a newly supported scenario. AD FS can still be used to support your Active Directory users who need access to a service in a partner network.

- The AD FS console in Windows Server 2012 has been redesigned and includes new nodes in the console tree and new wizards.

- AD FS requires three certificates. Before you can configure AD FS, the Service Communications certificate must be obtained as a Web Server certificate from your enterprise CA and installed as an SSL certificate on the local, default website. The remaining two certificates (Token-decrypting and Token-signing) are automatically created as self-signed certificates by default, but they can be replaced by Web Server certificates received from the enterprise CA.

Objective review

Answer the following questions to test your knowledge of the information in this objective. You can find the answers to these questions and explanations of why each answer choice is correct or incorrect in the "Answers" section at the end of the chapter.

1. You are establishing a federated trust with a partner organization. An IT administrator at the partner administration asks you to send her your federation metadata XML file. Your AD FS is running Windows Server 2012. In which of the following nodes in the AD FS console would you be able to determine the location of the metadata file?

   A. Endpoints

   B. Claims Provider Trusts

   C. Relying Party Trusts

   D. Attribute Stores

2. You want to replace the default Token-decrypting certificate in AD FS with a certificate issued by your enterprise CA. You request a certificate and are prompted to select a certificate template. Which certificate template do you choose?

   A. Computer

   B. Domain Controller Authentication

   C. Kerberos Authentication

   D. Web Server

3. You want to replace the default Token-signing certificate in AD FS with a certificate issued by your enterprise CA. Into which certificate store should you import the certificate?

   A. Current User\Personal

   B. Current User\Enterprise Trust

   C. Local Computer\Personal

   D. Local Computer\Enterprise Trust

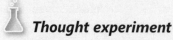

Thought experiment

You are an administrator for Cpandl.com. The Cpandl.com company network includes 60 servers running a combination of Windows Server 2008 R2 and Windows Server 2012.

Cpandl.com employs approximately 300 field workers who connect to an in-house application while visiting various sites. Currently, the application is supported by two servers that are hosted on the company premises and are running Windows Server 2008 R2.

Your IT manager has expressed an interest in moving the in-house application to a cloud service to reduce the administrative overhead associated with hosting the application on the company premises. Your manager wants your Active Directory users to be able to sign in to the cloud-hosted application by using their existing company credentials, but he doesn't want to store a copy of the Active Directory database on the premises of the cloud hosting company. To explore this scenario further, your manager has asked you to research what is needed to implement AD FS on your company network.

With this information in mind, answer the following questions:

1. Does the scenario described require you to install AD FS on Windows Server 2012, or can you use a server running Windows Server 2008 R2?

2. What are two ways you could install AD FS 2.1 on a server running Windows Server 2012?

3. After you install AD FS, which wizard should you run to perform the initial configuration of AD FS? Which wizard should you run to establish a trust with the cloud hosting service?

4. You perform a test installation of AD FS. During initial configuration, you receive an error message indicating a missing server certificate. You then request a Web Server certificate from your enterprise CA and install it in the Personal certificate store of the local computer. What should you do next?

Answers

This section contains the answers to the Objective Review and the Thought Experiment.

Objective 14.1: Review

1. **Correct Answer:** A

   A. **Correct:** The Endpoints node includes paths to services and metadata, including the federation metadata file.

   B. **Incorrect:** This node shows claims provider trusts, not federation metadata. Claims provider trusts are trust objects typically representing a resource partner that is providing claims information.

   C. **Incorrect**: This node shows relying party trusts, not federation metadata. Relying party trusts are trust objects typically created in partner organizations that consume claims information from the local instance of AD FS.

   D. **Incorrect**: This node shows attribute stores, not federation metadata. Attribute stores are directories or databases that an organization uses to store its user accounts and their associated attribute values.

2. **Correct Answer:** D

   A. **Incorrect:** The Web Server template is needed. The Computer template allows a computer to authenticate itself on the network

   B. **Incorrect:** The Web Server template is needed. The Domain Controller Authentication template is used to authenticate Active Directory computers and users.

   C. **Incorrect:** The Web Server template is needed. The Kerberos Authentication template offers enhanced security capabilities for domain controllers authenticating Active Directory users and computers.

   D. **Correct:** AD FS communicates with other parties through a local web server. The Web Server template is used to prove the identity of this web server.

3. **Correct Answer:** C

   A. **Incorrect:** You want to import the certificate into a store for the local computer because the certificate will be used by the computer in general, not by your user account.

   B. **Incorrect:** You want to import the certificate into a store for the local computer because the certificate will be used by the computer in general, not by your user account.

C. **Correct:** The Local Computer\Personal certificate store is used to store certificates issued to the local computer and associated with a private key. A private key is needed to sign objects such as tokens.

D. **Incorrect:** The Local Computer\Enterprise Trusts certificate store is used to store certificate trust lists. A certificate trust list provides a limited way to trust self-signed root certificates from other organizations.

Thought experiment

1. You can use Windows Server 2008 R2 if you download and install AD FS 2.0.

2. You could use the Add Roles and Features Wizard, or you could run the following Windows PowerShell command: `Install-WindowsFeature AD-Federation-Services`

3. First run the AD FS Federation Server Configuration Wizard. Then run the Add Relying Party Trust Wizard.

4. Install the certificate as an SSL certificate on the default website of the local instance of IIS.

Index

A

ABE (access-based enumeration), 50
access control
  claims-based, 249–250, 259–262
  DAC support, 245
access policies, 259–264
access rules, 246
account policies, 178
Active Directory
  configuring domain controllers, 163–171
  installing domain controllers, 89–105
  maintaining, 171–178
  objective summary and review, 101–102, 104–105, 178–179, 182
  restoring deleted objects in, 172–178
  updating file and folder objects, 252–253
Active Directory Administrative Center
  about, 171
  Active Directory Recycle Bin feature, 171-174
  Central Access Rule page, 260–262
  manipulating resource properties, 251–252
  opening, 173
  restoring deleted objects in, 174–176
Active Directory Certificate Services (AD CS), 335
Active Directory Domain Services Configuration Wizard, 91–94
Active Directory Domain Services Installation Wizard, 91
Active Directory Domain Services server role, 90, 94, 99
Active Directory Federation Services. See AD FS (Active Directory Federation Services)
Active Directory Recycle Bin feature, 171–174
Active Directory Rights Management Services (AD RMS), 335
Active Directory Users and Computers, 224
AD CS (Active Directory Certificate Services), 335

AD FS (Active Directory Federation Services)
  about, 335–336
  Certificates node, 338–339
  Endpoints node, 337–338
  installing, 340
  new features of console, 336–339
  objective summary and review, 340–341, 343–344
  Service node, 337–339
  Trust Relationships node, 339
AD FS Federation Server Configuration Wizard, 336
AD RMS (Active Directory Rights Management Services), 335
Add-ADDSReadOnlyDomainControllerAccount cmdlet, 95, 99
Add-ADGroupMember cmdlet, 165
Add Authorization Entry dialog box, 285
Add-DAAppServer cmdlet, 139
Add-DAClient cmdlet, 130
Add Or Edit Server dialog box, 316–317
Add Relying Party Trust action, 336
Add Relying Party Trust Wizard, 336
Add-RemoteAccessLoadBalancerNode cmdlet, 125
Add Roles And Features Wizard
  accessing, 10
  Confirm Installation Selections page, 4–5, 11
  Graphical Management Tools and Infrastructure, 14–15
  Installation Progress page, 11
  installing domain controllers, 90–91
  installing IPAM feature, 311
  installing Remote Access server role, 127
  installing Storage Spaces, 24
  Select Destination Server page, 10
  Select Installation Type page, 10
  Server Graphical Shell and, 14–15
  Before You Begin page, 10

B

C

F

G

H

Q

Quality-of-Service for Hyper-V, 81
quick migration feature, 228, 231–232

R

RADIUS protocol, 150
read-only domain controllers (RODCs), 99, 169
Receive-SmigServerData cmdlet, 3
recovery points, 288–290
Register Server Wizard, 273
registering
    servers in Windows Azure Online Backup, 273
    WSMT, 3
regular expressions, 257
reinstalling
    feature files, 4–5
    server roles, 4
relying party (RP), 336–337
Remote Access configuration wizards
    Application Server Setup Wizard, 129, 139
    Client Setup Wizard, 129–132
    Configure Remote Access page, 128–129
    Infrastructure Server Setup Wizard, 129, 135–139
    Remote Access Server Setup Wizard, 129, 132–135
Remote Access Management console
    advanced configuration options, 140
    Application Server Setup Wizard, 129, 139
    Client Setup Wizard, 129–132
    Configure Remote Access page, 128–129
    Enable Load Balancing option, 125
    Infrastructure Server Setup Wizard, 129, 135–139
    Remote Access Server Setup Wizard, 129, 132–135
    Update Management Servers option, 139
    verifying configuration, 140–142
Remote Access Server Setup Wizard (DirectAccess)
    about, 129
    Authentication page, 134–135
    Network Adapters page, 133
    Network Topology page, 132–133
Remote Clients Wizard (DirectAccess). See Client Setup Wizard (DirectAccess)
Remote-Desktop-Services role, 13
Remote Event Log Management group, 42

remote Group Policy update feature
    about, 185–190
    firewall rules for, 190–192
remote management
    configuring servers with earlier versions of Windows Server, 46–49
    domain controller options, 39–40
    enforcing settings with Group Policy, 47–49
    Group Policy update with, 186–192
    of multiple servers with Server Manager, 38–46
    objective summary and review, 50–51, 53
    Remote Server Administration Tools for Windows 8, 49
Remote Scheduled Tasks Management rule group, 191
Remote Server Administration Tools for Windows 8, 49
remote servers
    deploying roles on remote servers, 7–11
    managing with Server Manager, 8
    opening PowerShell prompts on, 39
    Windows Server 2008 and, 46–47
remote updating mode, 207
Remote Volume Management rule, 42
Remove-GPLink cmdlet, 193
Remove-GPO cmdlet, 193
Remove-GPPrefRegistryValue cmdlet, 193
Remove-GPRegistryValue cmdlet, 193
Remove Roles And Features Wizard, 16
Remove-VMFibreChannelHba cmdlet, 69
Remove-VMNetworkAdapterAcl cmdlet, 76
Remove-WindowsFeature cmdlet, 7
Rename-GPO cmdlet, 193
replica servers
    configuring, 283–286
    configuring VMs, 286–292
    failover clusters and, 300
    performing failover, 294–297, 300
replica virtual machines, 282
replication. See Hyper-V Replica feature
Reset-VMResourceMetering cmdlet, 61
Resource Metering feature, 60–61, 76
resource pools
    about, 108
    creating, 108–109
    metering, 108–109
resource properties (classifications), 246, 251–259
Resource Properties container, 251
resource property list, 251–252
Resource Property Lists container, 251

X

About the author

 JC MACKIN (MCSA, MCSE, MCT) is a writer, editor, and trainer who has been working with Windows networks since the days of Windows NT 4.0. He has authored or co-authored more than 10 books about Windows administration and certification, including the Self-Paced Training Kits for Exams 70-642, 70-643, and 70-685. You can follow him on Twitter @jcmackin.

What do you think of this book?

We want to hear from you!
To participate in a brief online survey, please visit:

microsoft.com/learning/booksurvey

Tell us how well this book meets your needs—what works effectively, and what we can do better. Your feedback will help us continually improve our books and learning resources for you.

Thank you in advance for your input!